# PARTIES WITH A PURPOSE

## LAYING THE GROUNDWORK FOR DISCIPLESHIP & EVANGELISM

*Marlene D. LeFever*

*Dedicated to*
*five of our favorite guests*
Gaile & Jim
and
Rosemary & Gary
and
Marc

*Recipes by*
Jack Richard Risley

*With special appreciation*
*to some of his favorite cooks*
Carol Risley
Sandra Fenton
and
Sue Barr

*Special thanks to*
Doug Schmidt, Isabel Anders, Sonya Duckworth, and Lisa Barnes
for editing and designing this book.

These party ideas have worked for my husband and me—some before we
were married, and some after. Our goal in sharing our collection is that
each idea will be reproduced in other Christian homes. If an idea works,
why should it be one of a kind? Unlike great works of art, the more
reproductions made of a party, the greater the value. May new hosts
among us take these ideas and explore them creatively in our homes and
churches, until our communities know that Jesus can be found there.

ISBN O-7814-5470-0, paper
Copyright © 1980, 1998 by Marlene LeFever
Printed in the United States of America

Portions of this book were previously published under the title
*Creative Hospitality*.

1 2 3 4 5 6 7 8 02 01 00 99 98

# Contents

The hospitality ideas in this book are not just intended to encourage a group of friends to have a dandy time together.

Instead they are designed to meet one of the following objectives:

*To give Christians tools to reach out to our unbelieving friends and neighbors, to open the possibility of Jesus Christ to them through planned hospitality events in our homes and churches.*

*To grow friendships among church people through hospitality events in our homes and the churches, building up the family of God.*

# My Church, My Family

*Be close enough to people
to see God transform lives.*

—Cynthia Herald

THE DOXOLOGY ENDED. There was a moment of quiet reflection while the organ played. And then the pastor made his announcement.

"I'd like to apologize for the crush of people in the foyer during the transition from the second to third services," he said. "Let's try a new traffic pattern. Those over here should file out the side door to the parking lot while those coming to the next service will use the rear doors."

His plan made sense. On recent Sundays, the meeting and greeting of crowds going two different directions had caused a terrible jam. But I felt incomplete as I followed the others in my row, duck-like, out that side door. Why? *There was no space for friendship to happen.* Once out the door and into the cold, we scurried to our cars. The planned exit underlined a deeper problem in many congregations. We might rub shoulders on tight pews, but we are not rubbing lives. During the services we might fellowship with God in a special way. But unless we're deepening friendships and making the opportunity to meet new friends, the Christian experience isn't whole.

Christian fellowship must mean that I am growing in my understanding of my Lord, becoming more in tune with His thoughts regarding life. In addition, fellowship with God also means that I am demonstrating and receiving love from other Christians in my family—the family of God.

While I was a child, church family time was Sunday afternoon. Lunch conversation would usually center around the question, "Who should we visit this afternoon?" Quite often that question would answer itself when we heard a car pull into our driveway and we would rush out to see which friends had decided to spend their Sunday with us.

My favorite family to visit was the Gehmans. They had kids just the right age, and they had a barn where we could build tunnels in the hay. When we were tired, we could sit in the living room or on the porch and listen to our parents retell stories, share recipes, or talk about the weather's effect on crops.

Looking back I realize I took for granted one of the unique aspects of these visits—people always seemed glad when we drove up. Visiting and sharing our lives was the right thing to do. Everyone visited—families with children, singles, elderly couples. How else would people spend a Sunday afternoon?

Christian fellowship was easier back then in Lancaster County. We all came from a Mennonite background. For several generations, our lives had woven themselves around and through each other's. Farming and its support occupations made common topics easy to find. And of course there were always the memories of courting days.

In my quiet Sunday corner, I sat and allowed my history to catch up with me and soak in. I know how Ira, the fire chief in Bird-in-Hand, was burned. And then there was the day my father showed up at my mother's door wearing knickers and she called the date off. And the stories of Jake and Nellie's misadventures with their horse and buggy. Now I'm several decades and thousands of miles from my homogeneous community. Church seems less like a word for family and more like a building I frequent in the center of a small Colorado community.

Realistically, I know I'll never reproduce the types of church friendships my parents had—friendships that lasted from the cradle to the grave. Today most people move once every three years. Has the transient church killed the possibility of church family? I find myself involved with a few close friends, but

what about the other 100 people who sit in my church's pews?

Have you ever had my experience of walking up to someone after the service and saying, "Good morning. Provocative sermon, wasn't it?"

"Yes."

"You're new here, aren't you?" I rattle on, "I do hope you'll come back again next Sunday."

Nervous laugh. "I've been coming for three months."

My turn for a nervous laugh.

Sound familiar? But how can we get to know each other's faces and at least enough about each other to feel comfortable talking—or even disappointed when we miss seeing each other in services?

I grappled with that question, and the place I decided to start was with parties—planned occasions in our home which are designed to help church people feel like family.

In fact, church parties were one reason my husband Jack and I decided to get married in the first place! We had both been happily single for over thirty years, so we approached our joining in a bit less emotional way than we might have if we had been younger. We made lists! Seriously! We listed all the benefits of our possible marriage and all the benefits of remaining single. After prioritizing the lists, we had a good idea how important marriage was to us. High on our list was church hospitality. We both loved get-togethers, and even felt gifted in hospitality. Jack admits, "As a single man, I didn't look at welcoming guests so much as a gift as a necessity. I'm such a bad housekeeper that I'd schedule company at my apartment at least twice a month to force me to clean up the mess."

As singles, Jack and I did lots of church hospitality with other singles, because sharing the work lightened the load. On our marriage list, we both liked the idea that we would have a regular partner for our events. Don't get me wrong. Throwing parties together was certainly not our only reason for getting married. We love each other and grin a lot in our approval of God's choice for us.

Over the past decades of our lives, Jack and I have had dozens of parties, some as singles, some as a married couple, and some as "singles" when our spouse was out of town.

Both Jack and I travel a lot on business, and we often plan events when the other one is gone. Jack was on his own for two weeks while I was in Alaska leading Christian education events. I'd been so thrilled to be asked that I'd said "yes" without realizing I'd be gone over his birthday. He made me feel guilty for a while, but then he sent out birthday announcements to all the men in our church, inviting them for a spaghetti dinner. About twenty came. Most had never been to a birthday party for a guy who planned and cooked it himself. Every year since then, I've heard about what a great evening it was from those who attended. "Are you going to go away this year?" they ask. "Why don't you forget his birthday again?"

Hospitality events come in all sizes. I've planned little ones for three or four people right up to an enormous Thanksgiving party that had somewhere between fifty and seventy guests (there were a lot of children!). No, we didn't rent the civic center for the Thanksgiving event. At the time, we lived in a four-room apartment. When our neighbor across the hall saw the crush of people, she opened her doors and increased our capacity to eight rooms. Then the woman on the next floor opened up her apartment, and the number of rooms swelled to twelve. But more about that later.

# My Community, My Family

*This "insider world"
is not our home.*

—Eugene Peterson

MIYOKO SCHEDULED an overnight "American" experience at my home as part of her first tour of the United States. I crammed as much into her time as I possibly could: tours of scenic areas, a visit to a neighborhood chili party, dinner with an American family that spoke some Japanese—and church. "I'm an American," I explained, "and I'm also a Christian. Would you be interested in coming to church with me?"

She was excited. "This is great . . . I've always wondered what people do in those buildings." Sunday morning, I listened to everything with new ears—ears that tried to understand our songs, testimonies, and sermons with absolutely no background. There was so much that would be totally foreign to anyone who had never been in church. To Japanese and American alike, much of the service might as well have been Greek. After it was over, I asked Miyoko if there was anything I could explain further. "No," she said. Then she fumbled for the right word to identify a woman who had stood up front and given her testimony. "That church . . . that church . . . well, that church *mother*. She certainly did get excited about her Jesus person."

Many more people than we realize have no more experience than Miyoko with the message of Jesus. Unlike her, most won't get excited about an opportunity to visit your church. They may, however, respond to hospitality in your home. Have you heard the quip, "Many Christians know more about the trees that grow in their neighborhoods than they know about the people who live behind those trees"?

Let's part those trees and visit with the secular people who live behind them.

To do this, I'm going to divide people by their life experiences by roughly placing them into demographic groups. These are artificial boundaries, but they will open discussion on how to reach different groups of people who live in our neighborhoods.

## Demographic Groups:

1. First, people who are headed for or just beginning retirement—The Silent Generation.
2. Second, people who are labeled Boomers, generally those born between 1946 and 1964.
3. Third, people who are just starting life on their own—Generation X.

4. Finally, we look at today's teens—Generation Next, who are also called the Millennial Generation.

I will be using a collection of research about each generation, and presenting that information through one *secular* representative of that group of people. According to George Barna, a leading evangelical pollster, obviously nobody will fit the exact profile we assign to a particular generational group. Generational labels are usually more convenient than accurate, and trying to define an entire generation is an inexact science. Barna suggests that individuals within a generation usually fit somewhere on a continuum of certain characteristics.

The following compilation may help you better understand the real people in your neighborhood and free you up to interact with them. We need to accept the challenge of moving out to people instead of expecting them to come to our churches. I like Eugene Peterson's paraphrase from Hebrews 13 on the necessity of moving out.

*In the old system, the animals are killed and the bodies disposed of outside the camp. The blood is then brought inside to the altar as a sacrifice for sin. It's the same with Jesus. He was crucified outside the city gates—that is where he poured out the sacrificial blood that was brought to God's altar to cleanse his people.*

*So let's go outside, where Jesus is, where the action is—not trying to be privileged insiders, but taking our share in the abuse of Jesus. This "insider world" is not our home.*

*—The Message*

We will be doing what John Stott calls "double listening"—listening to God's still, small voice as you listen to the voices of the world. Stott says, "We listen to God in order to obey Him; we listen to the world in order to understand its pain and its questions. And, the way we should be presenting the Gospel. Double listening leads to relevant communication."

You will find a list of sources used to write these monologues, along with additional reading suggestions, at the end of this chapter.

Billy Graham said, "Every generation is strategic. We are not responsible for the past generation, and we cannot bear full responsibility for the next one; but we do have our generation. God will hold us responsible as to how well we fulfill our responsibilities to this age and take advantage of our opportunities."

## A Secular Member of the Silent Generation Speaks (age: 55 and older)

"I've reached an age where I can totally appropriate humorist Dave Barry's feelings about flying. 'If I'm going to risk my life and valuable carry-on belongings in a profoundly heavy machine going absurdly fast way up in the air over a place such as Arkansas, where I don't even know anyone, then I want whoever is operating this machine to be much older and more mature than I. But now I routinely get on planes where the entire flight crew looks like it's raising money for its class trip.'

"I'm getting older, and I'm thinking more about God, and yes—I'll admit it—death. All my life I've been into religion . . . in moderation, of course. I haven't missed Easter in years. I did what was expected. I give a fair amount of money to my church just to keep it in running operation. That's what my generation does—keeps the stuff that our parents built from falling down. My father was part of the generation that built big business, big unions, big govern-

ment, big cold wars, AARP, and big church denominations. I'm doing my best to keep what his generation built from crumbling.

"I feel caught between my father's generation that built this world and the Boomers who insist on rebuilding it. My father got a red, white, and blue world, and I've recast it as salmon, gray, and mauve. Figures! I'm part of the first generation that never put a president into the White House. I say about so many things, 'Well, it's too late now.'

"I'm disappointed and a little angry at life—and God, too. The world is rushing on and leaving me behind. I was off to such a great start. By 20, I'd exceeded my parent's level of education; by 25, my parents' level of housing; and by 30, their level of income. Now as retirement looms, I feel like I've missed something. My inner person, maybe. I've had good fortune on the outside, but only turmoil on the inside. I've missed all the big markers in life. Now, a lifetime behind me, I suspect God is also a marker I've missed. My life is irrelevant.

"I know the old adage, 'You can't teach an old dog new tricks,' but I disagree. I'm learning all sorts of new things—how to retire, how to deal with the deaths of people I love, how to watch my children leave—and return when their lives fall apart. I'm under a lot of stress, and stress makes people open to personal change. I am open to change.

"I'd like to share who I am, my doubts, and my fears with a small group of people—but I don't have the nerve. My grandkids think I have it all together, and I'm scared to disappoint them. They think of me as the great mediator—helping them and their parents understand each other. Family fighting, any kind of fighting, unnerves me. That's one reason I don't feel good about the church. People are always fighting about little details that can't be all that important. I've got a load of church jokes that I use to entertain my golfing partners. Yes, I know; I'd rather laugh at religion than give up on it entirely.

"I've followed the rules all my life. I'm a good person. I work to make society work. I help the church pay its bills. So why do I feel so guilty—like there is something in life that's undone and I just can't get my arms around whatever it is? The world I started with is not the world I have to deal with now. I can say the same thing about God. I thought I knew what He required. I had the God-compartment of my life filled. But when I open the door to that compartment, there isn't anything there—only an empty echo. I'm scared. Life has no meaning."

## Thought Questions on The Silent Generation

### A member of The Silent Generation fell into a pit.

A Pharisee came by and said, "Only a bad person would fall into a pit."

A man without love came by and said, "You deserve your pit."

A New Ager said, "Maybe you should network with other pit-dwellers."

A self-pitying women said, "You haven't seen anything until you've seen my pit."

A realist said, "That is a pit."

An environmental inspector said, "Do you have a permit for that pit?"

An idealist said, "Things could be worse."

The pessimist said, "Things will get worse."

Then a Christian came along, took the man by the hand, and lifted him out of the pit.

(Adapted from Henry Brinton's sermon, "Sanctify the Congregation," *The Christian Ministry*, Jan-Feb, 1997.)

- If this person lived next door to you, what are some ways you might open up conversations about God?

- What type of hospitality events in your church and home might help this person fill up that empty God-compartment?

- What secular people do you know who are almost at or starting retirement? What Christians do you know who could help expand the views of Christianity of these secular people without turning them off?

Consider the following hospitality events as ones that could be easily adapted to The Silent Generation:

"Hay There" (pg. 75);
"Neighborhood Drop In"
    (pg. 83);
"Having Wonderful Time—
    Wish You Were Here"
    (pg. 98);
"Pass-Along Skills" (pg. 123);
"Project: Mission
    Awareness" (pg. 152);
"Passover" (pg. 202).

(This is only a sampling. Some of these would be appropriate for secular groups. Others are aimed at church family.)

## A Secular Member of the Boomer Generation Speaks (age: 35 to 54)

"I've visited a number of churches, and my favorites are those that have services at a decent time of the week, like Thursday or Saturday night. They usually have great music, and they don't embarrass people like me who show up—okay, I'll admit it—only once in awhile. Frankly, I think of churches like shopping centers. There are lots of them. They provide products that I'm free to buy or not buy. I just go from one store to another. I haven't found any church 'store' that has a product I'm willing to take home.

"I do sort of wish my kids went to church. They need the moral and character education that the church claims it can teach. But at the same time, I don't want the church indoctrinating them with weird things and all that stuff from the Bible. What a catch-22!

"My family is very, very important to me. So is my community. That's why I coach little league, even though my kids have outgrown its programs. I went through the flower-child hippie, draft resister, Jesus freak, and yuppie eras. That was enough adventure for me. Now I'd rather stay home. I spend a lot of time with my kids, but I've got no models on how to do this. Goodness knows my parents weren't into modeling. I did have two parents though. People used to ask me, 'What does your daddy do for a living?' Now people ask my kids, 'Does your dad live with you?'

"I'm tired of hearing people say that watching Boomers age is like watching a pig move through a python. There are 76 million of us, and we're a lot more important than digesting pork. We're the most important group in the world today, and we're going to leave a positive legacy. We'll do our best to put this country back on track. My generation is putting morality back on the public agenda. We'll remodel government to fit our beliefs. We've seen how it shouldn't be done—the Cold War, the JFK, MLK, RFK assassinations, Vietnam, Kent State, Watergate. Now we'll do it right. Call me an idealist. Or even a raving moralist. I grew up with an idealized image of what our world should be, and in my youthful arrogance, I assumed we would realize that image. We didn't, but I'm still a visionary. We're not finished yet.

"I want to remodel religion, too. I feel the need to look inward—to have a well-ordered inner life. I'm me-centered. I admit it. If that makes me selfish, so be it. I'm looking for good people who are good for me, people who will help me through my life passages, people who make sense and contribute positively to how I feel about myself. Deep down, I think I have the potential to be god-like. (I wouldn't say this to just anyone.) New Age Religion makes sense to me. It presents an ultimate reality—you know, that the whole world, us included, is one organic whole. It has no independent parts. All is one, and God is in everything and is everything. Doesn't that make sense to you?

"I believe that we humans need to see ourselves as expressions of God. Sin is any offense against ourselves. I heard a New Age speaker say, 'You do have a soul, and it lives on after this lifetime—many times. You will live forever and have control over your life. God is not dead. You are God.' Now *that* appeals to me a lot more than what I've heard from some Christian preachers. It fits me better than the Christian concept of God standing over what He created. It fits me better than believing that Christians possess the only objective truth about God and that there is only one God who is the source of ultimate truth."

## Thought Questions on the Boomer Generation

*Head-in-the-sand ignorance about our mission to the world is one thing. Fiddling while Rome burns is quite another. With the insights God is giving us about the harvest fields of the world, we incur great accountability when we do not respond to the need.*

—Bill Stearns

- You've got a group of neighbors sitting in your backyard and someone shares some of the New Age teaching. As a Christian, how would you respond to the statements the way you suspect Christ might respond if He were physically in your backyard?

- What type of events has your church had in the last year that would have been appreciated by this Boomer?

- What secular people do you know who are Boomers? What Christians do you know who could help expand these Boomers' views of Christianity without turning them off?

Consider the following hospitality events as ones that could be easily adapted to Boomers:

"All Under One Roof" (pg. 35);
"Roots"(pg. 40);
"Neighborhood Drop-In" (pg. 83);
"Picture Perfect Scavenger Hunt" (pg. 117);
"Family Communion" (pg. 178);
"Passover" (pg. 202);
"Recycled Christmas Party" (pg. 208);
"Thanksgiving" (pg. 237);

(This is only a sampling. Some of these would be appropriate for secular groups. Others are aimed at church family.)

## A Secular Member of Generation X Speaks (age: 20 to 34)

"Church is just not in my world. My parents never went and I don't think my grandparents did either. Church is just a stage for performers—big choirs, big bands, big buildings, big budgets. I don't respond to frills and a dog-and-pony show. I don't want God-packaging. Show me authenticity. Show me real! I've had my fill of these hypocrite drivers cutting me off and speeding by, leaving me with a great view of the Christian fishes on their cars. Frankly, what I've seen of the God-people isn't worth a fish gill. The whole thing can be wrapped up in their bumper sticker, 'Jesus is coming. Look busy!' Well, I am busy, trying to make the most of what Boomers left of the world, and I have no time for people who are nothing but show.

"I don't want to be too harsh. I'd have respect for Christians, I think, if they were honest and shared their mistakes and failures. I'm filled with questions and doubts, and parts of my life are a mess. How can I relate to Christian leaders who have no questions and no doubts? I've read some of Ralph Waldo Emerson, and I agree with some of his negative feelings about pastors. Things haven't changed since he spoke at Harvard Divinity School in 1939. He said that for most pastors, there was 'no hint in anything they said that they had ever plowed, and planted, and talked, and bought and sold; there was not a surmise, not a hint in anything they said, that they had ever lived at all.' Ministers I've heard seem to specialize in what Emerson called 'thoughtless clamor'; I need someone who can relate to what I face every day—real life.

"Something in me resonates with the songs of the band, Soul Asylum. In one song they sing, 'I'm homesick for the home I've never had.' Me, too. I'm looking for genuine relationships—home, family, friends. Don't stop me in the street and hand me a tract. Don't give me six easy steps to put joy in my life. I know life isn't easy. I'm aware of the decay of my entire planet—nuclear waste, ozone depletion, lying politicians, jailed pastors, AIDS, and global warming. This is the world I inherited. The national debt I inherited is so big that even if every sesame seed on every Big Mac ever sold was worth a dollar, the money wouldn't pay off the $4.4 trillion debt. I know Christians want me to ask, 'What must I do to be saved?' Instead, given my generations' 'McJobs' with no security or benefits, I'm asking, 'What must I do to survive?'

"My parents may have grappled with the question, 'Is there a God?' My question is 'Which God?' I pride myself in being pluralistic and not disrespectful about what other people believe. The story of Jesus is a great story, but what about the stories told by all the other great religious leaders?

"If you want to tell me about your God, invite me to a Mexican Pile-On at your place. Get to know me. Hear my story. Tell me yours. I'm looking for something to believe in. I'm just not sure what. I'm open to Christianity, to Buddhism, to New Age—anything that has some answers. When it comes to God, well, who knows? All religions are equally valid. 'Different roads, same destination'—that's my creed.

"I relate to Douglas Coupland who speaks for a lot of us twenty-somethings. He wrote, 'God is dead, but if you miss Him—hey, at least you know you're still half alive.' I'll admit it; I'm looking for the other half."

## Thought Questions on Generation X

*There is hope for new success in evangelism if today's believers will learn to listen before they speak, if we will learn to hear the questions contemporary culture is putting to us.*
*—Jerry Harvill*

- If this person lived in the apartment next to yours, what traditional ways of witnessing would you not use?

- Make a list of the ways this person's thinking differs from how a Christian thinks. Roleplay how you might engage this person in these areas.

- What secular people do you know who are between the ages of 20 and 35? What Christians do you know who could help expand these Gen Xers' views of Christianity without turning them off? Think of people who are part of The Silent Generation. Many Generation X people relate to this group better than to the Boomers.

Consider the following hospitality events as ones that could be easily adapted to Generation X:

"All Under One Roof" (pg. 35);
"Roots" (pg. 40);
"Scrabble Marathon" (pg. 70);
"Do-It-Ourselves Evening" (pg. 89);
"Raise the Banners High" (pg. 134);
"Sight and Sound— Scripture Alive!" (pg. 140);
"A House Dedication" (pg. 166);
"Family Communion" (pg. 178);

"New Year's Eve
    Dinner and Worship"
    (pg. 194);
"Tangram Shower" (pg. 255).

(This is only a sampling. Some of these would be appropriate for secular groups. Others are aimed at church family.)

## A Secular Member of Generation Next Speaks (age: 11 to 19)

"Would you believe there are more than 34 million of us? Welcome to my world, the first generation to come of age in the 90s. It's no picnic, let me tell you. Boomers feared the bomb and the draft. Generation X fears dead-end jobs. Me—I fear stray bullets and AIDS.

"I'm a good kid. So is every kid I know, at least when you compare us to Generation X and the Boomers when they were my age. My friends volunteer. We buy from marketers who advertise that they are making the world better. We're not rebellious like kids of the 70s or materialistic like kids of the 80s. Hey, compared to other generations, we're heroes.

"I'm amazed at how many adults think my age group is dumb. I know we score low in standardized tests. But I think my generation is the transition between old thinking and new thinking. We're moving from a traditional linear style of thinking that my mom does—do A, and then B, and then C. That's real organized and it bores me. It's not the way I think. My mind clicks like a computer, identifying and sorting information in all sorts of nonlinear ways. Then I integrate everything into a pattern that makes sense to me. My mind process is probably more like a mosaic than a straight line.

"I love computers. Life may be complicated, but computers aren't. I visited a chat site about God a couple nights ago. Interesting. It was the first time I thought seriously about people my age believing in God. It was a high-energy conversation, not just words out of the old black book. One guy talked about God changing his life and the power he'd found in prayer. I debated with him for a while. I wouldn't have listened to a preacher in church, but this guy talked my language—you know, more like a mosaic than in a straight line.

"I've been brought up to think for myself. My mom and I may disagree, but she doesn't tell me what to believe and what to think. It's nice not having boundaries and having to think for myself. Like God. I'm pragmatic. If ecology is in trouble, clean it up. If you feel the need for God, go to church. I just don't feel the need for something I can't see or can prove exists. I start in reality, and I think God is fantasy. Or, maybe God's just a word for reaching my full potential. If so, then I'm god.

"This is not to say I won't give church a try sometime, but my mother lived without it and I probably will too. I just can't think of any religious people I really admire. I'd rather meet Michael Jordan than Billy Graham any day, or our local radio and TV personalities than any of the pastors or youth leaders in this town. I'm not very trusting. For example, I don't believe advertising can be trusted. It's all such a put-on. I feel the same way about what most religious people say. They're just advertising the way they make a living, and it's probably just as much a put-on as most ads. Hey, we live in an irrational world, and I just don't think Christianity provides enough answers.

"I think a lot more about growing up and getting married than I do about God. I don't think I'll marry, especially since people don't have to get married to have sex. Faithfulness is a joke. I'm handling my parents' divorce better than my mom. She's depressed and that means I have to do more stuff around the house—be more independent. Sometimes I feel like the parent. This is my time to be a kid. Oh, well, everything is changing and I can't do much about it, so I might as well relax and let it happen."

## Thought Questions on Generation Next

Ring in nose, weird lingo, and the clothes! Many adults are afraid of these kids. Consequently, they make no attempt to get to know them, even when they live next door or down the street. Dwight Ozard provides an excellent context for building relationships with this cyber-suckled generation

"The greatest mission field we have is not in some faraway land. The strange and foreign culture most Christians fear is not across the ocean. It's barely across the street. The culture most lost to the Gospel is our own . . . it's a culture that can't say two sentences without referencing a TV show or a pop song, and that can't remember what it was like to have to get up and change channels. It's a culture more likely to have a body part pierced than it is to know why Sarah laughed. It's a culture that we stopped evangelizing, and have instead declared a culture war upon.

"Yet we do want to reach them. But we want to reach them without listening, without the hard work of straining to hear what lies beyond the interminable racket and crass immediacy that is their language, without being touched by their fears and without understanding the roots of their rebellion and cynicism. We are more likely to be scandalized than brokenhearted by their rootlessness and self destructiveness, blinded by their promiscuities to the hungerings beyond them. We trivialize and demonize their language—and thus, their very person, in part because they offend and confuse us; mostly because they threaten us, all the while wondering why they won't listen.

"As Jesus might have said, 'Let those who have ears to hear, shut up and listen.'"

(Dwight Ozards in *Prism*, July/August 1996)

- Do business with how you feel about Generation Next. What things don't you understand? What things frighten you? If God has put members of this generation into your life, read George Barna's book, *Generation NEXT*.

- If this unchurched teen lived next door to you, what are some ways you might open up conversations about his or her life, and thoughts about God?

- What type of hospitality events in your church and home might appeal to teenagers?

Consider the following hospitality events as ones that could be easily adapted to Generation Next:

"Roots" (pg. 40);
"Come as You Aren't" (pg. 60);
"Hay There"(pg. 75);
"Picture Perfect Scavenger Hunt" (pg. 117);
"Pass-Along Skills" (pg. 123);
"Sight and Sound— Scripture Alive!" (pg. 140);
"Project: Mission Awareness" (pg. 152);
"Recycled Christmas Party" (pg. 208).

(This is only a sampling. Some of these would be appropriate for secular groups. Others are aimed at church family.)

## Resources for Further Study

Information for these generational introductions came from the following sources. Secular sources are marked with an asterisk (*).

*BOOKS*

**Barna, George.** *Generation NEXT.* Regal Books.

**McIntosh, Gary L.** *Three Generations.* Fleming H. Revell.

**Regele, Mike.** *Death of the Church.* Zondervan.

* **Rushkoff, Douglas, ed.** *The GenX Reader.* Ballantine Books.

*ARTICLES*

**Belcher, Jim.** "It's the Gospel Stupid—Generation X and Religion." *Regenerational Quarterly,* Spring 1995.

**Borthwick, Paul.** "What Is the State of Youth Ministry Around the World?" *Christian Education Journal,* Spring 1996.

**Catucci, Thomas F.** "With a Little Help from My Friend . . . Teenagers Find God." *The Catholic World,* June 1994.

* **Coupland, Douglas.** "'X Marks the Schlock: Slacking Toward Bethlehem." *Vanity Fair,* March 1994.

**Groothuis, Douglas.** "Technoshamanism: digital deities in cyberspace." *Christian Research Journal,* Winter 1997.

* **Hornblower, Margot.** "Great Xpectations." *Time,* June 9, 1997.

* **Mitchell, Susan.** "The Next Baby Boom." *American Demographics,* October 1995.

* **Peterson, Karen S.** "Life in the Slower Lane." *USA Today,* March 7, 1997.

**Posterski, Don.** "Keeping Up in Our Changing World." *Decision,* May 1996.

**Tapis, Andrew.** "Reaching the First Post-Christian Generation." *Christianity Today,* Sept. 12, 1994.

**Zander, Dieter.** "The Gospel for Generation X—Making Room in the Church for Busters." *Leadership,* Spring 1995.

# 3

## *Hospitality Goals*

*The believers weren't jumping up and down saying, "The Great Commission—we're so excited! Let's go reach the world." Nor did they hear a voice out of heaven saying, "Go." They were simply running scared, but they accomplished what God wanted them to do—spread the word.*

—Bob Sjogren and Bill and Amy Stearns

**P**LAN AHEAD. Remember, it wasn't raining when Noah started to build the ark!

The hospitality ideas in this book are not just intended to encourage a group of friends to have a dandy time together. Instead they are designed to meet one of the following objectives:

1. **To give Christians tools to reach out to our unbelieving friends and neighbors, to open the possibility of Jesus Christ to them through planned hospitality events in our homes and churches.**

This will require prayer, planning and follow-up. It will not be easy. Harry Emerson Fosdick, in a sermon called "Christianity at Home in Chaos," used the story of Brer Rabbit and Brer Fox. Remember how Brer Rabbit saved his life by talking Brer Fox into throwing him into the brier patch? Brer Rabbit had convinced the fox that the brier patch was the worst possible place he could be thrown. What Brer Fox didn't know was that the rabbit was born and bred in the brier patch. Fosdick drew a comparison between Brer Rabbit and Christianity. He preached, "Christianity, far from feeling strange in a troubled time, was born and bred in a brier patch like this" (Mark Yurs, "Preaching in the Brier Patch," *The Christian Ministry*, Jan-Feb 1997).

If you open your home or your church to people who don't know your Lord or who are antagonistic toward the Gospel, you've entered the Brier Patch. In contrast to being scratched to death, you may feel the exaltation of knowing you're where today's Christians need to be.

2. **To grow friendships among church people through hospitality events in our homes and the churches, building up the family of God.**

In order to reach these objectives, I'll give complete directions for each event. By following these directions, it will be possible for you to duplicate each special event. However, you'll have a lot more fun if you tailor what you do to what the Lord wants *you* to accomplish. Add original ideas; augment mine. If you're like I was, you'll be scared half to death the first time you invite people you don't know very well. Things will get progressively easier as you coax your church family toward the pleasure of knowing they belong together, and as you show the attractiveness of a Christ-centered life to non-Christians.

One of the most important parts of a hospitality event is to identify your objective or goal for the event. You can use the broad objectives above or, perhaps more effectively, write a goal that is specific to you. The goal is the reason for the evening—what you want to see happen during those hours with your friends. Talk about your goals with a prayer partner. Consider writing them down before the event and coming back to them afterward.

Each idea here has a suggested goal, but this goal might not perfectly fit what you want to happen. So rethink each one. If it's right, guide your guests toward it. If something in the objective doesn't quite fit, have fun rewriting it.

Writing goals is not difficult. Follow this sequence:

Talk and pray about an idea with a Christian friend. What needs to be done? Who might need just this sort of activity about now?

Write what you want to have happen, but be careful here. What you write has to be measurable. At the end of the event, you have to be able to say, "Yes, that happened," or, "No, that goal was not reached."

A poor goal might sound great. For example, "I want the sixteen people from my new Sunday school class to have fun together." But that goal is almost impossible to measure. It would be better to say, "I want everyone in my Sunday school class to spend time talking with everyone else." That's a goal you can measure. If a tight group of special friends is open enough to include all sixteen people, everyone will have fun together.

Realize that you also have some control over the group reaching a measurable goal. For example, you might see the "football four" gathering in a corner to talk over the season's possibilities to the exclusion of other guests. If your goal is total group mixing, you could bring an unathletic person over to the group and introduce him into the conversation. You can note the shyness of another and spend time alone with that person, helping her feel at ease before you work her into a larger group.

Sometimes I've set fantastic goals, and the events have been flops. As I looked back on what happened, I realized that my events and goals didn't mesh. I should have asked myself if my plans could ever produce the results I wanted. A careful look at the activities and the mix of people there would have told me no.

If I want my guests to talk with people they have never talked with before, it's best to begin with a de-icer that will encourage them to mix in nonthreatening ways. If I want singles to enjoy the evening, I have to plan my activities with their interests and needs in mind. If there are children at the party and my goal is to help families meet families, I must make certain that the activities are fun across age levels.

All this is programmed. I have picked the direction I think things should go. Interestingly, events sometimes surprise me and take off in directions I never dreamed. I try not to chase a party with my goals, but rather to follow the party's enthusiasm. Even though things are not going according to plan, people are interacting and having fun. Great! This type of switch, however, rarely happens. In fact, it almost never happens in a group of church people who don't know each other well. Things usually start stiffly, and I need to make an effort to program that stiffness out of the evening.

Have you ever wondered why so many non-Christians know how to add life to group situations, while Christian friends stick closely to their cliques? On the whole, non-Christians seem more at ease than Christians in social situations. They often start conversations; they include newcomers in groups; they are more skilled at small talk. Now, remember, I'm talking about that first encounter—the party encounter—the let's-get-acquainted evening. I know many party-imperfect Christians who are fantastic conversationalists one-on-one. I have shared my deepest doubts with them and have felt their empathy and love. Of course, a genuine concern for the individual is more important in the long run than carrying on a good conversation with a group at a party. However if people don't mix, few of these kinds of deep friendships will be started. And Christians will continue to complain, "My church is so cold and unfriendly. It just isn't meeting my needs." And non-Christians will continue to believe, "Christians are dull, even downright unfriendly. The only thing they care about is getting me to think the way they do."

Nancy, a person I'd never met, accepted my invitation. Her name had been on a church list of two-visits visitors. When I met her at the door, we actually had to introduce ourselves to each other.

I got her involved in a small group, and then, in the rush of the evening, I didn't have much more contact with her.

As she was leaving, Nancy told me, "In this one evening, I have met more people than I have in several months of Sundays. To be honest, I haven't been real pleased with the church and was considering church hunting again. But after tonight, I guess I won't be looking anymore."

Nancy and I never became best friends. Perhaps that evening she found others who would eventually become very good friends. However, I did become part of her larger circle of "just friends." And that "just friends" circle can never be too large.

## Conversation Starters

How do we get conversations started among people who are not used to talking to one another? Many of them may have the same neighborhood or the same church in common, but nothing else.

I've used lots of techniques, many of them described in detail with these hospitality ideas. For example, at one party

where everyone in my apartment building was invited, I built a mound of construction paper, glue, tape, material scraps, sequins, and anything else I could find. As people arrived, I sent them to the pile to make name tags that told something about themselves. Before dinner, each person was to find out all he or she could about four people's name tags.

Of course, the tags were totally unimportant. What was important was the part they played in getting people to walk up to strangers and say, "Tell me about your name tag." From that line, they were only minutes away from, "What do you think about rezoning the open space for apartment buildings?" or "Do you have any idea how much attic insulation my brother's new house ought to have?" Great friendships from ridiculous name tags grow! The name tag makes the first approach easy—that first step many people are not willing to take without it.

Another frustrating but effective way to mix people at the beginning of an evening is to give everyone ten toothpicks when he or she arrives. Explain that the objective is to get everyone else's toothpicks. People do this by taking one toothpick from anyone who says the word

"I." The person with the most toothpicks at the end of a specified time (no more than twenty minutes) wins. Of course, to win each must engage others in conversation. How else will a person collect enough picks to win? It's a funny and stupid game. But the point is, it works. It gets strangers involved with others, and forces church people to mix beyond their comfortable circle.

## Who To Invite

There are any number of ways to mix people. It all depends . . . where is your heart?

1. People in the neighborhood, apartment complex, etc.

2. People who would find the group mix stimulating (for example: they work in similar areas; they have attended church once or twice; they are involved in comparable volunteer work).

3. Church groups might also be divided:

   A. *Singles* ("A" group—college students; "B" group—other singles).

   B. *Mixed groups* (singles and marrieds, and perhaps even children).

   C. *Christians and non-Christians* (or new Christians and older Christians).

I've spent a lot of time and energy on the B group of singles. I know personally how many of my single friends in the church felt. In fact, the first of these quotes is mine.

"I overheard one of the ladies of the church saying, 'I don't have any single friends. I don't think we'd have a thing to talk about. Actually, they scare me.' What am I! Some sort of freak?"

"I feel like a misfit. Always an uneven number."

"We're not accepted by the married people in the church. I would give anything to spend an evening with little kids—just playing with them like an uncle would. Short of just bluntly inviting myself over, this isn't going to happen."

"I'm more at home in singles bars than at most church functions. There people don't place me in a category labeled different. In fact, I feel like my stock goes up at a bar."

I want my home to be a place where singles can come and meet each other—comfortably, without necessarily pairing off, but with the opportunity to talk socially with other men and women. Sue Kline, managing editor for a Christian magazine, wrote in one of her editorials, "In my late 20s, I encountered the hospitality of the Prigels. To this day I think of them as a huge family, even though they had only four kids. Sunday dinners, however, seemed to embrace a cast of thousands—mostly singles who might otherwise have spent a boring Sunday afternoon alone. Instead, we squeezed around the giant dining room table in their rambling farmhouse for a rowdy meal and an afternoon of tramping about their dairy farm" (*Discipleship Journal,* Issue 98, 1997).

Social contact is extremely important to the single adult. When I first came to work in Illinois after spending three years as a missionary teacher in Japan, I didn't know anyone my age. I suffered from peer starvation! Sure, I would have enjoyed dating, but my need was more basic than that. I didn't have a single friend my age—male or female—with whom I could talk.

I'll never forget the first Sunday I visited Circle Church in Chicago. Two single women greeted me and asked if I would like to go out to lunch with them. Would I! I felt like the famine was over. I would have willingly paid for their complete dinners, including dessert, just to express my appreciation.

"Always singles at our parties." That rule has been rather strictly enforced by Jack and me in our apartment, and now, in our home.

We often mix married couples and singles—a less-than-earth-shakingly creative idea. And yet, for some people, it represents the first time they have ever crossed the lines between the groups.

Sometimes we will mix our church friends with others who are uncomfortable with the church. Of course, this can be ticklish. In no way do we want our secular friends to feel we have invited them in order to propagandize them. Yes, Christ is a part of our home and our marriage and the lives of many of our friends. That's no secret. We want our other friends to someday share our enthusiasm willingly—not because they were invited to a social occasion and buttonholed into a decision.

One evening we had a game party going on in three of the four rooms of our apartment. By drawing names, guests had chosen two other people as opponents in board games. Suddenly in the middle of the second game, one of the women screamed an expletive that hadn't been heard in that home since we moved in. Her teammate had made a wrong move, and she had uttered her normal response.

Later a friend who is uncomfortable with the church said, "I was impressed by what happened. Here was this swearing dame sitting across from this guy I'd call a big-time Christian. No one fainted or delivered a sermon."

It was this woman's first time in our home. Perhaps there will be another time more appropriate for sharing how we feel about the name she used so lightly. But that time was definitely not in the middle of a board game.

Much of our hospitality is aimed directly at the people who attend our church. Some of the names come from the membership and church directory list. Others are first timers who sign a visitor's card. Still others are students who attend only when school is in session.

"I was amazed when I got your invitation," Julie told us. "It read that you had invited a group from your church. I'd only visited twice—the two times I've been in church during the year my divorce became final. I was hurting and God seemed far away.

"At the party, people talked and laughed. They included me. That evening I met people who are now my best friends. More important, God and I smiled at each other again."

Julie verbalized her feelings at a time when I was wondering if it were worth all the effort. She is living proof that God was affirming the gift of hospitality.

## *The Bigger The Better*
### *(and not necessarily more work)*

*Ambition says,
"You could be doing great things for Christ."
The balanced voice says,
"Christ is doing great things for you."
That's contentment.*

—Marshall Shelley

HOLD IT! If you're going to whip right past these ideas because you've got a limited budget and a small home, don't.

Never underestimate the number of people who can have a great time in a small place. Most of the ideas in this section were tested in a four-room apartment. Of course, I'm talking wall-to-wall people, but no one seemed to mind. In fact, people mixed more easily at these large parties than they did at smaller ones.

I think the noise level has something to do with it. When a room is filled with a number of different groups, all talking at once, my individual pauses aren't noticed as much. I can relax and have a better time. Noise makes me less self-conscious. Years ago I worked as a reporter. My desk was in the middle of unwalled space in the city room. Twenty typewriters all going at once, and I could work. Every once in a great while, everyone would hit a stopping point at the same time and the room would be silent. People would look up nervously and we would all lose several minutes before we could build up the level of comfortable noise again. Big parties usually have comfortable noise built right in.

I also like the casual fun of a large party. There are never enough chairs, so people just drape themselves all over the place. When I first started giving parties, I would count the number of chairs I had and invite just enough bodies to fill them. That didn't work. Have you ever looked at a room full of people all sitting on chairs? They tend to place the chairs in lines around the wall—twelve people hugging the wall. It's awful. In that setup, everyone becomes part of the whole conversation— after all, we're all in this square circle. That means with my twelve guests, I get to talk 1/12th of the time. That's a lot of quiet. Dreary party. So now I take half the chairs I own, stack them somewhere, and force people to break into comfortable conversation groups. And I like it; I get to talk more.

Big parties can cost money, but there are ways to get around that. Covered dishes, dessert only, poor box at the door (yes, I've done this). Cutting the cost down to what people can afford—$2 in a poor box or an inexpensive Jell-O salad—allows many Generation X guests to participate financially. They don't have to feel like free loaders; they are making a contribution to the success of the event. Don't assume young people have enough money. Half the debtors seeking professional help at the National Consumer Counseling Service are between the ages of 18 and 32 with an average outstanding credit card balance of over $1,700.

Be careful not to let food become the main purpose for the evening. If you're a gourmet cook, great! Once in awhile, you may want to share the fruits of this hobby, but food should be kept in proper perspective. Use it to help you reach a goal. It's easier to talk with someone you hardly know when you're cracking and eating peanuts together.

For almost all big parties, I spread the food responsibility around. I write something on the invitation like, "Please bring some butter," or "I'm planning a smorgasbord of desserts," or "I can hardly wait to taste what you bring."

Sharing the work means I survive to enjoy my own party. But it also means that my guests will be more committed to having a good time because they have a small investment of their time and money in the evening.

I remember one bachelor who said he was baking his mother's best chocolate cake as his contribution to a party. He had called Maryland to get the recipe, and everyone was going to be green with envy because he wouldn't share the recipe. The party was half over when he finally arrived carrying a squatty boxed cake straight from the baker. "I almost didn't come," he said. "My cake turned out soupy and I was mortified. But then I remembered this great Swedish bakery across town. So I rushed over and bought this." Sure, I was sorry that he didn't feel free enough to show up without his soupy offering. But I was also pleased that he was so involved with his party contribution—even to the point of figuring that the party just couldn't get by without a cake from him. And, by the way, the town he drove across to get the cake was downtown Chicago!

## The Easy Ways

**Do things the easiest way possible.**

Judith Couchman wrote, "God weaves miracles into our hearts. In my case, it's the miracle of offering a simple, flawed hospitality instead of striving for the proverbial 'hostess with the mostest' award. A hospitality that—in a hectic and complicated world—nurtures guests without overwhelming and depleting the host. . . . Hospitality centers on inviting people into our lives and sharing from what we have, on helping guests feel relaxed and part of the household. Instead of dazzling people with our social skills, we pour God's warmth into their souls. This approach patterns after the early church when believers shared everything in common and eschewed the need to 'perform' and impress one another" ("Hospitality in a Hectic World," *Discipleship Journal*, Issue 98, 1997).

*Cleaning*—Do the heavy stuff in the early part of the week so that on the day of the big event, all you need to do is pick up. With some hospitality events, I was so exhausted by the time the guests arrived that I enjoyed nothing about the evening except the closing of the door behind the last guest on his way home. That was silly. If I had paced myself, what a difference it would have made!

*Lists*—Once again, lists make things easier because you aren't plagued with last-minute flashes of things that absolutely have to be done. I make lists for everything—perhaps I overdo it a bit. I start with my objective for the event and then build lists of ideas for the event, lists of people who might enjoy coming,

lists of people who RSVP'd, lists of food everyone will be bringing, and lists of the week- and day-before chores. I even make a list of the food that ought to be out on the table. I can count in double digits the number of times I opened the oven after the guests have gone to find unserved baked potatoes or opened the refrigerator to find an untouched gelatin mold.

Pair up with a girlfriend, boyfriend, or spouse. Divide the work and share the evening's fun. When I was single, two other friends and I made a Japanese dinner for about forty people from our church. It was a mammoth job, but we divided the work three ways and the feat was no longer amazing. Now, Jack and I plan together, work together on the ideas, and in the end enjoy the party together. It makes the whole process easier when one person doesn't have to do everything. I clean better than he does. Somehow he has never considered the fact that baseboards get dusty and it makes sense to clean them with all those guests coming to sit on the floor. On the other hand, I don't enjoy cooking as much as he does. He takes that responsibility out of my hands. It's really OUR party. Hospitality is not a feminine word.

## All Under One Roof

### An Unusual Progressive Dinner

What follows is an outline of an All-Under-One-Roof progressive dinner. Follow this pattern exactly if you wish. Or, use it as a starting point for ideas, and jump off from here into your own unique party.

*Objective:* To be a friendship starter between strong Christians and people in the church neighborhood. This idea is also an effective way for church groups to get to know one another better.

*Basic idea:* Plan a progressive dinner in your own home. People will progress from one room to another for each course. With each table or room change, they will eat with a different group of people.

An All-Under-One-Roof Progressive Dinner cuts down on the amount of time people spend driving from one house to the next. The party is ecologically sound! It also puts people into groupings they may not choose on their own.

This progressive dinner took place in three rooms of a four-room apartment. Two small tables were set in the living room, a larger one in the bedroom, and of course, we used the dining room table. My friend Caroline, Jack, and I each took a room that would be ours to serve. We three couldn't participate in the meal since our jobs involved serving our tables and running back and forth to the kitchen for refills.

But our primary goal was to encourage people to interact. Before the party, the three of us went over a number of gimmick topics we could use if it was obvious that a table group wasn't working. We would throw out questions like these:

"What's your opinion of house churches?"

"Share a compliment that someone has given you that has helped you define who you are. Anything you say will not be considered bragging."

"What kind of animal have you always thought you were most like! Why?"

My invitation mix was half singles and half married people, all from my church. In the group was a mix of people I knew were Christians and others who were probably seekers. At each table I wanted some married people and male and female singles. My party limit was determined by how many tables I could set and how much food a small kitchen could hold.

**INVITATION IDEA**

# ALL UNDER ONE ROOF

**PROGRESS WITH US FOR DINNER**
from the Living Room to the Bedroom to the
Dining Room

WHEN:

WHERE:

WHY: To build friendships in our community.

ALL UNDER ONE ROOF, we'll supply the food,
and you supply the noise.

When a person arrived, he or she was given a program indicating where that person would sit for each course. Each person might change tables or rooms or stay in the same room and have the table people change. It was great fun trying to put the whole pattern together. A program card would look like this:

> *ROBERT RICHARDSON*
> *Soup and Salad—Bedroom Table*
> *Main Course—Dining Room Table*
> *Dessert—Small Table in the*
> *Living Room.*

There were three courses and three moves for each person. The courses were soup and salad, main course, and dessert. We allowed about a half hour for each course, and about five minutes between courses for people to figure out where they were to go next.

I did not arrange who would sit where at each table. How the group placed itself was the group's decision. It was interesting that for the first course, most married people grouped themselves at one end of the table and the singles at the other. By the main course, people were a little more mixed, and by dessert, the mix was complete.

At our party, the first course was supposed to include home-

made cauliflower soup. Jack was taking a soup course at a cooking school and this was to be his one creative touch for the meal. To this day, he has no idea why the soup turned bad, but just minutes before the guests arrived, he discovered it tasted slightly carbonated. We three discussed how many might die if we served it, and decided not to take the chance. We flushed it, and as the front doorbell rang, Jack was dashing out the back door to the supermarket for cans of soup.

He had chopped onions for garnish on the cauliflower, and it went into the canned soup. Would you believe he got all sorts of compliments on his soup—and he accepted every one!

Depending on your group, you may want to implement these ideas.

1. With a church group, why not pray after each course? The people at each table would elect someone to thank God for the food that had been eaten and especially for the fellowship at the table during that half hour.

2. You might want to put questions for discussion under different plates.

Here are some ideas for questions:

"Share something you like about our neighborhood. Then pick someone else at your table to do the same."

"If you were starting a church in this neighborhood, what programs would you include?" (This question works effectively with both Christian and secular guests.)

"What would be some of the benefits and problems if our government decided to tax churches?"

"If you could pick your ideal age, what age would you be? Why?"

"Go around your table telling everyone's name. If you can't remember the name, tell something that you've picked up about the person during this course."

Conversation starters like these are easy to write yourself. If the question can be answered in a single word, it's probably not a good one—the answer will be over too quickly and doesn't force the person to share much about himself or herself. Try to think of questions that call for paragraph answers, and pick

subjects that might spark conversation.

Just because you're mixing Christians and non-Christians, don't assume a "churchy" question would be a turn-off. Just structure it so that opinions can be shared without sparking arguments. Think through how secular people might view the question, or how Christians might react negatively to it.

You may not need conversation starters at your tables, but when I am mixing people who don't know each other well, my motto is "Be Prepared." When a group of people is eating in dead silence, I get the urge to serve that cauliflower soup.

Just remember . . .

# *Be Prepared*

## PROGRESSIVE DINNER RECIPE IDEAS

Meal designed to serve 24

## First Course— Soup and Salad

### CAROL'S CORN CHOWDER
*12 large onions, chopped*
*8 medium potatoes, diced*
*4 cups chopped celery with leaves*
*1-1/2 teaspoons salt*

12 cups milk

4 cans cream style corn

Cover onions, potatoes, celery with water. Add salt. Cook until tender. Add milk and corn, and reheat. Add salt/pepper to taste.

### HERBED SALAD

4 heads lettuce, torn

1 package fried bacon (crispy), crumbled

1 dozen hard-boiled eggs, crumbled

Place bacon and egg crumbles over the torn lettuce.

### Dressing:

2 cups salad oil

4 small onions, sliced

2 cups white vinegar

3 Tablespoons mustard

1 cup sugar

3 Tablespoons lemon juice

Salad herbs

Mix ingredients and add herbs to taste. For example, add 2 Tablespoons of oregano or 2 teaspoons of dill weed. Refrigerate four days to allow flavor to penetrate.

## Main Course

### APRICOT CHICKEN

6 chickens cut in pieces

3 large jars apricot preserves

3 large jars French dressing

4 packages dried onion soup mix

8 Tablespoons Worcestershire sauce

Bake chicken in a buttered, uncovered baking dish for 1 hour at 350°. Mix the rest of the ingredients together, and at the end of the hour, add the sauce to the chicken. Cover tightly and cook 20 minutes longer, or until fork-tender.

### RICE

4 cups uncooked rice

4 5-ounce cans of water chestnuts, drained and sliced

8 cups hot water

4 Tablespoons butter or margarine

Toast rice in a shallow casserole at 350°. Stir occasionally so rice browns evenly. Blend remaining ingredients; stir into rice. Bake covered until rice is tender and liquid is absorbed (about 30 minutes).

Add a vegetable and rolls and butter if you wish.

## Dessert Course

### RASPBERRY ANGEL CAKE

4 angel food cakes

2 pudding mixes—vanilla is best

1 large jar of raspberry jelly

butter frosting

Carefully slice each cake horizontally to make three layers. Fill the first layer with pudding and the second with raspberry jelly. Frost with butter frosting.

# Roots

## Covered Dish Dinner

*Objective:* Participants from a church or a neighborhood will share backgrounds to build a basis for closer friendships.

*Basic idea:* Invite adults to bring a covered dish that says something about their historical or geographical roots. Plan the whole evening around the sharing of backgrounds. As people share recipes, childhood stories, facts about grandparents, they add enormous amounts to the little most of them know about each other. The more people share, the more a feeling of family and trust develops.

I have found that for parties that are this unusual, I need to give people some ideas of what I want them to do. This encourages them to think creatively. On this invitation, I've included my sample ideas. Feel free to delete mine and include your own.

The number of guests you have is limited only by floor space. You may want to supply coffee, tea, and punch, and your own Roots contribution, but the dinner will come walking through your door with your guests. (When I did this, most people brought a dish for six to ten people; I had more than enough food.)

When the guests arrive, have them write their names on slips and place them in a hat for a drawing after dinner.

Give them ROOT SHEETS. Before dinner and up to the time of the drawing, they are to talk to ten different people. From each they should get the answer to one question on the ROOT SHEET. Obviously the goal of this activity is to get people to talk. What they find out about the person's answer to a sheet question is not as important as what they say after the question has been answered.

Here are some sample items for a ROOT SHEET. Adjust yours. You'll probably find it necessary to push people a little at the beginning. Let them know that there will be a time of accountability for what they have learned!

## ROOT SHEET

- Find out an interesting story about someone's grandparents.
- Talk with a couple who each came from different parts of the country.
- What background quirks did they bring to their marriage?

## INVITATION IDEA

### ROOTS COVERED DISH PARTY

Share your roots. Dig into your personal history and come up with a dish that tells something about your ancestral or geographical background.

WHEN:

WHERE:

*For example:* Marlene is French, so she could bring French pastry. She and her brother grew up in Pennsylvania Dutch country, so he could bring pickled eggs.

Label your dish with its name and origin, and your name. Bring along copies of your recipe to share.

- Find someone who has a famous or infamous ancestor.
- Talk about a childhood experience a person would like to pass on to future generations.
- Share the funniest experience you can remember about a relative.
- Find someone who has a relative who could have been rich or famous if he had followed through on an opportunity. (For example, I have an uncle who had an opportunity to buy the property on which Disney World now stands for only a few dollars an acre. He didn't buy because he was sure an investment in a swamp would never pay off!)
- Find the person here who has the most living relatives he or she can identify by first names.
- Find someone who has lived in at least three completely different places. Which did he or she like best and why?
- Find someone who comes from the longest line of people who are in a similar trade.
- Find a couple who, without checking with each other, can give the maiden names of the other's mother and grandmother.

- Find someone who has an amazing childhood story and listen to it the whole way through.
- Ask someone to dig back into his or her middle school or junior high past and come up with something important that happened.
- Get someone to share something from his or her personal past that made that person blush.
- Ask someone who grew up in a Christian home to share the history of his or her parents' or grandparents' conversion.
- Ask someone to share a game he or she has played that originated in a geographic root area.

**ROOTED IN CHRIST**

At least a half hour before you want people to begin eating the ROOTS meal, ask three Christians to prepare "Rooted in Christ" prayers—just a sentence or two. The 30 minutes will give them time to think about what they will say, and perhaps even to write the prayer. Ask one to center her prayers on thanksgiving for this neighborhood's roots. Another should praise God for his family roots. The third should thank God for any friendship roots that deepen or begin to grow this evening.

If approached correctly, non-Christians will not be turned off by prayer. Recently I was at a large tourist ranch where several thousand people were served beef and beans on a tin plate. Before the meal, the master of ceremonies announced that he would pray a simple grace for the meal. He said, "I know this isn't the politically correct thing to do, but it's part of our heritage and part of the roots on which our country was built. We believe a lot of our problems would be solved if we could return to those roots." The largely secular crowd clapped.

Sample prayers are included here. If the people you have asked to pray don't understand what you're asking them to do, then allow them to read these samples. Encourage them to put their prayers into their own words.

### Thanksgiving for the Neighborhood's Roots

"Lord, thank you for the people who make up this neighborhood. We especially thank you for the children who will someday look back on this place as their roots. May they be happy and safe here, and may they feel our love for them and your love."

### Praise for Family Roots

"Thank you for our families—mothers, fathers, brothers, sisters—and also for those people who we consider family, because they have added immeasurably to our lives."

### Praise for Friendship Roots

"Thank you, Lord, for parties, for the times when we can get together, say hello, smile, and get excited about one another. Keep your hand on our conversations tonight. Guide the growth of our friendships."

Give people plenty of time to eat. Don't rush. Just the amazing array of foods should provide interesting conversation. Encourage food refills and exchange of recipes.

After the meal, draw three or four of the names you collected from all the guests and placed in the hat. Ask those people to share an interesting thing they discovered about someone in the ROOT SHEET conversations. This type of accountability is fun and no one will be embarrassed since each person is allowed to pick anything from the list to share. If Carl never got to number 7, no one else need know about it. He'll just share the answer he got to number 3.

At my ROOTS party, I gave prizes to the people whose names were drawn. I had small plants that had been rooted in water, so all their roots were exposed. They were silly extras that made the evening more fun.

After the planned ROOT activities were over, our guests stuck around for hours. They had no trouble at all growing friendships once the ROOTS had been planted.

## ROOT RECIPES

Once in a while, you'll find that someone will draw a blank on personal roots. So be prepared with a few recipes that cover large geographic areas. Supply these only when necessary—you wouldn't want someone not to come simply because he or she doesn't have a clue about what to bring. These recipes are simple, since usually the people who have trouble thinking of what to bring are not used to cooking.

### STEWED APPLES
(Good for anyone who comes from the northern sections of the United States.)
*6 apples, cored and quartered*
*1/3 cup sugar*
*lump butter*
*cinnamon (to taste)*

Add all ingredients except cinnamon to a small mount of water. Boil at low heat until apples are soft. Add cinnamon.

### BANANA WALDORF SALAD
(Good for anyone who comes from the southern sections of the United States.)
*3 large apples*
*1/2 cup celery*
*1/2 cup salad dressing*
*2 bananas*
*1/2 cup crumbled walnuts*
*lettuce*
Mix ingredients and serve on lettuce. Serves 6.

### FISH STEW
(Good for anyone who comes from a seacoast region.)
*1 Tablespoon cooking oil*
*1 clove garlic, chopped*
*1/2 cup chopped onion*
*1/3 cup chopped green pepper*
Sauté in a Dutch oven or a large saucepan.

*1 - 1-1/2 lbs flounder or white fish, cut up.*
*1/4 pound mushrooms, sliced (optional)*
*2 cups cooked tomatoes*
*3/4 cup tomato paste*
*1 cup chicken broth*
*1 Tablespoon lemon juice*
*1 small bay leaf*
*1/2 teaspoon dried oregano*
*1 teaspoon sugar*

*3/4 teaspoon salt*

*1/8 teaspoon pepper*

Add these ingredients, excluding the fish, to those you have sautéed. Cook uncovered for 20 minutes. Add fish and cook 10 to 15 minutes longer, or until fish flakes easily.

Serve over rice or spaghetti. Serves 6.

## Trifle

(Good for anyone with English background.)

*1 package yellow or white cake mix*

*1 can fruit cocktail (any combination of fruit can be mixed here—bananas, strawberries, blueberries, etc.)*

*1 cup vanilla pudding*

Bake cake. When cool, cut into large bite-sized pieces. Add the fruit, including juice, and the custard to the cake. Stir gently. Chill several hours. Can be served with a garnish of sweetened whipped cream.

## Corn Bread

(Good for a person with farming background or ancestors.)

*3/4 cup cornmeal*

*1-1/2 cup flour*

*5 teaspoons baking powder*

*1 teaspoon salt*

*1/4 cup sugar*

*2 large eggs*

*1 cup milk*

*1/4 cup melted butter*

Grease and flour a 9" x 9" pan. Sift dry ingredients together. Beat eggs one half minute. Add milk and beat another half minute. Add liquid to dry ingredients. Blend. Add melted butter, and mix only until blended. Spread in pan. Bake at 375° for about 15 minutes or until golden brown. Cool about 10 minutes before loosening and cutting into squares.

# Yawn!

### A Board Party

***Objective:*** People across age levels (church group or a Christian/secular mix) will have opportunities to build friendships as they compete in simple board games.

***Basic idea:*** Bring back a few of the old parlor games, and structure round robin games around them. After games, serve do-it-yourselves soup and salad.

If your group will include younger Generation X and Generation Next people, throw in a few computer games. This will give the younger people in the group an opportunity to teach the older. Teens often see computers as their pen and paper, lifestyle, and religion.

One teen said, "I live to plug into my real community on the Internet. I feel closer to friends there than I do to the kids who live next door. Most older people I know approach computer skills as if they are from an ancient planet." As these under-25s teach the less computer savvy to play games, face-to-face friendships may develop. *Youth Markets ALERT* reported that 96% of today's young people are computer literate.

## PREPARATION

*Collect games.* I never have enough, so I ask other guests to bring some along. If your friends are like mine, you might want to line up more boards than you'll need. People often forget.

I set up the games everywhere—on window seats, tables, and floors. And I've never been a purist about the board angle of the party. Pick-Up-Sticks is a great game. So are Jacks. Tiddlywinks can also help adults rid themselves of inhibitions.

I number each game location. When people come, they draw one number out of each of three bags—a red bag, a green bag, and a grocery bag. For the first game, everyone goes to the board with the number on the red tag; for the second game he or she goes to the one numbered on his green tag; finally comes the grocery bag tag.

Be careful setting this up. You have to be certain you know the number of people coming so you'll have the right number of numbers and games. You also have to be careful to have the right number of tags in each bag to successfully play different games. For example, Chinese Checkers only takes two people. So if that game is number six, you should have no more than two number six cards in each bag. You'll want four people for Sorry. So you'll need four slips for this game in each bag.

(Exception: If you use computer games, assign one person who knows how to play each game. If a teen plays a computer game for one setting, she should draw cards for the other two.)

This party mixes people beautifully, and since numbers are drawn, people rarely will play the same people twice. It's also a great party for mixing people of all ages, from high school kids right up to people of grandparent age.

I allow about twenty minutes for each game. There are just three scheduled games in an evening, and that allows about an hour for the soup to simmer. After the soup and salad meal,

**INVITATION IDEA**

# YAWN!
# A BOARD
# PARTY

---

### YAWN—WE'RE "BOARD"

Come and be "board" with us.

We're planning an evening of good, old-fashioned board games. Come play!

WHEN:

WHERE.

Food? Sure! We're making Whatever Soup. We'll have the stock simmering and you bring something to add to the stock. The soup will be what you make it.

Or, bring something to add to the lettuce.

We promise you won't be bored!

the planned part of the evening is over. The games are only the excuse around which hospitality is extended.

## FOOD SUGGESTIONS

This party is limited only by the size of your soup kettle! Provide the soup stock to which your guests will add the extras. Dry bouillon (dehydrated cubes) or chicken broth make excellent stock.

You may have guests ask for ideas of what to add. For the soup, suggest carrots, potatoes, noodles, rice, chicken pieces, turnips, corn, celery—and the list goes on.

For the salad, suggest beets, bean sprouts, cheese, croutons, garbanzo beans, sunflower seeds, crumbled hard-boiled eggs, green pepper, bacon bits, turkey or ham slices, shredded carrots, olives, cauliflower—and the list also goes on.

## IDEAS

Before soup is served, ask a Christian guest to thank God for the diversity in the foods He made. Ask another Christian guest to thank God for the diversity in the people he made.

*Sample Prayers*

On diversity in food: "We have all brought something to add to the soup and salad, Lord, and with each addition we are reminded of how much we have. What a creative God you are! Thank you for the texture of the turnip and the fine hardiness of the potato. Thank you for the common sense of lettuce and the taste of excitement the tomato adds. What fun you must have had making all these foods. We appreciate you, God, and praise you for your creativity."

On diversity in people: "Thank you, God, for the many different people you have brought together in this room— for people who can talk easily, for people who giggle, for those who can bear prayer burdens, for those who preach and teach. Not one of us is a carbon copy of another. And like our additions to the soup and salad, each of us adds texture and unique taste to your creation. Thank you that I am part of this mix."

*Name the Soup*

Why not sponsor a little contest! Everything needs a name. The group will have created a unique and totally original soup and salad. What in the world should people name their creations? Give everyone three-by-five cards and ask those who wish to participate in naming the creations to put suggestions in a box. Choose some perfectly partial judges to pick the winning names! Perhaps these winners could take home some of the leftovers.

## A Word About Cupid

I'm all for the little fellow! But with common sense.

I have often invited people I thought would enjoy each other to my parties, but what happens after they get there is up to them. Dating is healthy. If two people can meet and talk and enjoy each other at a hospitality event, and later also enjoy dating, that's grand. What better place for people to meet than in a Christian home?

Jack and I were happy single. But part of our contentment can be traced back to our friendships with other singles. Friends —girl friends and boy friends— are a part of healthy single life.

My friend Karen introduced Jack and me. She told him that I was the type of girl he might enjoy dating. I doubt that he would have noticed me if she hadn't pointed. But she cared enough to point. And he trusted her judgment enough to ask me to a play. We talked through the entire evening, and we haven't stopped talking since. She pointed us in the direction

of friendship.

I'd even go so far as to suggest Christian obligation in this context. Whole businesses are built around providing secular places for singles to meet. My single Christian friends don't belong in a singles bar. But if the alternative is sitting at home alone, can I blame them for heading in that direction? A local country western radio station encourages singles to submit their requirements to a computer dating service and the computer will guarantee the perfect date. I've made some funny blunders when I tried matchmaking, but I still think I'm more effective than a computer.

I have a set of rules that I usually follow in my self-appointed task of dating yenta.

First, let things happen. It's usually enough just to invite people to the house. I provide activities that allow them to come with or without dates and not feel left out or different.

Second, don't hesitate to bring up the subject of dating. So two people never did meet at a party but they would enjoy dating—or at least I think they might. Why not suggest it? If either says no, what has been lost? What have I lost? And, they rarely say no.

Recently I was talking with my girlfriend Dale. "I think you might enjoy meeting Skip. How would you feel about going out to dinner with him? Maybe a double date."

"I'd be scared to death," she said.

"Does that mean no?"

"It means yes. I'd be scared, but I'd do it. It's just one evening out of my lifetime, and I think once I quit shaking, I'll have a good time."

As far as I know, not one person has ever met a mate because I opened my home for hospitality. That's fine with me. But I do know many, many who have built friendships with other singles, and enjoyed being single more because of it.

"I haven't dated since my divorce," Jean said. "I'm lonesome, and frankly, I feel ugly. Last night I ended up playing Pick-Up-Sticks with Phil, and for the first time in ages I was laughing and feeling less like a loser."

"I lost the crazy game," she admitted. "But it was important to know that someone of the opposite sex was having a good time with me."

Third, move out of the picture. Once I've done my introduction, suggestion, or first double date, it's over. I pull out. It's important for people not to feel pressured into friendship or somehow guilty if it's obvious that my dating match was a mismatch. What happens in their relationship has nothing to do with the friendship I've built with them as individuals. Meddling can be manipulative and dangerous.

Single is wonderful. It's a lifestyle some people choose, and others, for one reason or another, are part of. And it can be a lot more fun when it includes friendships with other singles, married couples, and families.

On the lighter side, an unattributed article on the Internet suggested ways for a guy to find a wife, patterning how several men in the Bible did it.

- Find an attractive prisoner of war, bring her home, shave her head, trim her nails, and give her new clothes. Then she's yours. (Deut. 21:11-13.)

- Find a man with seven daughters, and impress him by watering his flock. (Moses, in Exodus 2:16-21.)

- Have God create a wife for you while you sleep. This will cost you a rib. (Adam, in Genesis 2:19-24.)

- Become the emperor of a huge nation and hold a beauty contest. (Xerxes, in Esther 2:3, 4.)

- A wife? . . . hmm . . . bad idea. (Paul, in 1 Cor. 7:32-35.)

## Mystery Bag Supper

*Objective:* To encourage each person from our church to talk with a large number of others, getting to know them in a casual, non-threatening alternative to the traditional church supper.

*Basic idea:* Everyone will pack a bag supper and include in his or her bag an identity clue. The host couple will mix up the bags before everyone picks one at random. The meal activity involves each person discovering whose bag supper he or she is eating.

This inexpensive party is limited only by the number of people the host can pack in. The host is responsible only for punch and coffee, and everything else is part of the bag. This idea also makes a great replacement for the traditional covered dish supper. I like church suppers, but often the food is cold by the time my group gets

served, and more important, we sit at long tables—usually with our friends who are saving us seats. So I'm limited in the people I can get to know better.

"Sandy's a new Christian," her friend told me. "The monthly church supper was her first experience with a Christian social. She was so excited, but when we got to the church, everyone seemed at home with friends. It was as though the circles were closed. We ended up sitting with the one lady in the whole church we already knew. She's great, but we had looked forward to the evening as an opportunity to increase the number of people we could greet by name."

"I wish we could have moved around a little," Sandy said. "It was almost like sitting in the pews and eating—nice long rows of Christians munching!"

Obviously an important clue to the success of the Mystery Bag Supper is being in a place where you can move about a little to check with people throughout the room about their clues. When I tried this supper, I had most of the people sitting on the floor in constantly changing groupings. There were little footpaths people followed as they searched for the person behind their bag's clues.

**INVITATION IDEA**

# MYSTERY BAG SUPPER

### Shhhhh! Follow these directions.

1. Pack a great bag supper
2. Include a clue to your identity in the bag

WHEN:

WHERE:

**Mystery Question:** *By the end of this evening, what new friends will you have made?*

Clues are important. Encourage people to write reasonable, but not easy, ones—clues that could possibly be discovered by people at the church.

For example, I'm a high school Sunday school teacher, so my first clue for our church might be:

"Before the doxology has been sung, I get a taste of feeling young!"

Now that clue doesn't give me away, but it does put me in the Sunday school somewhere, and even someone who has no idea who I am would have a starting place. He could ask others, "Are you in the Sunday school? Do you teach? Did you pack this supper?"

## EXPANDING THE SUPPER

Mystery Bag Supper can be the total activity of the evening, especially if it precedes the Sunday evening service. Or it can be expanded. Here are some ways to expand the mystery supper into a total mystery evening. Pick the ideas that would work best in your group. Add your own special touches of creativity.

### Mystery Speaker

Announce that there are going to be three mystery speakers. In fact, the mystery is so deep that the speakers don't even know who they will be.

The mystery speaker idea has a getting-to-know-you flavor, adding a rather unique Christian emphasis. For your three speakers, pick guests who have little trouble talking in front of the group. Interview each person, using questions that will encourage paragraph answers. Some ideas follow.

Ask the first mystery guest speaker these questions (be sure to pick someone you are certain is a Christian):

1. Share your name. Tell how you came to have your first name(s).
2. If you could have one contemporary person as a mystery guest in your home, who would you choose and why?
3. What might you serve this person for dinner? Why?
4. If you had about an hour with this person after dinner, what questions would you ask?
5. If Jesus were coming to your house for supper, what three very recent happenings in your life would you like to thank him for?

Ask the second mystery guest speaker these questions (pick a person you know has a strong Christian witness):

1. Share your name and give a little background on your last name.
2. If you were on a mystery plane ride and you knew you could have the plane land anywhere in the world, where would you want to land; why?
3. What are some of the things you would like to do after you land?
4. Suppose you discovered that most of the people in this country knew nothing about your God, but they all spoke your language. What things would you share with them?
5. Suppose Jesus gave you an envelope in which he had placed the mystery location where he wants you to serve Him. He tells you not to open it until you are certain you are willing to be a living testimony for him. You pray, and make the decision to open the envelope. Inside is your home address along with the addresses of most of the people in your immediate area (block, apartment building, small town). What things would you immediately get busy doing?
6. You get such a good response that you decide to ask God for additional helpers in your area. What qualities would you want these new workers to

have? Why is each quality you mention so important?

Ask the third mystery guest speaker these questions (pick someone who is active in the church):

1. It's always been a mystery to non-Christians why we give up Sunday morning sleep to go to church. Pretend I'm a non-Christian neighbor who has just asked, "Is church really worth all the trouble you go through to get there?" Answer assuming that I'm really interested in a serious answer and it could make a difference in my life.
2. Suppose you are the mystery speaker at our Sunday evening service. No one knows you'll be speaking, but you want to do your best to get everyone out to the meeting. What things would you do to attract people's interest in the service?
3. Why do you like our church?
4 Suppose someone in your neighborhood says, "People who go to church are dull. Name me one who isn't." Go the second mile and name him three people in our church who aren't dull, and share what makes these people exciting. Share two things about our church you think we should praise God for.

*Some help for the interviewer*

Of course, you will pick mystery speakers who talk easily in front of people, but you still carry a lot of responsibility for keeping things light and moving. Most of the guests' questions will be easy to answer. But suppose someone has been asked to share three things and he or she draws a blank after two. That's fine. You can add a third, or simply move onto the next question.

Often an extemporaneous speaker will not fully develop an idea. You can help by asking, "Can you tell us more about that?" Or, "How might you go about that?"

Encourage your guest speakers. They are answering in difficult, unprepared situations. Affirm them. Saying things like this will help: "That's a very creative answer"; "What a good idea; I wish some of us would try it"; "For an off-the-cuff speaker, you're excellent."

Look at the guest when that person is talking. Know the questions that you will ask well enough to get involved in the speaker's contribution. Smile when it's appropriate. Encourage when necessary. Add something if you think it would be helpful, but be careful not to steal the show from the guest.

After all, you've had time to think about the questions, and he or she has not.

You can involve the audience. After the mystery speaker has given some good ideas, you could turn to the whole group and say, "OK, here's your chance. What would you add?"

If you get an overly-talkative speaker, you may want to interrupt with the next question. Each speaker should be on stage for no more than five minutes. This allows for fifteen minutes of speaking—the length of the average adult's listening limit.

*Mystery Games*

Why not use basic game plans with which people are familiar, but add a mystery twist?

**MYSTERY RHYMES**

Write one line of double couplet rhymes on slips of paper. Hide these slips throughout the church. Each guest should hunt until he or she finds one slip of paper. That person then begins searching for others who found lines that rhyme with his or hers. There are four slips in each rhyme, so there will be four people in each group. (You may also want to number each slip so people will find it even easier to decide who is in their group.)

When all four people in a

group have found each other, they should arrange their rhyme in an order that makes sense and prepare to recite it to the group.

The first group to find all four of its people wins. If you have an uneven number, announce that a group may discover that all people have rhyme slips and it's still missing one or two. The whole group searches for the missing slips and will then read more than one line per person when it shares with everyone.

Use as many of these rhymes as you need. Or if you need more, make up your own.

1. *We want you all to know*
1. *When high winds gust and blow*
1. *When falls the rain and snow*
1. *To church we still will go*

2. *It's not the living end*
2. *The rules we want to bend*
2. *It's not a sin to lend*
2. *Nursery duty to a friend*

3. *I go to hear what's written*
3. *It seems quite right and fittin'*
3. *I squirm like a baby kitten*
3. *I think I'm tired of sittin'*

4. *What is that awful wail?*
4. *The church all turns pale*
4. *The choir has missed the trail*
4. *That note's not on the scale*

5. *We've got a goodly hunch*
5. *Hashed preacher's had for lunch*
5. *Things would improve a bunch*
5. *If we'd pray before we crunch*

6. *No trouble when it's light*
6. *Sunday brings the church in sight*
6. *But something's not quite right*
6. *We can't find it Wednesday night*

7. *Gossip is the word I fear*
7. *It can burn and it can sear*
7. *But would it cost so dear*
7. *If we remembered God can hear*

## MYSTERY CHARADES

Follow all the rules for charades, but set the idea around the word *mystery* rather than the more normal categories of song titles, plays, or books.

If the two sides have difficulties thinking of mystery topics which the other side must act out, get them started with these few suggestions:

*Ah, Sweet Mystery of Life*
*Sherlock Holmes*
*Agatha Christie*
*Murder on the Orient Express*
*The Hardy Boys*
*Nancy Drew*
*The Mouse Trap*
*The mystery guest (or word)*

## I'VE GOT A MYSTERY

Ask a number of people to come prepared with a mystery to share. If they need samples, you could share these:

"I lost the diamond from my ring, and to this day I haven't found it."

"My son has an interest in mechanics, and there hasn't been a mechanical person in my family for generations. It's a mystery to me where he gets his talent."

"I'm teaching a class of ten senior high boys and two girls. It's a mystery to me why the girls don't just flock in."

Before the game write the mysteries on large cards so they can be shown to the audience, but not those guessing what the mystery is.

Model "I've Got a Mystery" after the old television program "I've Got a Secret." Choose four panel members at random from the guests. They each take turns asking the person with a question about the mystery. Each question must be answered with a yes or no. A panelist continues asking questions until that person gets a no. Then it's the next panelist's turn.

Panelists should start asking broad questions and work down to specifics. For example, "Does your secret involve a person?" "A person in your family?" "Your son Joshua?"

At any time during the questioning, the host may yell "CLUE!" At this point, the person with the mystery must share a substantial clue.

When a panelist guesses a mystery, award that panel member a small prize, retire that person, and choose another member.

## MYSTERY COLLECTION

Ask guests to put their Christ-centered project ideas into a bag. Explain that one of these projects will be chosen and the offering will go to that project. These projects might include special church-related projects or special gifts to missionaries, etc.

After the offering has been taken and counted, have someone draw a project, sight unseen, from the bag and read it. Appoint someone to make sure the donation is delivered.

# Slightly Smaller
## (and not a bit less fun)

*God weaves miracles into our hearts.
In my case, it's the miracle of offering a simple,
flawed hospitality instead of striving for the
"hostess with the mostest" award.*

—Judith Couchman

RUTH WAS THE MOST amazing hostess I've known. She lived in a tiny one-room apartment, just barely big enough for a bed and chair and hot plate. But she believed in hospitality. Even though she had no table, she invited two friends from her church family for dinner. While the two sat on the bed and she on the chair, she served dinner—complete and delicious and all done on her hot plate.

Since Ruth's dinner party, I've believed that there is no space too small to allow friendship and Christian community to happen.

After a Scrabble Marathon in our apartment, a woman told me, "I've never done any entertaining. Perhaps I've been waiting to get married and have a home and the trappings before I got involved. But I think the time has come." She explained that she was telling me about it so that if she chickened out, I'd remind her of her obligation and hold her accountable.

Her first party was a great success. Once people catch on to the excitement of laughing together, the enthusiasm for body life multiplies. And some of that enthusiasm can be life changing.

"I met a lot of people tonight," a guest told Jack. "I talked in depth with several of them. For the first time, I'm sure I would be missed at church if I didn't show up next Sunday."

I had a friend in college who shared, "I always feel a little guilty when I have too much fun. Somehow, it doesn't seem quite Christian." That's sad. A party can be a gift from God. It can be the refresher that makes it possible for us to go out and try again. There have been times when I've been so dead tired, so washed out, that I would have dropped if I had had the energy to fall. Sometimes what I needed was two consecutive nights of eight hours' sleep. Other times it was my soul that was weary. Those times, what I needed was an opportunity to laugh.

Playing times can be very Christian times!

## Come As You Aren't

*Objective:* To provide an opportunity for non-Christians and Christians to enjoy their creativity, and in the process, to encourage non-Christians to rethink their stereotypes of church people.

Many people have never known any Christians, and many

of today's teens and young adults have never been in a church. They don't know what Christians mean when they talk about "the sanctuary." They've never heard a sermon. Rev. Jana Childers quoted poet-theologian Amos Wilder at the American Guild of Organists' Region VIII convention in Portland Oregon. Wilder says that going to church should be like "approaching an open volcano where the world is molten and hearts are sifted. The altar is like a third rail that spatters sparks. The sanctuary is like a chamber next to an atomic oven; there are invisible rays and you must leave your watch outside" (reported in *Context*, Feb. 1, 1996). Yes, I've been to sermons like that, and I pity Christians who haven't and non-Christians who have defined the Christian life from clichés, news of litigation, and TV portrayals.

A pastor at a Baptist church I visited in Anchorage, Alaska, told me that he had sponsored an open house for the church and invited the community to walk through. "We wanted people who have never been inside a church building to walk through. We wanted to diminish the scare factor," he said. "We didn't play organ music or hand out tracts. We just invited people

to walk through and see what is inside. One woman who took the tour told me, 'I like this place. It's peaceful and I'll consider coming back. But what I don't understand is why a building this small needs a Jacuzzi.'"

***Basic Idea:*** For this party, every Christian guest should invite someone he or she believes needs this type of evening, this type of demonstration that the Christian life includes creativity. This is a costume party—the type of costume will be determined by the type of party you choose. Each guest or couple must be prepared to give a two-to-four-minute reading that explains or expands the costumes. Guests will be asked to be creative visually and vocally.

Come As You Aren't is an opportunity for a fun party, and in the process, Christians may discover new talent to use for God. When someone dares to speak aloud at a party, she might also be willing to read a poem on Sunday morning that fits with the worship aim the pastor has established.

A friend told me recently that her pastor in St. Louis dressed as King David, and delivered his whole sermon on the Psalms from David's first-person perspective. It made the

## INVITATION IDEA

Your invitation will have to change to suit the type of party you pick. Here's one idea:

# COME AS YOU AREN'T

## VALENTINE COSTUME PARTY

TIME:

PLACE:

*Occasion-Valentining!*
*All costumes strange and*
  *shining*
*Fashion redefining*

*Great couples symbolizing*
*In costumed look devising*
*A first-night show arising*

*Come as a famous pair!*

**Bring along a 2-to-4-minute reading about your pair.**

PAIR EXAMPLES:
**Romeo and Juliet**—*read a bit from the play*
**Abraham and Sarah**—*do a dialogue based on the Bible story*
**Mashed Potatoes and Gravy**—*Do a reading from Betty Crocker*

experiences of the shepherd, outlaw, and king come alive in a new way. She was so excited about the effect the costume had on the congregation that she talked the pastor into giving the sermon again on a child's level in Children's Church.

One little boy's mother called the week after her son had heard the David-clad minister. "What are you doing at your church?" she asked. "My little boy is totally convinced that a Bible character came to life and talked on Sunday. He can't wait for next Sunday."

I wish our costume party had been held a little closer to St. Louis. I'd have invited that pastor to the party. I'd have asked him to help us spot hidden talent, those who have never been asked to participate in our church service because we never thought of them. And more importantly, we may discover people who gain enough confidence in their creative skills to say yes the next time they are asked to glorify God in a special way in the church.

## COSTUME PARTY DIRECTIONS

Here are some costume theme ideas:

*Famous pair*—this makes an interesting Valentine idea, and this is the one I chose.

*Famous book character*—especially good if you'll be inviting a lot of college students.

*Biblical characters*—for an event that involves just church attendees. I can't remember where I saw the cartoon that depicted a totally naked kid running around a room full of other children in biblical costumes. The Sunday school superintendent was telling the teacher, "There's no way you could have known, Mrs. Jones, that when you planned a biblical costume party Jamie would come as Adam before the fall!"

*Childhood heroes or nursery rhyme characters*—enter Batman!

*Costumes from a specific historic period*—perhaps 18th Century.

At the Famous Pair party we attended, the invitation gave several examples of costumes people might use. This helped get their ideas flowing, and it also told the guests that this was not a totally sophisticated party. How in the world would any pair come as mashed potatoes and gravy? No one picked up that challenge, but two friends came as an egg and bacon.

Jack and I went around and around on our costumes. It made the pre-party time fun, and we never dreamed we could have come up with so many great—though mostly unworkable—ideas. For example, we talked about being the yellow pages and fingers—playing on the ad, "Let your fingers do the walking through the yellow pages." I could have made a dress made from the yellow pages of an old directory. Jack could have gotten a pair of long johns that we would paint. His body would be the partial fist and his legs could be the two fingers walking. What fun! We finally settled on butler and maid costumes—typecasting for our roles that evening.

## WHO TO INVITE

This is a very demanding party, and we invited people we thought would enjoy the challenge. We began with several who are life-of-the-party-type people. We knew they would help carry the evening and make everyone less self-conscious because they would be so free and self-assured.

To this we added a number of people we thought might enjoy this kind of party. If we were wrong, they could always RSVP with, "Sorry, but that's the evening I always cut my cat's nails." In a way, it's these people who make the party special. When they get excited and

share, it's as though the lights flash, and we yell, "Discovered! New talent! How can this talent be channeled for Christ?"

Recently I was asked to put together a choral reading for Sunday worship, and all the people I asked agreed to participate. We even had a practice session. But twenty-four hours before the service, the people began backing out. I was new at the church and had involved everyone I knew. I learned that when friends fail, you ask total strangers! I called Robert. He said yes, and what a job he did! Later he told me how pleased he was with this opportunity. "I have always been afraid to get up in front of people. That's silly, so I've been taking a speech course. I was praying for an opportunity to test how much I was learning."

Funny how God lets us stumble onto people He needs!

Idea: each person from the church is required to invite someone who doesn't go to church. The church person and the person he or she invites work together as a famous pair. Make certain singles know that pairs can be same-gender. Two girls, for example, could come as the kitchen cleanser, Spic n' Span.

Be open to the possibilities.

## READINGS FOR PAIRS

Since these readings are short, people usually enjoy them rather than panic over them.

At our party, one couple pantomimed their Sesame Street characters' voices as a record played. Others came as "Two Peas in a Pod." They read directly from an encyclopedia, and were very clever in emphasizing certain portions so the reading was actually hilarious. (For example, did you know that several hundred years ago, it was considered very poor taste to eat peas in a public place?) Samson and Delilah read from a children's story book, and Delilah actually cut Samson's hair as part of her reading.

Jack and I couldn't find anything on a butler and maid, so we developed the following sequence.

JACK:
The stage lights grow dim.
Drama's plans are laid.
The Master's been shot;
It's the butler or the maid.

MARLENE:
Tiptoeing through time
We're fully aware
That history's not made
Without them there.

JACK:
Who cut the apple
On which Eve fed!
Who gave Jael the nail
For old Sisera's head!

BOTH:
The butler and the maid!

JACK:
Who opened doors
For all Caesar's life!
Who cleaned up the mess
From friend Brutus' knife!

BOTH:
The butler and the maid.

JACK:
Who saddled elephants
For Hannibal's ride?
Who dusted Cleo's face
By Anthony's side?

BOTH:
The butler and the maid.

MARLENE:
Who steeped the tea
While Luther wrote!
Who made the meals
He ate writing notes?

JACK:
Who knows their names?
Only a few.
There's Hazel and Jeffery;
There's me and there's you.

BOTH:
Life's front stage fills
With many an actor,
But the maid and butler
Are its one stable factor.

### A COSTUME VOTE

Ask all guests to rate the other guests' costumes and readings. You may want to use ballots that are like this.

### VOTE FOR SECOND BEST

Tell the group, "We know that your costume is obviously the best one here. No doubt! So we would like you to vote for the second best in the following categories:

(1) Second best total costume;
(2) Second funniest costume;
(3) Second best reading."

Just hearing that they have won will probably be award enough for the lucky couple. But you might want to go a bit further.

Adjust your prizes to the type of party you have chosen. For example, if you have a valentine party, give boxes of valentine candy. To the Second Best Total Costume, we, the butler and the maid, awarded a free dinner at our favorite restaurant—with us along, of course. This gave us a chance to get to know two guests from the party even better.

If you are doing famous book characters, you might award famous paperbacks or new Christian books that you're sure most people have not yet read.

If you do biblical characters, you might give study guides on famous characters in the Bible. There are some excellent books out there on Paul, Abraham, Moses, Mary, and others.

### PRAYER BEFORE THE FOOD

Ask three guests to pray, each concentrating on a specific aspect of the night's fellowship.

*Person 1:* Thank God for His gift of creativity.
*Person 2:* Praise God for our voices—to use in fun and in service for Him.
*Person 3:* Thank God for His provision of food beyond our needs.

If you wish, share the following prayers with Christians who will be praying. It may help them focus on what you want to do. Or you may want to copy these prayers and have them read. If so, make certain the reader is in full agreement with what is said. Do not ask people to share anything that may ring hollow.

*Person 1:* Thank God for His gift of creativity.

You created the world, God, and all the intricate and enormous parts of it. How can we doubt Your creativity when we hear that You never repeat a snowflake design or when we watch an autumn woods put on its coat of many colors? And how can we doubt Your creativity when we look around this room? Thanks for the fun of the evening, and for the creative minds You gave us that allow us to play. May I be willing to put as much effort into the more serious creative tasks that You put into my path.

*Person 2:* Praise God for our voices.

Thank You, Lord, that You made us with the power to communicate. Not only can we use an exciting variety of words, but we can give them expression and accent and tone. What fun to have a voice! Thank You for the voices that were part of this evening. And I pray that You will use our voices, and my voice, effectively in the more serious matters on Your agenda. Tonight was easy, Lord, and fun. I'm glad You were here and part of our activities. Tomorrow may not be as easy, Lord. But I want You to know how happy I am that tomorrow You will be there, and part of everything I do.

*Person 3:* Thank God for His provision of food beyond our needs.

Food is very special, Lord, and sometimes I miss that fact as I rattle through predictable thanks. Tonight let me pray with thought. Thank You for the food You've made. Not one of us would starve without it tonight, and perhaps we would never even feel terribly hungry. So it's a special extra from You. How loving of you to provide it for us. Thank You for party foods. What a creative gift for You to give.

**FOOD IDEAS**

Why not have any great dessert you are good at making!

Or you could follow your party idea straight through the food. For example, in the famous book characters, ask each pair to bring a dessert they think their character would enjoy. Each dessert should be labeled with the name of the character. For example, if someone came as a Hobbit from *The Lord of the Rings*, he might bring along Hobbit Seed Cakes.

## Hobbit Seed Cakes

*1 cup butter*
*1-1/2 cups sugar*
*1 can poppy seed filling*
*4 eggs, separated*
*1 teaspoon vanilla*
*1/2 teaspoon nutmeg*
*1/2 teaspoon cinnamon*

1 cup sour cream
2-1/2 cups sifted enriched flour
1 teaspoon baking soda
1 teaspoon salt

Cream butter and sugar until light and fluffy. Add poppy seed filling. Add egg yolks one at a time, beating well after each addition. Blend in vanilla, nutmeg, cinnamon, and sour cream. Sift together flour, soda, and salt. Add to poppy mixture, beating well after each addition. Fold in stiffly beaten egg whites. Pour into greased muffin tins.

Bake in a 350° oven for about 20 minutes or until done. Allow cupcakes to cool about 5 minutes. Remove from tins.

For a Valentine pairs party, all desserts could be either red and/or white, for example, red and white Jell-O cake.

### RED AND WHITE JELL-O CAKE

3 packages (3 ounces each) red flavored Jell-O (vary the shades of red by using cherry, raspberry, black cherry)
3 cups boiling water
2 cups cold water
1 cup cherry juice
1/4 cup sugar
1 package raspberry Jell-O
1 cup cold milk
1 teaspoon vanilla
2 cartons whipping cream

Prepare the first three flavors of Jell-O separately, using 1 cup hot water and 1/2 cup cold water for each. Pour each into a shallow pan; chill overnight.

Mix cherry juice and sugar; heat until sugar dissolves. Remove from heat and dissolve raspberry Jell-O in hot liquid. Add 1/2 cup cold water. Chill until syrupy.

Combine milk, vanilla, and stiffly whipped cream in a bowl. Blend until mixture forms soft peaks. Fold into syrupy Jell-O.

Cut the three red shades of Jell-O into small cubes and fold into the raspberry mixture. Pour into a 9-inch angel food cake pan. Chill 9 hours. Unmold. Spread top and sides with whipped cream and coconut. Decorate with red candy hearts. Serves 14 to 16.

If you have a biblical costume party as a church hospitality event, you might encourage people to bring recipes that have some Bibleland flavor. When guests arrive, you might serve stuffed dates.

### STUFFED DATES

Stuff pitted dates with walnuts, marshmallows, cream cheese, candied fruits, or anything else that sounds like it might make an interesting bite-sized goodie.

Or what could be more appropriate than Heavenly Hash!

## HEAVENLY HASH

*1/2 pound dates*
*1 medium can chunk pineapple*
*1 medium size jar maraschino cherries*
*1 cup miniature marshmallows*
*1/2 pint whipped cream*

Cut dates into small pieces and mix all ingredients together with the stiffly whipped cream. (Do not use a ready mixed whipped topping.) Sprinkle the top with ground or chopped nuts. Serves 8 to 10.

If you are doing costumes from colonial days, you might consider a blueberry pudding that can be served either hot or cold. Ask guests to bring other desserts.

## BLUEBERRY PUDDING

*1 quart blueberries*
*2 cups sugar*
*3 Tablespoons butter*
*1/2 teaspoon salt*
*1/8 teaspoon cinnamon*
*3/4 cup water*
*1 loaf bread*

Combine blueberries, sugar, butter, salt, cinnamon, and water in a saucepan. Bring to a boil and simmer 10 minutes, stirring occasionally. Remove crusts from bread and cut slices into 1-inch squares. Lay half of the bread squares on the bottom of a 9-inch square serving dish. Pour half the hot blueberry mixture over the bread. Repeat process with remaining bread squares and blueberry mixture. Chill for two hours. Serve plain or with a dollop of whipped cream. Serves 8.

If you are a gourmet cook, you may realize that most of the recipes here are simple and make use of ingredients that are easy to find. I've chosen them because I can make them. This means even someone who isn't a great cook—me, for example— can be successful. If an untried cook asks you for an idea for what he or she can bring to an event, you can safely suggest most of these recipes.

Cooking has always scared me. When I got my first job as a newspaper reporter, I was terrified to discover that one day a week, I was the food editor. Luckily, all I had to do was page through the recipes that various food companies sent and pick the ones that made me hungry. A year later when I left the job, the managing editor told me that the paper had gotten a number of calls over my tenure from people in their twenties who were just realizing that life included knowing how to turn on a stove. They appreciated my simple choices. "But," he added, (before I had time to bask in the joys of simplicity), "our next editor will be someone who knows what tarragon is just so we don't lose the other half of our circulation."

## Scrabble Marathon

*Objective:* Church and non-church people will be randomly matched in a game situations, giving them opportunities to converse and build friendships.

*Basic idea:* Pairs will combine their Scrabble skills to get the highest score. Each game is twenty minutes long; three games complete the marathon.

You will need one Scrabble game for every four people attending. When I sent out my invitations, I did it in groups of four so I would end up with an even number of players for a complete game.

Develop clever ways to mix people for games. For example, you decide that the first two people to arrive will play the seventh and eighth. You don't know who those people will be, so it's a rather fun, chance

thing! Make sure people know how they were chosen to be together that first game. They will stay together for all three games.

For the second game, you could have the pairs whose combined ages are closest play each other. Allow ten minutes between games for people to complete the higher mathematics!

For the third game, people could couple with a pair with whom they share some common number—same year graduated from high school, same number of remaining car payments, same starting number in their ATM code—whatever they discover.

Set a timer when each twenty-minute game starts. When it goes off, the person playing may put down the final word, and at that point the game is ended. Only the earned score is counted. Remaining letters are not subtracted.

Make certain each pair knows that the higher their added scores at the end of twenty minutes, the better the chance of winning. It is to the players' advantage to move quickly.

Throughout the three games, each pair keeps its own score.

To add interest, give each pair this scoring card.

---

*SCRABBLE MARATHON*

Names: _____

**Combined score—**
  game one _____

**Combined score—**
  game two _____

**Combined score—**
  game three_____

Total score:_____

*Both pairs in your game should agree on the following items before they are recorded on both your score cards.*

**Game one—**
  the longest word: _____

  Person scoring it:

  _____

*(The final version is the one that counts. For example, if someone just adds an "s" to make piglet piglets, the person who adds the "s" gets the longest word score. If there are two longest words, the word worth the most points wins. Still the same? Toss a coin.)*

**Game two—**
  funniest word:_____

  Person scoring it:

  _____

**Game three—**
  most unusual word: _____

  Person scoring it: _____

---

After the games have ended, choose two judges to determine the winners. In the last two categories, the decision will be totally up to the judges.

At one Scrabble party, I gave silly prizes in keeping with the fun of the evening. You can probably top me, but just to get you started, here's what I did.

The highest scorer got a tape measure.

For the longest word, the \winner got the world's longest pickle. (Actually, this was a restaurant-sized jar of sweet pickle slices.)

The funniest word won its creator a great joke book.

For the most unusual word, the winner took home a terrible print of an abstract painting.

**THE PEOPLE MIX**

For several reasons, we chose the Scrabble Marathon as a party to mix our friends who are excited about God and church with those who are not. It's healthy for each group to know what the other is thinking. What is our church's reputation in the community? How can we as church people become more involved with the concerns of people who are not with us each Sunday? Both groups have a lot to share, and very few opportunities to do so. The game is common territory. Nearly everyone can play Scrabble. Game related conversation is easy. "I can't do a thing with five *e*'s." "Does anyone know how to spell the plural of *ditto?*" "Who knows a *q* word that doesn't need a *u?*"

Second, the marathon angle

**INVITATION IDEA**

# SCRABBLE
# PARTY

**S**ure, it's a party
**C**ome to our house
**R**ound 7:30 P.M. on (date)
**A**nd
**B**e prepared!
**B**ecause we're gonna play
**L**ots of Scrabble
**E**very game for prizes and fun

**RSVP**

allows people to move around a lot, and actually to spend twenty minutes with six other people. The marathon is pretty much confined to an hour, so after the games, people can regroup and conversation can continue for real. Because they have had the mutual game experience, they have some common conversational starting point.

In a way, this party is dangerous. You've heard that religion and politics should be off-limit issues at social occasions. I disagree, but even if I didn't, I have some friends who are so excited about what God's doing in their lives that it just spills over naturally.

When people share what is important to them, great things can happen. For example, a neighbor asks a church member about one of the outreach programs of the church and why people are willing to put so much time and money into it. The conversation turns to God. There is no polemic involved. Two people are talking naturally, the one sharing what Christ was doing through people who serve Him, and the other sharing his ideas and observations about this project and the church. What a concept—people meeting so they can learn to care about each other!

Philip, recently separated, attended a Scrabble marathon. When everyone else was eating, Jack noticed that Philip and Paul, another guest, were missing. Paul later explained, "He told me that this was the first time he'd been anywhere since the separation, and he wanted to bolt. I'm probably the only guy here who has been through a similar experience. We walked around the block several times, and he talked it all out."

A very serious thing to happen at a party. And absolutely appropriate.

## DESSERT IDEAS FOR SCRABBLE MARATHON

A friend suggested alphabet soup, but for what it has in cleverness, it lacks in dessert flare!

You could make sheet cakes, cut them in strips, and position the strips to form letters. Ice the large letters.

### CHOCOLATE ROLL

*5 egg yolks*
*1 cup powdered sugar*
*3 Tablespoons cocoa*
*5 egg whites*
*whipped cream*
*thin chocolate sauce*

Beat egg yolks until thick. Add sugar and beat thoroughly. Add cocoa, fold in stiffly beaten egg whites. Spread on buttered, floured cookie sheet and bake about 15 minutes in a 350° oven.

Turn out on floured cloth. Cover with a damp cloth. When cool, spread with whipped cream and roll. Serve slices with chocolate sauce. Serves 8.

## AMBROSIA FLUFF PIE

   *1 package (3-1/4 ounce)*
      *vanilla pudding and pie filling*
   *1 package (3 ounce) orange-*
      *banana flavored gelatin*
   *2-1/2 cups water*
   *prepared whipped topping mix*
   *1 unbaked coconut crust*

Combine pie filling mix, gelatin, and water in a saucepan. Cook over medium heat. Stir until mixture comes to a full boil and is thick and clear. Remove from heat. Chill until mixture begins to set.

Prepare whipped topping mix as directed on the package. Thoroughly blend into the chilled pudding mixture. Spoon into unbaked coconut crust.

Chill until firm (at least three hours). Garnish with a large puff of whipped topping and a sunburst arrangement of orange sections. Serves 8.

## CHOCOLATE MERINGUE PIE
**Filling:**
   *1 cup sugar*
   *1/4 cup cornstarch*
   *1/4 teaspoon salt*
   *4 Tablespoons butter*
   *3 ounces unsweetened chocolate*
   *1-1/2 cup warm water*
   *3 eggs, beaten*
   *grated peel of 1 lemon or orange*
      *or 1 teaspoon vanilla*

**Meringue:**
   *4 egg whites*
   *1/2 teaspoon cream of tartar*
   *6 Tablespoons confectioner's sugar*
   *1 teaspoon vanilla*
Crust:
   *8-inch pie crust*

Mix 1 cup sugar, cornstarch, and salt. Set aside.

Melt butter in a heavy three-quart saucepan over low heat. Add chocolate, stirring to melt. Remove from heat. Stir in water and sugar mixture; then stir in eggs. Stir over low heat for about 15 minutes, until slightly thickened and smooth. Stir in lemon peel (orange or vanilla). Cook, stirring occasionally.

Pour into cooled pie crust (8-inch baked crust or crushed chocolate cookie, gingersnap, or graham cracker crust).

For the meringue, beat egg whites until frothy. Add cream of tartar and continue beating until you have soft peaks. Beat in sugar, one tablespoon at a time. Do not overbeat. Whites should stand in peaks, but should not be stiff. Add vanilla.

Spread in a decorative design over the chocolate and bake 10 to 15 minutes at 350° until peaks are slightly browned. Cool the pie and refrigerate. Filling will set to firmness as pie is chilled.

### FUNNYCAKE

You've heard of Pennsylvania Dutch shoofly pies with the gooey bottoms. This recipe is an adaptation. It consists of a sauce baked in a pie shell and topped with cake.

In this cake, develop your own sauce ideas. Why not try apricot jelly or butterscotch or blueberry? Or, here's a recipe built around a chocolate base.

**Chocolate syrup:**
*3/4 cup granulated sugar*
*1/2 cup cocoa*
*3/4 cup water*

*1 Jiffy white cake mix*
*9-inch pie crust with*
*high fluted edges*
Prick bottom and sides of pie crust. Bake in 400° oven for 12 to 13 minutes. Cool. Reduce temperature to 375°.

To make syrup, combine sugar, cocoa, and water. Boil about 10 minutes or until slightly thickened. Cool.

Prepare white cake according to package directions. Pour chocolate mixture into the pie shells. Pour the cake batter over the chocolate. Bake for 35 minutes at 375°. Serve topped with whipped cream or ice cream, if desired.

## Hay There

*Objective:* To work with two other people in party planning. (You'll want to pick people who have not been as involved in church hospitality as you have. In a discipling relationship, you will be sharing what you have learned from your experience.)

To invite three different sets of church friends and mix them. (This event makes an effort to break up church cliques.)

*Basic Idea:* Plan a hayride and "hay" activities to follow the ride.

### WORKING TOGETHER

Pick two other people who are interested in helping the church grow together. Perhaps they have never organized an event like this, but they have dropped clues indicating they might be willing to try. Good clues: "I would like to do something like your last party someday." Or, "When I finally get my act together, I'm going to have you over to my place."

**INVITATION IDEA**

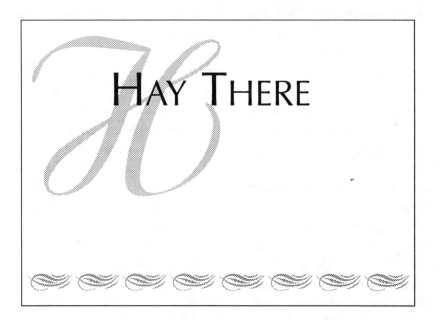

# HAY THERE

**GALLOP OVER TO (PLACE) ON (DATE),
AND CLIMB INTO THE HAY WAGON.**

GIDDY-UP TIME (TIME)

SING 'TIL YOU'RE "HORSE"

RACE AROUND PLENTY

TROUGH PROVIDED

**WHOA:**
BRING (COST). WE'VE GOT A HIGH HORSE!

Each partner in the "Hay There" trio is responsible for inviting an equal number of people. When I worked with two girlfriends on a party like this, we each invited ten, limiting the size of the party to the limitations of our resources and the facilities.

Each of us chose people from our small circle of special friends. In a way, we were sharing circles, and in doing so, enlarging each circle of friends and acquaintances. As we worked together the party became so much more than it could have ever been with one of us working alone.

## HAY RIDE

It is possible to plan a hayride almost anywhere in the country. This particular party happened in Chicago. I've also lived in Providence, Rhode Island, Lancaster, Pennsylvania, and Colorado Springs, Colorado. In each of these cities, it is possible to have a hayride. Look in the yellow pages. You'll be surprised! And if you divide the cost among all those who will attend, the evening can be an event without a mortgage!

Most places that have hayrides also have a barn or large garage for activities after the ride. So plan for a total evening.

## ON THE WAGON: SOME ACTIVITY IDEAS

*Sing*

Start with songs everyone knows and just sing through the bunch. Ask someone who plays the guitar to bring it along. A harmonica would be a great addition. Ask an enthusiastic person with a strong voice to take the lead. Ban all transistor radios!

*Joke*

Start a can-you-top-this-joke session. But only if you really know your people! Someone who thinks the wrong joke is just hysterical can change the tone of the party and ruin the evening.

*Share*

If the group is small or has been divided into several wagons, things will get more "groupy." You might suggest people share a bit about their first or funniest date.

*Constellations*

Bring along a constellation book. As a group, pick out the ones in your sky. Bone up on the mythical stories behind them and share with the group. Or select your own groups of stars, name your original constellation, and make up a story to go with it.

## OFF THE WAGON: PARTY ACTIVITIES FOR A BARN, GARAGE, OR BASEMENT

Barn activities will depend on the makeup of your group. Pick from these suggestions, and add your own ideas.

### Folk Games

These games provide great exercise, and if you have an area big enough, they are a perfect end activity for a "Hay There" evening. At our party, the three of us hired a caller for the evening. We told him that few of us knew anything about folk games or square dancing. He was great. He brought his record player and a microphone, and in a few minutes we knew enough to skip and twirl following his commands. Most of us were pretty awful, but we had a great workout. Limit this activity to an hour or two. We hired a caller for three hours and by the end of the second hour most of us were gasping and looking for an empty chair.

Be honest with the caller. Tell him this will be a Christian group. Let him know the goals of the party. He might not totally understand, but he will probably respect you for it and adjust the tone of what he's planned to meet your needs.

### Circle Games

Play some of the circle games you haven't played since you were in summer camp. I'll suggest a few here just to get you tuned back to your past. For additional help, you may want to interview a fifth grader.

In my games, I've changed the traditional names to ones more suited for a "Hay There" party.

### Flying Wagons
(Better known as Flying Dutchmen)

Everyone, except one pair, holds hands in a large circle. The excluded pair runs around the outside of the circle, and at any point, hits the hands of another pair. That pair will then run like crazy the opposite direction around the outside of the circle from the original hand-hitting pair. The only object is to get back to the broken space in the line first. The two who arrives first grab the hands of the people there, completing the circle once again. The slower pair runs around looking for two other hands to hit. No big deal, but it's fun!

### Horse Around
(Better known as Dodge Ball)

Divide the group in half. One half stands in a large circle

around the other half. The object for those in the large outer circle is to hit the legs of the people in the center with a large, soft ball. The people in the center should do their best not to get hit by the ball. When someone in the center is hit, he or she takes a place in the outside ring and tries to get those who are still left out of the circle. Nasty game! The winner is the final person left in the center. That person is probably also in the best condition.

*Horse and Stall*
(Better known as Musical Chairs)

The people are the horses and chairs are the stalls. Place the chairs (stalls) in a circle, one less stall than the number of horses playing. The seats of the stalls should face out. Everyone marches around the stalls in time to the music. When the music stops everyone lunges for a stall. One person will be left without a stall. That person is out. Remove another stall, and keep going until you have one stall and two horses left. The winner is the one to get that last stall. Watch out for some really bloody collisions. I've always felt it was more fair if the person controlling the music could not see the horses.

*Horse and Mule*
(Better known as Ducks and Geese)

Horse and Mule was a third grade recess favorite of mine. Regression can be fun. Horses line up on two parallel sides of the building. A mule is in the center. The horses must run from one side to the other. The mule's job is to tag as many of these running horses as possible. When a horse is tagged, that person becomes a mule and helps chase the remaining horses. The winner is the last untagged horse.

*Gallop*
(Better known as Rhythm)

Everyone sits in a circle, a very wise thing to do if you've just finished playing all those running games. Each person is given a consecutive number—1, 2, 3, and so on. The leader will establish an easy four-beat rhythm. Beat one is measured with everyone slapping his lap. Beat two, everyone claps. Beat three, snap of the right hand; and beat four, snap of the left hand. So the rhythm goes:

Slap Clap Snap Snap

On the Slap, Clap, people should say the word Gal—lop. On the first snap of the right hand, the leader will say his own number. On the second snap, he will say anyone else's number.

For example:

> Gal
> lop
> 1-4

Number four will then keep in tune with the Gal—lop, his or her own number 4, and anyone else's number. The object is to concentrate in order to stay in time and not get the numbers mixed up.

Some people have an awful time with this game. Anyone who messes up with a number or timing is out of the game. Keep speeding things up until only a few really rhythmic people are left galloping and snapping.

You can make things harder by setting up the chairs in a horseshoe pattern. One end of the horseshoe is the top, the other the bottom. Every time someone misses, that person goes to the bottom—instead of being out of the game. Everyone below that person moves up a chair and everyone's number changes. The object, of course, is to get and stay at the right end of the horseshoe.

## Horse Laugh

The object of Horse Laugh is not to laugh. Everyone begins with a straight face. One person is "it" and his or her job is to get the others to laugh by doing anything but touching them. Some people can't go ten seconds before they are howling. As soon as a person laughs, he or she joins the "it," trying to make all the others laugh. The last to laugh wins!

## Relay Games

Relays are easily rediscovered by adults with straw in their hair. Once again, use those you played when you were a youngster. You may want to change them slightly to make them just perfect for a Hay There party. Here are some examples:

## Straw Saver

Divide your group into teams. Everyone should find a piece of straw—perhaps off the wagon. Then people line up in team lines and put their straws in their mouths. Place a Lifesaver candy on straw of the first person in each line. When you yell, "Start!" that person must pass it on to the next person's straw. No hands allowed (unless the Lifesaver drops). The first line to get the Lifesaver to the end wins. If lines are short, you may want to make the winner the first line to get the Lifesaver to the back and up front again.

*Root the Boot*

Each person in the team should spend time studying the shoes of the other farmers in the group. Then each person should take off both shoes and place them in a pile along with all the shoes from all the other groups. Mix the pile. The first group to find its shoes and have them back on all feet wins. One little thing. No one may find his or her own shoes. Don't add this rule until immediately before the game begins. The group must find each other's. And no telling. The team members must be observant.

*How Does Your Garden Grow?*

Place a large bag of dried beans as far away from the teams as possible. Give each team a bottle. Once again, teams line up. At the signal, the first member of each team rushes up to the bean bag and scoops out as many beans as he or she can—on the back of the hand. The player rushes them back to his or her team's bottle. The object is to get the most beans in the bottle in the shortest amount of time. As soon as one team finishes with all its players, the game is over and the beans should be counted. The team with the most beans wins. It would be possible for the first team done

not to have the winning bottle of beans.

*Whistling Farmer*

Teams get into lines again. Place a box of crackers at the far end of the room. The object of the game is for each team member to take turns dashing up to the crackers, eating one, and whistling. Each person must whistle before he or she can return to the line and the next person begin. The first line finished munching and whistling wins.

*Dress the Farmer*

For each team, have an outfit of farm clothing—work boots, coveralls, flannel shirt. At the starting signal, the first person in each line must put the clothing on over his or her own clothes, including buttoning all buttons, and take everything off. Then the second person does the same thing. The first team completely dressed and undressed wins.

*Farmer's Almanac*

Make an identical picture list for each team. Place stacks of magazines at the far end of the room. The first person in each team dashes to find the first item on the list in the magazines. The second finds the second after the first person has returned with his or her picture to the line. If a team doesn't have enough players to finish the list, people should just go twice. The first team with a complete list of pictures wins.

You'll have to adjust your list to the type of magazines you've got, but here are some ideas to get you started:

—A lady the farmer would whistle at

—A lady the farmer wouldn't whistle at

—An animal for the farm

—A money-making crop

—A replacement for the old horse

—A five-syllable word the farmer doesn't know

—The farmer's daughter (under ten years old)

—Something the farmer's wife could use in the kitchen

—Something the farmer would have no use for

—Something the farmer would love to eat before noon

## PRAYER BEFORE REFRESHMENTS

Prayer fits perfectly before the food is served, but it doesn't have to be limited to thanks for the food. Encourage people to thank God for others they have met tonight, for the fun they are having, and, of course, for the food. You might ask people to limit themselves to sentence prayers and use the pronoun "I" rather than "we." It makes prayers more personal. For example, the prayer, "We thank you for the amazing array of stars, Lord," becomes "I thank you for the amazing array of stars, Lord." What a difference a word can make.

## "HAY THERE" FOOD

Can you have a bonfire? Why not build the food around it? A first thought is hot dogs and marshmallows, but vary that a little. Try stick kabobs.

Everyone should find a stick and fill it with kabob pieces that you have cut earlier. Kabob pieces can be all sorts of things. For example:
*pieces of hot dog*
*cut green pepper*
*water chestnuts*
*onion chunks*
*pineapple chunks*
Tomatoes get too juicy and fall into the fire.

## VEGETABLE BAGS ON A GRILL

Make individual vegetable packets and place them on a grill about one hour before eating. Use wide heavy duty foil to make the bags. Grease the foil well and allow some butter to melt on top of the vegetables. In the packets, you could place:

*thin sliced potatoes*

*carrots*

*celery stalks*

*green peppers*

*onion pieces*

*cabbage pieces*

Add salt and pepper.

## BANANA BOAT

For each banana boat, peel one strip from the banana, keeping the skin intact. Cut out a wedge of banana. (Use the wedge as one of your kabob chunks.) In the hollow put chocolate squares and marshmallows. Add other things—cherries, nuts, peanut butter. Cover with the peeled-back banana skin. Wrap in heavy duty foil. Place in coals for several minutes to allow the chocolate and marshmallow to melt.

## BARBECUED BEEF

This recipe is for ten people. Add multiples to meet the needs of your "Hay There" party.

*3 pounds browned ground beef*

*2 large onions, grated*

*1 green pepper, grated*

*1 large bottle catsup*

*1 can tomato soup*

*2 teaspoons sugar*

*2 Tablespoons dried mustard dissolved in 3 Tablespoons vinegar*

*1-1/2 teaspoons meat seasoning*

*1 celery stalk cut in small pieces*

Mix all ingredients and simmer for about 1-1/2 hours.

## MOCK ANGEL FOOD

*1 loaf white, unsliced bread*

*1 large can of condensed milk*

*1 package shredded coconut*

Divide loaf into 10 pieces. Dip each piece of bread quickly into condensed milk. Roll in shredded coconut. Stab the slices with the sticks and toast them lightly in the fire.

# Neighborhood Drop-In

*Objective:* To meet and talk with neighbors, offering them your friendship.

*Basic idea:* People who live in close proximity will get together for a short period of time—sharing food and a bit of their lives.

When Jack and I moved into our first apartment, we were so wrapped up in the wonderful little world we were creating that we never got around to meeting the lady across the hall. For three months, she was just five steps away from our front door. One night the ambulance came and took her away. We never saw her again.

We didn't even know she was sick. An elderly woman living alone, no doubt she was afraid of us unfriendly, younger people. If we had known—if we had taken the time to know—we could have driven her to the hospital and surrounded her with caring love as she left her familiar surroundings.

The red light on the ambulance wasn't out of sight before Jack and I promised God that we wouldn't repeat our performance. God had placed us in our church, but he had also put us in an apartment building surrounded by people who might need friends.

"Help us to know and love and help the person who moves in next," Jack prayed.

## PLANNING A NEIGHBORHOOD DROP-IN

Pick a weekday evening—Tuesday or Thursday seemed best for us. This helps to keep the evening casual. On the invitation state the time limits for the drop in. We limited ours to an hour and a half. This announced ahead of time to the older guests that it would not be a late evening, and it told everyone that the evening would be too short to be tedious.

Hand-deliver the invitations. Jack and I delivered them together. We wanted both the men and the women to feel welcome, although we always had many more women than men at our Drop-In Parties.

Ask people to bring something. We had our first Drop-In around Christmas, so we asked everyone to bring six cookies. What a selection we got, but the cookies were just a means to an end. When people participate, they feel more a part of things—a commitment to make the evening work. They weren't just coming—they were coming and bringing. Other things people might bring would be six pieces of their favorite candy, three pieces of fruit, six slices of cheese (you supply fruit and crackers). Match the season.

Make certain people feel welcome. A short conversation when you give the invitation can cover this. A recent widow told me, "You don't want me. I've just moved in and wouldn't have a thing to talk about to anyone." I named three other people in the building who had been there less than a year, and she could see that I really wanted her to come. She did.

**INVITATION IDEA**

# NEIGHBORHOOD DROP-IN WELCOME

We pass you in the hall . . . at mailboxes . . . in the laundry room . . . on the steps . . .

So how about stopping to say hi?

## NEIGHBORHOOD DROP-IN

7—8:30 on *(Date) (Place)*

Bring six cookies

We had neighbors who never came, but they were more friendly after our invitation. It was as though we had offered a sense of community, and no one ever completely rejected that.

## THOSE AWFUL FIRST MINUTES

No one knows the others, and people are wishing they had never come. So break the ice.

I provided a pile of construction paper and straight pins. People were asked to tear name tags that told something about themselves.

Some tore and pinned most of their life history. One lady who lived above us tore a green leaf and announced that her name was Fern. Another tore a roller skate and said that was her favorite sport. Jack, always the artist, tore a paint palette and pinned dabs of all colors to it.

No scissors. This is not an opportunity for people to demonstrate artistic skill. It's just a silly little thing to keep people busy for about three minutes after they arrive and give them all a common place from which to start a conversation.

Conversation can be slow at Drop-In parties. You want people to talk, yet many of them may have nothing more in common than the block or the building.

Jack and I go over good topics of conversation before the guests arrive. Sometimes we even write lists, and when there's a lag, we remember something we wrote and ask a question to get things moving again. Here are some good questions for us; you'll want to edit the questions for your own situation.

- Who's lived here the longest? What was the place like when you came?

- What do you do for most of the day? Don't stop with some thing like, "I lay tile." Find out what that involves. What kinds of tile does he lay? Does he free-lance? Has he ever worked on any famous buildings? What was his hardest job?

- Where are you going on vacation this year? Again find out all you can about that vacation—ever been there before? Are you driving or flying? How do you keep the kids happy in the car?

- What's it like to be retired? I think the whole thing sounds wonderful, but I'm not sure I would know how to handle my time. Did you prepare for it before the day came?

- Where did you live before you came here? Do you have plans for buying a home? What kind of place are you looking for?

- How many children do you have? Where do they live? What do they do?

- Has anyone seen/read (insert a popular book, movie, TV program)? Encourage people to share their opinions.

Steer conversation away from any talk about neighbors who aren't at the party. Almost every neighborhood has its strange people—the ones who inspire the most amazing "did-you-know?" tales. But this type of conversation will ruin the friendliness of the evening. In an apartment, the same thing goes double for talking about the landlord. This isn't the time to get even, even if he or she does deserve it.

We had some amazing things happen at our first neighborhood meeting. We discovered that one of the ladies on the next floor was a retired missionary from India. She had served under the same mission I had served when I was a college short-term missionary. And the woman a few doors over had graduated from the same

Christian college I had. She was going through a divorce and was calculatingly cutting Christians and the church out of her life. The girl across the hall, the one who moved in after the ambulance took away the woman we had never met, was searching for reality in Christ. Since her divorce she felt unaccepted by those who up to that time had guided her spiritual growth.

**GOD TALK**

I find it easy to talk, but talk about God? That's always been difficult for me. Then I met a Christian who talked about her God as easily as the achievements of her four children. He fit there naturally. I never got the feeling Karen went around looking for places to dot her conversation with things about God, but He was so much a part of her life that she couldn't talk too long without including Him.

I can understand that kind of excitement. I'm that way about writing and my job working with Sunday school curriculum. I get excited about writing curriculum and all the wonderful ways of getting teenagers involved in studying the Bible. And sure enough, everyone who knows me knows I feel this way. If a person wants to be my friend, he or she is stuck listening to bits about my job. It's so much a part of me. What made God talk so different for me? Unless, of course, He wasn't as important to me as my writing—not as much a vital part of my life. I didn't want that to be true.

I began to follow Karen's example of talking about God when He fit into the conversation, rather than skirting around Him for fear of embarrassing or turning off the person I was talking with. I just forced myself to be more open about my feelings about my God. I remember one of the first times, I about scared myself to death! I was talking with a seat partner on a plane, and he asked what I did for a living. Previously when I was asked, I would say, "I write curriculum," but this time I told the whole truth: "I write Sunday school curriculum for teenagers."

"Really?" he said. "Isn't that awfully boring?"

"Not for me. I love it. I can point kids toward Christ and a reason for living," I said. "I don't just write curriculum; I believe in what I'm doing."

"That's great," he replied. "I've got a good job, but it's not a reflection of me. I take home the money and that's about all there is to it."

"What do you do?" And we were off discussing his job. My little affirmation of God hadn't cornered him or made him defensive. But God had been there. I had told that man something that was extremely important to me. And I had told him naturally and honestly. A little later we did come back and talk specifically about how an educated person in this scientific world could believe in God—a difficult conversation that never would have been started if I hadn't dared to fit God talk into my life naturally where he belonged.

Rev. Jana Childers talked about Baby Boomers during her presentation at the American Guild of Organists that I mentioned earlier. She pointed out the fact that Boomers are facing the three Ms—mortgages, menopause, and mortality. "They are hookable. All that is needed is the right worm. Radio, TV, direct mail, leader charisma, praise choruses, and a 'customer is always right' attitude may be distasteful to those of us whose vocations locate us in the traditional church, but we shouldn't turn up our noses at the bait bucket too quickly. If we were honest, many of us would have to admit that we are not averse to a little fishing ourselves. And there are those who say it comes highly recommended by a sagacious Galilean."

My "fishing" has the word *naturally* attached to it. I don't look for catchy places to inject God, but I try to be aware, with the Holy Spirit's help, of places where He belongs. Then I'm not inclined to switch topics or be careful not go places where God talk belongs—at least, not as often as I used to. Now I just talk Him through! And I have never found anyone who was offended by this. Never! Not at Drop-In parties or on airplanes or at secular educational conventions!

## Do-It-Ourselves Evening

*Objective:* To work as a team in preparing a total meal, building that sense of community into a do-it-ourselves (inductive) Bible study. (This evening is perfect for new Christians or a mix of growing Christians and seekers, people who already have some curiosity about the Bible.)

*Basic idea:* A group of six or seven people will meet to prepare dinner and participate in a do-it-ourselves Bible study. Keep the group small so everyone will fit into your kitchen. Cutting, peeling, and stirring together is part of the fun—and necessary for the success of the evening.

**THE MEAL**

Do nothing ahead of time but gather the ingredients and the pots and pans. When people arrive give everyone an apron and a supper job. You might choose to make something like crepes because they take a while and are a bit unusual. They are not difficult and can be the basis for an entire meal.

Men in the kitchen? Of course. Don't be sexist! Don't approach the event assuming anyone will be uncomfortable or not want to participate. I never make jokes about men in the kitchen. I do, however, give specific directions. "I'd like the cheese cut into cubes about the size of an olive," or, "Tear the lettuce after you wash it." I'd rather give too detailed directions than end up with a noncook staring at a head of lettuce and wishing he or she could throw it at me.

One evening I planned a mini do-it-ourselves party with three other people. Two of them, Bob and Rita, were planning to be married. The primary reason they wanted to come was to give Bob exposure to a kitchen. He knew all about TV dinners and fast food goodies, but he had never had the opportunity to learn the real skills necessary to make a stove work for him.

**INVITATION IDEA**

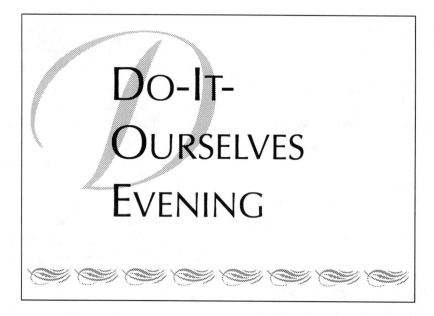

# Do-It-Ourselves Evening

**COME HELP US PREPARE DINNER**
*Slave for hours*
*Over a hot fire*
*You'll love it*
*Come join us in a Do-it-Ourselves Bible Study*
*Studying the Bible*
*Discovering what God says*
*You'll love it*

WHEN:

WHERE:

Everyone had a great time. Rita and I were in charge of the salad. Jack and Bob attacked the crepes. Jack mixed the crepe batter, and did the first few, before turning the task over to Bob. He did perfectly. Rita quipped, "Well, Bob, now you can cook. Let's set the date!"

At a do-it-ourselves evening, you might want to post a list of jobs and recipes involved to get things moving.

For example:

Rita: Wash and cut all the vegetables for the salad.

Roger: Make the salad dressing and crepe fillings.

Bob: Make crepes.

Jack: Mix crepe batter, supervise crepe fillings.

Marlene: Make dessert crepe filling.

## RECIPE SUGGESTIONS

### SPINACH Á LA _____
### (INSERT MAKER'S NAME)

*1 pound fresh spinach*
*2 celery stalks, diced*
*3 hard-boiled eggs, chilled, diced*
*8 radishes, sliced*
*addition of any other diced*
  *vegetables that look interesting*
*1/2 pound diced bacon*
*3/4 cup oil*
*3/4 cup red wine vinegar*
*2 teaspoons sugar*
*1 teaspoon salt*
*1/2 teaspoon dry mustard*
*1/2 teaspoon pepper*
*1/2 clove garlic*

Remove stems from spinach. Wash leaves carefully; drain. Cook diced bacon until crisp; drain. Put oil, vinegar, sugar, salt, mustard, pepper, garlic in electric blender or covered jar. Blend or shake until well mixed. Toss spinach lightly with dressing. Turn into a large bowl and top with radishes, eggs, bacon, celery, etc.

## BASIC CREPE RECIPE

This recipe is used by the Magic Pan restaurant that specializes in crepes.

### MAGIC PAN BASIC CREPE RECIPE

*3 eggs*
*1 cup all-purpose flour, unsifted*
*1/8 teaspoon salt*
*1 cup milk*
*1/4 cup water*
*2 Tablespoons butter or margarine*

Put eggs in bowl and beat well with fork. Add flour and salt and continue beating until batter is smooth. Gradually add milk and water, beating until smooth.

Melt butter or margarine and set aside. Before cooking each crepe, brush 8-inch crepe pan with a little butter or margarine. Heat pan over medium heat until just hot, not smoking. For each crepe, pour 2 or 3 tablespoons of batter into hot pan. Tilt pan from side to side instantly to cover entire bottom of pan with batter. Cook about 1 minute, shaking pan frequently to keep crepe loose. When bottom side is lightly browned, turn with spatula and brown on the other side—about 30 seconds.

When crepes come out of the pan, stack on top of each other and cover with a towel to keep moist and pliable. Yields 12 to 14 crepes.

I have a special crepe pan called "The Crepe Maker." The pan is a great addition since it makes my crepes look better. Any small, slope-sided heavy skillet will be fine.

There are a number of basic batter recipes. "The Crepe Maker" suggests this one for 16 to 20 crepes:

### THE CREPE MAKER BASIC BATTER
*2 fresh eggs*
*1 cup milk*
*1 cup flour (all purpose, presifted)*
*1 Tablespoon soft butter (melted)*
*pinch of salt*

In a mixing bowl, beat the eggs and add milk. Add the flour gradually, stirring constantly with a whisk until the batter is smooth. Add butter and salt and mix until the batter is as smooth as cream. If possible, refrigerate 24 hours before use.

Crepes can be filled with just about anything. Here we make some main course and dessert suggestions, but after you've made several dinners of crepes, branch out on your own with amazing, delicious original ideas.

### CHICKEN Á LA _____ (INSERT MAKER'S NAME)
*1 pound mushrooms, chopped*
*2 Tablespoons grated onion*
*2/3 cup butter*
*6 Tablespoons cornstarch*
*2 teaspoons salt*
*1/2 teaspoon white pepper*
*1 cup half-and-half*
*2 cups whipping cream*
*4 cups diced cooked chicken*
*1 cup chopped walnuts*

Sauté mushrooms and onions in butter. Blend in cornstarch, salt, and pepper. Add half-and-half, cream; cook, stirring until thickened. Add chicken and heat to boiling, stirring occasionally. Stir in nuts. Remove from heat. Spoon some of the chicken mixture on the center of each crepe. Fold two opposite sides over the filling. You'll have enough filling for 16 crepes.

### ALMOND DESSERT CREPES
To make the filling for 8 to 10 dessert crepes:
*1 cup sugar*
*1/4 cup flour*

*1 cup milk*
*3 eggs*
*1/2 cup chopped almonds*
*3 Tablespoons butter*
*2 teaspoons vanilla*
*1/4 teaspoon almond extract*

Combine sugar and flour and add to the milk. Cook, stirring until thickened and bubbly. Beat eggs slightly and add them a little at a time to the milk mixture. Cook until boiling. Remove from heat. Beat until smooth. Stir in chopped almonds, butter, vanilla, almond extract. Cover with wax paper and cool. When cool, spoon into the center of the crepe and fold over the sides or roll the crepe. Top with cherry sauce.

***Cherry Sauce:***

Use prepared cherry pie filling and add a dash of nutmeg or cinnamon. Add lemon juice if the filling is too thick.

Crepes are quite filling. You might want to save dessert until after the do-it-ourselves Bible study.

## Do-It-Ourselves Bible Study

***Objective:*** Everyone will participate in a depth study of a small passage of Scripture and gain a working knowledge of simple inductive Bible study.

***Basic idea:*** Working in small groups, people will study the Bible for themselves and discover guidelines and principles for Christian living as they work.

In do-it-ourselves Bible study, the groups will go through the process many preachers do. First, they will become familiar with the content. Then they will look within the passage to decide exactly what it says—not what they think it ought to say or have heard someone else say it says. Their findings must be based on what is directly stated or indirectly implied in the passage. Groups will then share what they have found and end the study with prayer.

Follow this process. As much as possible, make certain each person has a copy of the same version of the Scripture passage. When everyone has the same words, long discussions over which word is really the most effective are eliminated.

Choose a short section of Scripture. From two perspectives, a good one to try is John 3:16, 17. First, if your guests are really familiar with the Bible but have never participated in an inductive Bible study, they may be amazed by the amount of material they have missed in these two verses. Second, if seekers have been invited to participate, this section hits right to the heart of the gospel. (Or you might try Peter's declaration about Jesus in Mark 8:27-31.)

Share with your guests a short secular story about inductive study in biology. This will make it easier for them to see what they will be doing in inductive Bible study.

The following story by Samuel H. Scudder is condensed from *Every Saturday,* April 4, 1874.

### In the Laboratory with Agassiz

*It was more than fifteen years ago that I entered the laboratory of Professor Agassiz, and told him I had enrolled my name in the scientific school as a student of natural history.*

*"When do you wish to begin?" he asked.*

*"Now," I replied.*

*"Very well," he took from a shelf a huge jar of specimens in yellow alcohol.*

*"Take this fish," said he, "and look at it: we call it Haemulon; by and by I will ask you what you have seen."*

*In ten minutes I had seen all that could be seen in that fish, and started in search of the professor, who had, however, left the museum. . . . I returned to my fish. Half an hour passed, an hour, another hour; the*

*fish began to look loathsome. I turned it over and around; looked it in the face—ghastly; from behind, beneath, above, sideways, at a three-quarter view—just as ghastly. . . .*

*I might not use a magnifying glass; instruments of all kinds were interdicted. My two hands, my two eyes, and the fish; it seemed a most limited field. . . . At last a happy thought struck me—I would draw the fish; and now with surprise I began to discover new features in the creature. Just then the professor returned.*

*"That is right," said he, "a pencil is one of the best eyes." With these encouraging words he added, "Well, what is it like?"*

*He listened attentively to my brief rehearsal. . . . When I had finished, he waited as if expecting more, and then, with an air of disappointment, "You have not looked very carefully. Why," he continued, more earnestly, "you haven't seen one of the most conspicuous features of the animal, which is as plainly before your eyes as the fish itself; look again, look again!" And he left me to my misery.*

*I was piqued; I was mortified. Still more of that wretched fish! But now I set myself to my task with a will, and discovered one new thing after another. . . .*

*The next morning I was able to ask, "Do you perhaps mean that the fish has symmetrical sides with paired organs?"*

*He was thoroughly pleased. "Of course, of course!"*

*I ventured to ask what I should do next.*

*"Look at your fish!" . . .*

*So for three long days, he placed that fish before my eyes, forbidding me to look at anything else, or to use any artificial aid. "Look, look, look," was his repeated injunction.*

*This lesson's influence has extended to the details of every subsequent study; a legacy the professor has left to me, as he left it to many others; of inestimable value, which we could not buy, with which we cannot part.*

You may want to quip that Bible study is a lot more fun than studying the dead fish, but the "look, look, look" principle is the same. In order to do effective looking, each person is to assume that this passage is the only one with which he or she is familiar. (This will help limit discussion to the passage under consideration.)

Ask each person to read the passage three times. Participants may feel this is unnecessary—after all, they may know the passage by heart. But insist. I use the following method when I'm leading simple inductive Bible study. I ask students to read the passage as if they were three different people.

*Person 1:* Read as if you were a newspaper reporter looking for something to report in your paper.

*Person 2:* Read as if you were an atheist looking for things to criticize.

These first two readings can be done very quickly without discussing how people responded. You will spend the bulk of the evening working with this third situation.

*Person 3:* Read as if you were on a desert island and had never read any Scripture before. Suddenly you see a bottle floating in on the tide. You grab it and inside is today's Scripture. What things could you know or assume about the subject (God, Jesus, love, the world, etc.) from this tiny excerpt?

Divide the larger group of six into groups of two or three. I like this because it forces a type of accountability that can be wholesome. Groups will be working on the same passage, and when they compare at the end of the looking-studying time, they can see just how different the two groups' studies were. So two good groups can double the benefits of do-it-ourselves Bible study.

Ask groups to pick a leader-recorder to write observations they find in their study. Observations are things that are found in the text or things that can be assumed from the text. Encourage people to try to diagram content, look for relationships between people—any type of creative search that will help them own the Scripture they are studying.

As a pre-study demonstration, I have found it helpful to give a few observations on the first two lines of this nursery rhyme, as if I were doing an inductive study on it. This gives first-timers a humorous sample to follow.

*Mary had a little lamb.*
*Its fleece was white as snow.*

From this I can state the obvious, and I can look for what I can assume in those two lines. I might suggest, for example:

Mary was probably a girl. Most people with the name of Mary are girls. She probably lived in a rural area since that's where lamb pets are usually found. Some lambs aren't white. If they all were, the poet probably wouldn't have wasted a whole line discussing its coloring.

Mary may have come from a good home. She seemed to know how to take care of a pet.

She may have been old enough to understand ownership because the word *had* is used. She owned the lamb. From this we could infer that she accepted the responsibility of the lamb.

Silly? Sure! You're looking for much more significant things in Scripture, but this illustration will help do-it-ourselvers get started. Encourage them to look a bit below the surface. If your guests are from your church, they probably already know the easy-to-find things.

Allow about twenty minutes for this inductive study and sharing.

I've done this type of inductive Bible study with high schoolers. Amazingly, the time often ends before they have completed their study. They'll ask, "Could we please have more time?" It's exciting to hear young people ask to study Scripture a little longer.

Your groups may do the same thing. But it's a good idea to cut off the group study while everyone is still into it. People will have a good feeling about the action of the group, and will want to try it again in their private study, or perhaps in their own duplication of a do-it-ourselves party.

*Extra Help*

If you think your guests won't really know exactly what you want them to do after you've done the above explanation, you might duplicate these simple directions for them to follow.

Write everything you can know or assume from this passage. These questions will help you find things:

*What do the difficult words mean?*

*What relationships are established here?*

*What laws, principles, or teachings are stated or implied?*

*Is there an outline?*

*Is there a progression of thought?*

*Is there repetition of thought or words?*

*What are the key words or phrases? What is the key verse? Why?*

*What does each verse mean? If necessary, paraphrase.*

*What title would you give this section to differentiate it from other sections of Scripture?*

*Briefly consider how this section applies to you today. How might you use it in your own life, in your witness to others?*

*Sample of John 3:16, 17*

Stop! Don't read further until you've tried the inductive study of John 3: 16, 17 for yourself. Then read the things I found. This list of observations is very incomplete. But it's a good start.

"For God so loved the world that he gave his only Son, that whoever believes in him should not perish but have eternal life. For God sent the Son into the world, not to condemn the world, but that the world might be saved through him" (RSV).

**OBSERVATIONS:**

- I found these attributes of God. He is loving, just, all-powerful, eternal.
- The Son was not personally condemned, because he could save others from condemnation. I can assume the Son was sinless.
- We must come to God through the Son—no other route.
- There are a lot of action words—God loved, gave. We believe, receive eternal life. God was not a passive; He was involved.
- There are some interesting contrasts—God, world; perish, saved; condemned, saved. It's an either-or situation. We can't sit on the fence in our relationship to God's Son.

There's a lot more to find here. It's fun to dig and see what amazing things God allowed his writers to communicate with us.

Be prepared for some off-the-wall comments, along with the serious ones. One young man said that he could relate to this situation. "If I only know about this verse, I can assume that God is a single parent. Jesus was an only child."

With simple inductive Bible study, I am reminded time and time again that I haven't even mastered the basic content of familiar passages, to say nothing of the principles that I have yet to honestly, consistently implement.

When your Bible study time is up, have groups share the three best things they have found. Encourage free discussion between groups.

*We-Can't-Do-It-Ourselves Prayers*

End the do-it-ourselves Bible study with we-can't-do-it-our-selves prayers. Suggest people pray for things that are outside their control. For example, someone might pray for an unsaved friend or family member. Another might bring a downtown street ministry to Christ. Still another could ask God for wisdom for world leaders as they deal with international conflict.

## Having Wonderful Time— Wish You Were Here

*Objective:* To encourage a feeling of family among church family members through the sharing of vacation experiences.

*Basic idea:* Everyone brings ten vacation slides and shares them with the group. The whole evening will be built around a vacation theme.

I prefer to wait for the middle of winter for this party. By that time, most of us need to remember that there is probably going to be a season of vacations some-day—if we can only wait long enough! (Of course, someone is bound to bring snow skiing pictures, complete with a slide of a car adorned with a "Think Snow!" bumper sticker. Forgive the person, and allow him or her to participate anyway.)

This party doesn't really have a people limit, especially if you have a covered dish supper to which others bring the food.

But most people get tired of slides after about an hour. So plan to adjust your crowd and the speed at which the slides are snapped to fit people's endurance levels. Some projectors automatically move to the next

**INVITATION IDEA**

# HAVING WONDERFUL TIME—WISH YOU WERE HERE

**We'll all come along on your vacation on (date, time, place).**
Bring ten slides from your best vacation and come prepared for the mini-vacation of your life.

*(OPTIONAL IDEA)*
**Bring a vacation covered dish—something you might have eaten on your most fun vacation!**

*Example:*
SEASHORE TRIP: fish dish
SOUTHERN SUN: fruit dish

picture every ten seconds—and although I wouldn't recommend using them for this evening, I do like the principle they implement—keep the show moving. One picture does not rate a fifteen-paragraph commentary. People are just giving the highlights of their days of leisure—not an entire diary account.

## SUGGESTED ORDER FOR THE EVENING

Before guests arrive, make up one "Traveler's Check" for each person.

On each check put a vacation question. Suggest that guests find the answer to that question from as many other people as possible.

While people are getting to know each other better through the Traveler's Check technique, load your slide projector with everyone's slides.

I've suggested twenty traveler's check questions. If you have more people, add your own. Remember the object here is simply to give people something to do in the first minutes when guests are arriving.

*Traveler's Check Questions*
- Tell me about the worst vacation you've ever had.
- If you've had a vacation to another country, tell me

about some of the cultural shocks you received.
- If you could vacation anywhere in the world, where would you go and why?
- If you have ever taken a weekend or mini-vacation, tell me where you went and what you enjoyed most.
- What's the cheapest vacation you've ever taken? How did you keep costs down?
- What things have you done on your vacations with your family that have made the times distinctly "family"?
- Tell about some interesting people you've met on one of your vacations.
- What are your plans for this year's vacation?
- What's the strangest luggage story you've ever heard?
- If you've ever taken a packaged tour, what advantages and disadvantages did you find?
- Have you ever had to make an abrupt change in vacation plans and found the change more fun than the original idea? If so, share.
- If you could take a vacation with your family and anyone else from all of history, what person would you choose and why?
- What interesting experiences have you had with food in

foreign countries?

- Suppose you couldn't go outside a hundred mile radius of here for vacation. Where would you go and why?
- What's something you've learned about yourself on vacation?
- Tell something that happened to you on vacation that was or could have been dangerous.
- When you travel with your children in the car, what things do you do to keep them from getting bored?
- Tell a little about your first airplane trip.
- What's the best vacation you've ever had and why?
- Tell about some of the treasures you've picked up on vacation.

After guests have had time to mingle, gather them for the vacation slide show. You might want to do this in two half-hour segments with food in the middle. Perhaps you should go first with your vacation slides. Show the speed at which you want guests to move along. The whole success of this part of your party will depend on the pep at which the slides move. Slow slides are deadly!

I once had a slide party that lasted too long, and when the

lights went on, two men were fast asleep.

## FOOD IDEAS

Carry out the vacation idea. If you asked each person to bring a dish that might be served on one of his or her vacations, you'll have a fine and unusual array of food.

I've found it's a good idea to have a few vacation recipes handy to suggest to people who say, "I can't think of a thing." Once I share a few ideas like those that follow, people usually think of several better ones and don't use my suggestions at all. So use these as stimuli.

Any southern vacation:

## ORANGE CUBE GINGER ALE DRINK

*2 cups sugar*
*2 cups water*
*2 cups orange juice*
*1/4 cup lemon juice*
*grated rind of two oranges*
  *(optional)*
*2-3 quarts ginger ale*

Boil the sugar and water for 20 minutes. Add all other ingredients and freeze in an ice tray. Pour ginger ale over the orange cubes to serve.

## FRUIT COCKTAIL CAKE

*1-1/2 cups sugar*
*2 cups flour*

*1 teaspoon soda*
*2 whole eggs*
*1 can fruit cocktail*
*1/2 cup brown sugar (optional)*
*1 cup chopped nuts (optional)*

Mix sugar, flour, soda, eggs, and juice from the fruit cocktail. Fold in fruit. Pour all into a greased, floured pan (large). You may want to sprinkle the top with a half cup of brown sugar and a cup of chopped nuts.

Bake until done—about 40 minutes in a 350° oven.

### Icing

*3/4 cup sugar*
*1/2 cup condensed milk*
*1/2 stick butter*

Boil all ingredients. While cake is still hot, pierce it with a fork and pour the icing over it.

Any mountains or woods vacation:

## CHEESE CONES

*3 ounce package cream cheese, softened*
*1/3 cup grated cheese*
*1/4 cup mayonnaise*
*parsley flakes*

Combine all ingredients. Chill. Shape to resemble pine cones and stick almonds into the cheese base to complete a very realistic looking pine cone. Can be served with fruit and crackers.

Any seashore vacation:

## TUNA LOAF

*2 eggs*
*1/2 cup milk*
*2 cups soft bread crumbs*
*1/4 cup minced onion*
*1 Tablespoon minced parsley*
*1 Tablespoon Worcestershire sauce*
*1 teaspoon salt*
*1 teaspoon dry mustard*
*1/2 teaspoon tarragon*
*3 cans (6-1/2 or 7 ounces each) tuna, drained*

Combine eggs, milk, bread crumbs, and seasonings in mixing bowl. Beat until blended. Add tuna and mix thoroughly. Turn into a foil-lined loaf pan. Bake in moderate oven (350°) for about 45 minutes. Lift out of pan; remove foil. Serve with parsley sauce.

Parsley Sauce
*1 can condensed cream of celery soup*
*1/2 cup milk*
*2 Tablespoons chopped parsley*
*1/2 teaspoon dill weed*

Combine undiluted soup and milk; stir over low heat until hot. Add parsley to dill weed. This seaside treat will serve about 8.

## PRAYER

Before the meal, ask two people to pray, thanking God for

their vacations, and two people to thank him for work that makes vacations possible.

Sample vacation prayer:

Dear Heavenly Father, we all had a wonderful time last summer at the seashore. It seems far away now, but we still benefit from the rest and renewed energy those days gave. I appreciate your gift of vacation!

### Sample Work Prayer

I sometimes complain about my job, Lord, especially when I have to get up early in the morning. But then I consider people who don't have jobs, and I realize how fortunate I am. I appreciate your gift of work, Lord. It makes me appreciate the special times of vacation. More importantly, it gives me a way to contribute to others who have needs and to do special things for those I love.

### Host Prayer

We welcome your presence tonight, Lord, at our vacation party. Thank you for never taking a vacation from caring and loving us. Thank you for making it possible for us to have vacation foods. Thank you for memories of the successful holidays you have given us in the past and for the anticipation of vacations still to come.

## VACATION GAMES

If your guests are game people, you may want to plan a few for after the dinner and slides. Actually, let the time of evening and the feeling of the group determine this. If everyone is having a great time talking to one another, don't interrupt with games.

### A Visit to China

Play Chinese Checkers. If you don't have enough boards and marbles to plan the game in its original form, play it on a checkerboard. Use ten checkers per player and arrange the board like this:

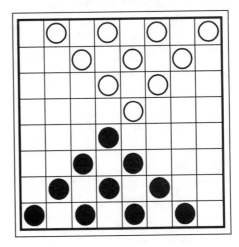

The object is to completely change sides on the board. The red checkers will end up on the same squares as the black checkers started, and vice versa. To do this players can jump their own and their opponent's checkers. Checkers jumped are not removed from the board. Jumps may be made both forward and backward across the board. The person with all checkers in place first wins.

*A Visit to Japan*

Jon, Ken, Poi is a quick, easy way to involve everyone. Each person gets a partner. Each partner makes a fist and moves it up and down while saying 'Jon, Ken, . . . " On the third word, Poi, partners make one of three symbols with their fists. They can symbolize a rock, scissors, or paper. The symbol each person makes will determine which partner wins.

scissors—two fingers extended
  like a scissors from the fist

rock—tight fist

paper—hand open, palm down

Winners:
  Scissors cuts paper,
    so scissors wins.
  Paper covers rock,
    so paper wins.
  Rock breaks scissors,
    so rock wins.

The person who has made the winning symbol finds another partner and plays again. This continues until two people are left. These two have a play-off. Since everyone playing is reduced by half each time Jon, Ken, Poi is played, the game moves quickly. If both players make the same symbol, they simply do the Jon, Ken, Poi again.

It might be fun to give fortune cookie prizes for this game and Chinese Checkers.

I often saw this game being played on the streets of Tokyo. Grown men would Jon, Ken, Poi as a simple way of making decisions. For example, one might say, "I'd love American food tonight." Another would reply, "I'd rather have sushi." No big deal. Just Jon, Ken, Poi and the winner chooses the food.

*Sand Castle at the Seashore*

Divide the group into pairs and sponsor a sand castle building contest. Use clay instead of sand. Set a short time limit and have a judging. The winning pair could take home a toy bucket and shovel prize.

*Piñata the Easy Way*

Explain that you tried to get a piñata from Mexico, but had to settle instead for some of the goodies that might be in one.

Put all these goodies on a tray. Show it to everyone in

the room for about twenty-five seconds.

Remove the tray and sing a song everyone knows. Then give people pencil and paper and ask them to list all the things that were on that tray. The person with the longest list wins.

Depending on what's on the tray, you might give its contents as the prize. If people tie, divide the spoils.

The tray might contain just about anything. For example, four different types of candies, a cupcake, a banana, a grape, a spoon, a napkin, beads, a greeting card, a pencil, a comb, an apple, an orange, a child's storybook, little toys. You'll need quite a few things to make the game as much fun as possible.

*Disneyland Postcard*

Everyone gets a pencil and an 8 1/2" x 11" sheet of paper. Everyone is to draw the castle at Disneyland or Disney World. If Jeff protests that he hasn't seen it, suggest he just draw the neatest castle he can imagine.

Then turn out all the lights. No one should be able to see what he or she is drawing. Allow several minutes for this creation. Turn on the light; everyone should sign the castle he or she drew. Judge the winners. Prizes could be comic books featuring any Disney characters.

# 6

## *Touch Another Generation*

*If your heart is not full of God,
you won't see God anywhere.
But if your heart is soaked with the sense of
God's presence, you will recognize that presence.
When we come together in very simple ways,
we sense the presence.*

—Henri Nouwen

HOW LONG HAS IT BEEN since your church's young people and adults had a good time together?

Church—The Christian institution that works hard to keep big people, little people, and the in-between people from meeting. Sunday school classes are age-graded. Many churches have youth and children's church. Teens sit with their peers during the worship service. Only the youth leaders get to come to youth activities. And my church completed its separation by having a youth prayer meeting.

Yes, in many ways being with our own age group is good. For example, as a child, I never would have prayed aloud in the adult prayer meeting. But still, by being kept apart, I was insulated from the needs, concerns, and joys of my church family's adults.

In these intergenerational parties, I would like to see the following things happen:

• Parents and young people will be provided with a neutral territory in which to get to know each other better and respect each other more.

• Adults in the church will gain a new appreciation for the abilities, talents, and gifts of the church's teens. Teens will gain a new appreciation for the abilities, talents, and gifts of the church's adults.

• Friendships, including accountability relationships, will be formed between young people and nonrelated adults.

Concerning this last point, it is true that often during the adolescent years, it's necessary for the young person to move away from parents in order to determine who he or she is and what he or she believes—as an individual—apart from parents. During this time, a teen tends to choose other adult confidants. Hopefully a Christian young person will choose Christian adults from the church—but that teen won't if he or she never meets them or has an opportunity to discover that they care.

A girlfriend of mine attended a church during her adolescent years in which she was totally separated from adults. Her family would part at the car in the morning when they arrived and return after church was over—often not seeing each other in the meantime. Sara was extremely artistic, but neither of her parents had skills in that area. Her father provided for her physical needs. Her mother tried to keep the lines of communication open, but she and Sara were so very different. So Sara pulled away from her parents and looked for another adult after whom she could pattern her life.

That listening, caring, artistic model that she needed could have come from an adult in her church—if she had known any. She didn't. Instead she chose as her model a non-Christian YWCA leader who taught classes in sketching and oils. Sara slowly drew away from the church. Today she is a model citizen, a perfect example of a community leader. A nicer, more helpful woman you could never wish to meet. She, like her non-Christian teacher, helps other young artists. She is careful not to dampen their enthusiasm. She lets them learn from her by example. She's always excited about their little steps forward.

But never a word about Christ. Months go by and she doesn't attend church. God is still a part of her life, but not a very big part. When she was growing up and needed to see how an artistic person like herself could live a life dedicated to Christ, there was no model available. What a difference a member of her church family could have made.

Of course there are positive examples of Christians living. This is what this chapter is aiming for. One pastor told of growing up in the church that loved him. He said, "My parents were alcoholics. I'm not sure they cared if I lived or died. I know they didn't care where I was or whether there was food in the house. A neighbor sensed there was something wrong in my house. She said, 'Every night at 6:30 there will be an empty chair and a place for you at our dinner table. Come any night you wish. You are part of our family.' At the same time, she invited me to Sunday school. I went and found Jesus Christ. Through my high school years, people from that church bought me jeans and shoes. After graduation a group of men told me that if I wanted to go to college they would pay my expenses. After college I knew God wanted me to become a pastor. Again those men offered to pay my way through seminary. Let me sing the praises of the Christians at that church. As a child, as a teen, they were the only people who loved me."

These party ideas are presented with the prayer that the men and women who implement them will make the Christian difference in the lives of the church children who participate in them.

A word about models. When you get involved with young people, you are putting yourself on display before them. That's dangerous.

First, you must be what you preach. Examine who you are on Sunday. Are you the same on Monday on the job—whether that job is in or outside the home? The answer is rarely an unqualified yes. We're all working daily at better patterning our lives after Christ. None of us has arrived. But the continuous struggle for a greater Christlikeness should be obvious.

One way I make certain growth is taking place is to ask myself the question, "What is there about me that I wouldn't want the young people in our church to copy?" I take the first answer that pops into my head, and with God's help begin to work on changing that area. One area I struggle with is putting products before people. I don't want the young people to copy that in me, and so I am working to make sure that I care as much about the people who work with me daily at my job as I do that the deadlines are met. I'm working on growing; I'm never full grown. I want my church's children to know this

and join me in this lifelong adventure.

You might try asking yourself the same question, and work on the first area that comes to your mind. Taking things one at a time makes it easier to measure results, and it's less depressing than trying to tackle the whole less-than-Christlike mess I am at once.

Second, don't be a surface friend. When I was growing up few adults ever shared their spiritual or personal struggles and problems with me. I wouldn't have been able to handle many of them, but I needed to know that those people hadn't arrived —Christ was still working in their lives. I needed adults to be honest with me.

Perhaps more than anything else honesty is the key to developing friendships with kids. Share a little of yourself as they are sharing themselves. Let them know that friendship works both ways. You'll listen and care and pray for them, and you expect them to do the same for you. You expect an in-depth friendship to develop.

I have tried this type of sharing friendship with the teens and younger children I've taught in Sunday school throughout my life. With no exceptions, I've found that they were willing to return that friendship. They were willing to participate in making a two-way relationship grow.

When I had a disease of the iris, my doctor told me, "The worst that could happen to you is that you'll go blind in that eye. Of course, you've got a mild case, and we're going to begin clearing it up immediately." I was a basket case after my visit. I kept waiting for my vision to dim. The problem struck Friday and on Sunday I told my class my fears about my eyesight. I shared with them my inability to let God take total control of the problem and to quit worrying. They understood, and we had a prayer time. Three or four of the guys prayed specifically about my eye—prayed with deep concern and without clichés. Right then that small group of teenagers was my support body in the church. I honestly feel that I couldn't have gotten better emotional support and continuing prayer support from any other group in the church.

I feel sorry that so many potential friendships go undiscovered because the church adult and the church young person never have an opportunity to meet and share.

What the ideas in this chapter can do is increase your circle of friends. Those friends may be young, but you'll find that they will enrich your own personal life—and their participation, creativity, and enthusiasm will increase the quality of life within your church family.

## Happy Birthday to Us

*Objective:* Christian teens and their parents will have an opportunity to share symbolic gifts, reaffirming their love for each other.

*Basic idea:* It's everyone's birthday all at once—one grand celebration for the entire year. Parents will be responsible for making and presenting symbolic gifts to their children; young people will be responsible for symbolically decorating and presenting cakes to their parents.

This party will be most successful if it is sponsored by people who are already involved with the young people at church—like youth sponsors and pastors, or Sunday school teachers.

Let both parents and teens know what your goals are. You might want to talk about them before the invitations are given. Keep things enthusiastic—after all, this is in part a tongue-in-cheek party.

## INVITATION IDEA

This invitation is written to the young person. Change the wording to appropriately direct a second invitation at the parents.

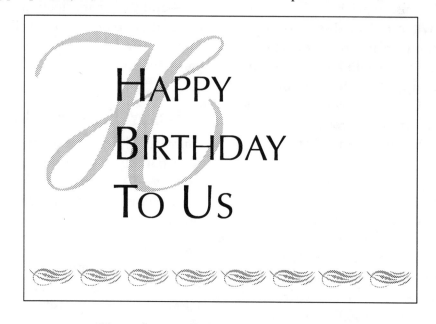

# HAPPY BIRTHDAY TO US

**FOR YOUR PARENTS.**

Don't bring gifts; just bring you.

And don't call and tell us it's six months 'til birthday time.

Everyone got born some date this year.

We just decided to celebrate all at once

**ON** *(date and time)*

**AT** *(place)*

Be sensitive to the feelings of young people who might not live with a natural parent. Encourage them to bring their guardians. Or there may be parents who want to come, but are unable. Suggest teens pick a parent-substitute from the church and come anyway. (The teen must check with Mom or Dad first. Parents should never feel the church is undermining them or pulling their children away from them.)

Some parents may not be part of the church program. Call these people with a special invitation and a rundown of the afternoon or evening activities. Parents who refuse to attend in-church events may be less hesitant about coming to something in a home or non-church building.

You may be surprised at who shows up for the birthday party.

### THE YEARS HERE

(This is a mixer designed to get people interacting)

Ask each person to write his or her age on a slip of paper and drop it into a box—no name necessary. Then each person is to guess the total number of years represented by the group, write it on a slip of paper, and give the guess to you.

Each person gets to ask three people a question from recent history that would help date him or her. If I were the host, a senior high student might ask me if I remember the bombing of Pearl Harbor. I would say, "No, I was too young." That doesn't tell him how old I was, but it gives him a clue. Or someone could ask an older parent, "Did you serve in Vietnam?" His answer, "No, but I was in the Army during the war," would begin to date him. Winner is the person who guesses closest to the correct number of years in your box.

The prize could be an inexpensive bottle of wrinkle cream or hand lotion.

### SHOW AND TELL

Each family should agree on one funny story about their family that might help the rest of the group get to know them a little better.

To get the thinking started, give an example of what you mean. I might tell the following story from my childhood: My brother Jim went fishing and caught a huge mud carp in the Conestoga River. He knew it couldn't be eaten, but he wanted to show it off to the rest of us, so he brought it home. Unfortunately, mud carp live a long time out of water and my mother couldn't bear to see the poor fish gasping. It was still flopping on our side porch ten minutes after Jim arrived home. Enough! My mother filled the tub with water and in went the fish. That evening every time we made any loud noises the fish would frantically race around the tub. Before morning it had died—of a heart attack, we think. Funny thing. Jim must have gone fishing other times after that, but never again did he bring his catch home.

## CAKE AND PRESENTS

Divide the parents and young people. During this half hour period, parents will create symbolic gifts for their children, and young people will decorate a birthday cake for their parents.

The cake: Make several sheet cakes and cut them into large pieces, each big enough to feed each parent attending and the teen. The more decorating materials you can provide, the better: candies, food coloring, icing, nuts, candles, construction paper. Each teen's assignment is to create a cake that tells something about how that teen feels about his or her parents. For example, Kesha could pile a huge icing mound on her cake and later explain to her mom, "I feel a mountain of love for you."

Encourage everyone to keep what they do positive and fun. They should know that they will be sharing the symbolism of their decorations with their parents before the group.

## LEMON PUDDING CAKE

Multiply the recipe to fit your needs:

*1 box lemon cake mix*
*1 Tablespoon finely grated lemon*
  *or orange rind*
*4 eggs*
*1/2 cup salad oil*
*1 cup cold water*
*1 box instant lemon Jell-O pudding*

Mix four minutes until mixture is smooth. Do not overmix. An electric beater is best. Grease pan and dust it with flour before turning batter into it. Bake at 350° for 50 minutes or until done. Cake is done when it springs back in the middle at the touch of a finger and does not leave a finger mark.

## BUTTERCREAM FROSTING

*4 Tablespoons flour*
*1 cup milk*

Mix into a paste and bring to a boil. Boil until thick. Cool.

*1 cup sugar*
*1 cup butter*
*1 teaspoon vanilla*

Whip ingredients. Add cooled flour mixture and beat with mixer 7 minutes.

## THE PRESENTS

Parents may have more trouble making symbolic gifts than young people have decorating their cakes. So be there with helpful ideas and encouragement.

Supply them with construction paper, scissors, tape, magic markers, material scraps, pins, and anything else that might go into the construction of a symbolic gift. Suggest parents think of some special gift that money can't buy—something they would like to give to their child. You might want to have one symbolic gift prepared ahead of time to give them an idea of what you're talking about.

For example, if I were making a gift for my teenager friend Peter, I'd make a great donut-shaped thing. Then I would attach to the circle other more unusual shapes, each with small holes in the center. When I gave it to him I would explain, "Peter, my gift to you is the development of your unusual creativity. Most people choose to go through life predictably. My large donut hole represents them. The other smaller, more unusual and perhaps more difficult shapes represent the directions open to you. You have the potential for doing many creative things for your Lord. My gift includes the prayer that you will dare to do them."

Encourage parents to choose symbolic gifts that can appropriately be shared in front of the whole group.

When both groups have finished, get them together again. You might want to draw family names from a hat to decide who goes in what order. Each young person should share what the cake means and parents what their symbolic gift means.

Be ready to ask parents or teens questions that will force them to elaborate on what they have created.

*Optional:* Take pictures of every gift and every cake. Use these as a reason for a follow-up note a few days after the party. Thank people for coming and sharing. You may want to share additional prints with people who are your church pray-ers. Suggest they pray daily for the family whose symbol you have given them.

## PRAYER TIME

When each family has shared, have a volunteer prayer time.

Keep the prayers optional. If you have non-Christians in your group, this part of the party may be difficult for them. You want them to feel a part of the group—affirmed, not threatened. But to leave out this personal response to God would be wrong. God is a part of the lives of most of the people who will attend this party, and he should be actively included.

People should thank God for other members in their families. Suggest they be as specific as possible. For example, I might pray for my father, "Thanks for Dad, Lord. I like the way he keeps track of my family history and shares interesting facts about my background with me."

## CAKE EATING PLUS

Young people should cut their cakes and share with their parents. Add to the cake any other goodies you wish—nuts, ice cream, candy, punch, coffee.

Suggest that people divide into groups of families—two families to each group. While the groups are eating they should be planning a humorous roleplay to present to the entire group after the cake is gone. In the roleplays the teens should play the parents and the parents the teens. Everyone in each group must be included.

Here are some roleplay ideas—enough for ten family units. If you need more, you can use one twice, or better still, develop some original ones.

*Roleplay 1*

You're in a van on vacation and have been traveling six days without any long stops. Roleplay your conversation. Keep it funny, and somewhat realistic. When you put on your roleplay for the whole group, line up the chairs as if they were van seats.

*Roleplay 2*

You are the modern version of the Swiss Family Robinson. Off you've gone to live in a tree. Roleplay some of your conversations including some of the fun and hardships of living in a tree. Be funny. When you share your roleplay with the whole group, you might stand in different parts of the room as if you were on different limbs of the tree.

*Roleplay 3*

You're all zoo animals—some are parent animals and the rest are teen animals. You're all behind the same zoo bars. Hold a conversation about the people watching you. Be funny. For the group you might want to line up as if you were all at the bars looking out.

*Roleplay 4*

You are part of a committee formed to ban chocolate in this country. You are presenting your case to the lawmaking body. Be funny as you give all the crazy ideas you can on why this makes sense. When you share your roleplay with the groups, you may want to sit in a horseshoe line.

*Roleplay 5*

You are part of a parent-teen baseball game. Make comments you might make to each other if you were really playing the game. Be as funny as possible as you mime the motions of the game. When you give the role-play, you may want to stand in a diamond shape as if this room were the playing field.

After the groups have put on their roleplays, follow the last one with a real parent-teen base-ball or volleyball game.

## Picture Perfect Scavenger Hunt

*Objective:* Church people who do not ordinarily have contact with young people will work as team members, getting to know them better, and building a wider church support base for the teens.

*Basic idea:* Adults and teens will participate in a photographic scavenger hunt.

Invite similar numbers of

church adults and young people to the hunt. With the adult guests, vary the ages. Some might be recently married; others could be grandparent-age. None of the adults invited should be parents of teens.

Make a special effort to let everyone know the goal of the party. Everyone is responsible for its success. You might even enlist the help of several teens in planning the adult guest list. Include two or three adults who already built friendships with the young people.

You'll need to buy a throw-away camera for each group of six guests. If the scavenger hunt teams get much bigger than six, there won't be enough group participation.

**PARTY PATTERN**
Everything is built around the picture idea:

*Give Away a Piece of Yourself*

You'll need to do something as guests arrive to break the ice and get teens and adults used to talking to each other. So try this idea. As each guest arrives, take a close-up Polaroid picture of his or her face. Cut that picture into four pieces with part of the face on each piece. Explain that each person is to give the pieces away to people he or

**INVITATION IDEA**

*(In this spot place a picture of yourself or your home.)*

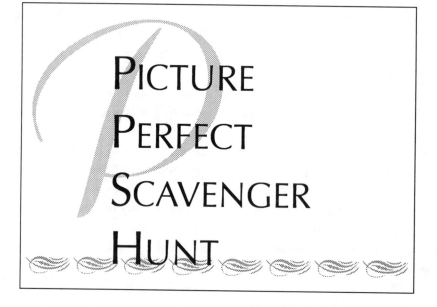

**P**ICTURE

**P**ERFECT

**S**CAVENGER

**H**UNT

**T**IME:  *(Remember you'll have to have daylight)*

**P**LACE: See picture for house (or host)

Come and team up with someone twice or half your age to take the pictures of a lifetime!

**B**RING **O**NE **I**CE **C**REAM **T**OPPING!

she doesn't know very well. Teens should give their pieces to adults, and adults should give their pieces to teens.

When they give their picture pieces away, they should allow the person who receives the piece to ask them three questions about themselves. Give a few examples of the type of questions that might be fun. For example, after an adult gives a teen a piece of his picture, the teen might ask. "What do you do for a living?" "What was the most fun party you ever attended as a kid?" "How do you feel about the young people in our church?" Each of these questions demands more than a one-word answer, and that's good for conversation.

A teen might give an adult a piece of her picture, and the adult could ask three questions of her. For example, "What's the most difficult thing about being in school right now?" "What are some of your favorite activities?" "Tell me something about the young people at our church that I probably don't know."

### Scavenger Hunt

After the mixer, divide the group into teams for the scavenger hunt. Try to have an equal number of teens and adults to send out on each team. Remember the old-time scavenger hunts when each team was given a list of things to find and bring back to home base first? A photographic scavenger hunt is exactly the same thing, but teams are given a list of pictures to bring back instead of a variety of other paraphernalia.

Give each team a camera and a list of the pictures it is to bring back. First team back wins.

Here's a starter list of pictures. Some of my ideas won't make sense in your area, but you could use this as an idea base.

### Photographic Picture List

1. Everyone in your team in one picture. Photographer may not be anyone attending this party. Photographer's name:

   _____.

2. Anyone standing on a roof.
3. A married couple not at this party holding hands.
4. A red car stopped for a red light.
5. Someone less than a year old.
6. A garage mechanic yelling.
7. A wildflower with a bug on it.
8. Something that doesn't make sense.
9. Someone over sixty laughing. Person laughing should not be from this party.

10. Someone doing something legal.
11. A father with an elementary child.
12. A green thumb.

When teams have returned with their cameras, take them for one-hour development. Use the "down time" for making and eating sundaes.

Half the fun of the evening will be groups sharing their shots. You'll want to make a display board. A long piece of paper—butcher paper or a paper tablecloth—would be perfect.

Make a great production of giving the winners a prize. For example, give each a cheap picture frame for a favorite scavenger hunt shot.

*Food*

Sundaes are easy and always popular. You supply the ice cream and have the guests bring different toppings. Encourage people to be creative. Here are some more unusual topping suggestions— just in case anyone asks for your ideas:

> *canned pie fillings*
> *honey and cinnamon granola*
> *chopped fresh fruit.*
> *(Try one of the new hybrids; for example, dinosaur eggs, a cross between a plum and apricot.)*
> *butterscotch pudding*
> *sunflower seeds*
> *all the regular goodies too*

*Picture games*

After the scavenger hunt and some snacks, the party may have gone on long enough. Or people may enjoy working together on some different types of pictures. Keep your ear carefully tuned to the tone of the party. Don't let things drag.

## MAKE-A-PICTURE GAME

You're the photographer.

Randomly divide the guests into groups to plan crazy pictures you suggest. Groups will have sixty seconds to plan and then everyone must stand perfectly frozen while you take a Polaroid shot. When all the pictures have been taken, the whole group will judge which are best and you'll award prizes.

You'll want to label each shot, so people will remember exactly what was being depicted in the shot.

One key to this game's success is choosing unique groups for each picture. Here are some ideas that you can try, again, in your own way:

1. Everyone in jeans. This means that everyone wearing jeans will be part of this

picture. You may have six in the shot or only two. However many are in this category will have to develop the picture you assign to them. A person may fit every category and be in every picture or be in just two or three. That's part of the fun. No one knows which pictures he or she will be in until you announce the group idea.

2. Everyone wearing purple.
3. Everyone with shoestrings.
4. Everyone who has played laser tag.
5. Everyone who remembers being jealous of a blond.
6. Everyone who knows the church telephone number by heart.
7. Everyone who would choose a butterscotch sundae over a chocolate one.
8. Everyone who is computer literate.

Add others. People who fit in these categories will develop the following pictures. Encourage people to be as funny about this as possible.

1. Picture of a farmer in his barnyard. Suppose everyone in jeans had to make this picture. One person would be the farmer and the others would be different animals. After the shot is developed, it can be labeled and placed on display. Later it can be judged against the others in some crazy categories.
2. Picture of a cow jumping over the moon.
3. Picture of the California gold rush.
4. Picture of the old woman in the shoe and her family.
5. Picture of a Ripley's "Believe It Or Not" exhibit.
6. Picture of a famous constellation.
7. Picture of two space ships docking.
8. Picture of a magazine ad for deodorant.

After all these crazy pictures are taken, display them for judging. Each person gets one vote in each category. Here are some categories you might use.

1. Picture that best illustrates the assignment: _____
2. Picture that shows the craziest amount of creativity:

   _____
3. Picture least likely to ever turn up in our church newsletter: _____
4. Picture with the most creative mix of young people and adults: _____

Since you really won't know how many will win in each

category, you'll want to have cheap, expandable prizes. For example, a handful of peanuts to everyone who was in the craziest picture, or a voucher for an ice cream cone at a local store.

If your church has an appropriate bulletin board, you might want to make a display out of these pictures and put them there for the whole congregation to enjoy.

## BABY PICTURES

If you can get baby pictures of each guest, display them on a board with a number beside each. Each guest gets a piece of paper, and the object is to tell the name of each baby pictured. The person with the most correct answers wins. The prize—how about a jar of baby food?

## PICTURE TALES

Before guests arrive, cut interesting pictures from magazines and put them on cards. For example, you could have a picture of a boy riding a bike, a ripe tomato, a mother at a supermarket, a teen playing football, a roast turkey, a couple fighting. The pictures should have no common theme.

Turn all the cards face down in the center of the room. To start, a volunteer will pick up any card, look at the picture, show it to the group, and begin telling a story about it. After about a minute of the story, you yell, "Switch," and that person will stop—even in mid-sentence. He or she will then point to another person who will pick up another picture and continue the story. Continue this way for several minutes. When one story has gone about far enough, you can start over with the pictures that are still face down. This is a fun, creative, and completely nonsensical game.

Here's how one story might start out. The first person picks up a picture of a girl holding roses. He might say, "Ellie was just thrilled. Her first roses. But she had no idea who had sent them. No card. You would think that the person . . ."

And you yell "Switch!" The person points to the next person to continue the story. She picks up a card of an old mule, and says, ". . . would have been more considerate. After all, she spent every day in the fields working with her old mule, who was actually allergic to roses. In fact, even a whiff of them sends him off kicking and braying. Ellie decided that she must . . ."

And so the game goes on.

## Pass-Along Skills

*Objective:* Middle-school children and the older people in the church will have an opportunity to become friends and share or learn a handicraft skill.

*Basic idea:* People with special needlework and other craft skills will teach them to young teens from their church. They will work together through the evening to teach and learn the basics.

This party idea had its conception back in my old junior high days in my Lancaster county neighborhood. The women for about a mile radius decided they would meet once a month to do their mending. Since I was the only half child/half woman in that area, I was invited to attend. It was great fun. I got to know and appreciate these women, some of them four times my age. The adult conversation was great. I learned some of their concerns and the things that they considered their successes. I learned to talk with them, and was thrilled when they listened and seemed to think that what I said made sense. They made me happy that I would someday be an adult woman.

Few of these women were strongly involved in a church and many didn't claim to be Christians. Yet because they lived in the same community, they seemed to sense that they should be important parts of each other's lives. I've rarely seen that type of support and caring duplicated by the local church. But perhaps this party will help change that.

Call or see each young person and explain in detail what you have in mind and what your goals for the evening are. Of course, before you can send out invitations, you'll need to get the support of all the older people in your church who are willing to be part of your togetherness activity so you'll know what crafts you'll be offering.

Stress that this is not a big achievement evening. Everyone will be having a good time even if kids never master anything as simple as the crochet chain stitch. The big thing is learning to know each other and to appreciate each other's abilities and skills.

There's a world of truth in Randy Raybrook's statement in *Discipleship Journal,* "Some people become better disciplemakers as they get older, not because they have learned more techniques, but because they know themselves better."

**INVITATION IDEA**

# Pass-along Skills

---

**Learn a skill taught by one of the people in our church.**

**Stretch your mind; stretch your fingers.**

When:

Where:

**Instruction available in:** *(change list to fit the skills of the people in your church)*

CROCHETING, MACRAMÉ, PIN STRIPING,

BREAD MAKING, KNITTING.

## NO FEAR FACTOR

You may be hesitant about trying this idea because you've heard horrible tales about young teens. A few of them are probably even true, but this evening has built-in safeguards which will eliminate the discipline problems that can be part of this maturation level. Middle schoolers, usually ages 11 through 14, relate extremely well to the generations older than their parents. So grandparent-and-older-aged people are often on their wavelength.

Many kids this age have not been exposed to traditional handicraft. It's something new, and its very newness will hold their interest. Their hands are fully developed and they have the mental skills to master patterns quickly. I remember the day my great-aunt Sarah came to visit. I was twelve. I couldn't tell you what she looked like, but I'll never forget the gift she gave me. She taught me to do the chain stitch and two other crochet stitches. I think I put edging around every handkerchief in the house. Of course, Kleenex soon became popular, and I discovered dating, so I never really learned skilled crocheting. But in that one day I had my only taste of "grandmothering" and I just loved it.

To this day I use the needles she gave me to catch tears in knits, and more importantly, I learned to look with appreciative eyes at the beautiful things craftspeople of other generations had made.

You're supplying grandmother and grandfather figures. Our mobile society and broken homes have robbed many young people of their grandparents, and our communities often do not have a good mix of older and younger people. Many young people have never even held a conversation with someone who remembers World War I. They have never touched the wrinkled hand of an elderly person and glimpsed a bit of the preciousness of life and how very short life can be.

On an evening like this, you'll see reflections of the type of woman and men these people will be in five years. It can be a very reassuring evening.

With this evening, you are also opening the way for turnabout occasions. At this party the older people are the teachers, but there are many things young people can teach and do for the older people. And these things may happen if you provide a friendship opportunity.

One local school system

started a grandmother adoption idea and had its young people plan an evening for senior citizens. Thirteen-year-old Billy told me about his elderly date. "I couldn't believe she agreed to come to our party, and was it ever interesting to listen to her talk! She was born and lived for twenty years in England and still has an accent. And she's lived in the same house in Oak Park for fifty-four years. That's a lot longer than my dad has even been alive.

"I don't think she had ever been around young people much before our school party. But now that it's over, she feels good about us.

"I brought brownies to the party, and she told me how much she enjoyed them. So I'm planning to make her some more. Maybe that one evening was the start of a real neat friendship.

"She belongs to a senior citizens' group," he continued. "They often make fun and interesting craft projects. She's promised to make me a monkey out of a sock. I've seen them in stores and I think they're kind of neat.

"You should have been at the party. Some of the people there told us stories that went clear back to horse and carriage days.

All together they had lived over 2145 years! And if I couldn't learn something from all that experience, I'd have to be pretty dumb."

If this evening works, turn it around completely in a few months and have the young people offer to teach their skills to older adults: computer games, playing on the Internet, making computer artwork, writing and laying out the Sunday bulletin on the computer.

## STRUCTURING THE EVENING
### Display

Consider having a little exhibition of the older people's work on display when guests arrive. Be sure to place the names of the people beside their handicrafts. In communities where there are fairs, some may have won ribbons. If so, display them with the crafts.

### Preparation

It will make things easier for you if you ask each person to supply all the materials one young teen will need. This would include the correct needles, yarn, thread, anything that is needed to practice. This doesn't mean that the older guests are to bring enough materials for the teen to complete a whole project. Just enough for him or her to learn on. (If you have more teens than older people, some will have to teach two or more kids and should bring supplies for them. If this would be a financial hardship, enlist grandparent-age people who will not be teaching to contribute money for supplies.)

*When Guests Arrive*

Have magic markers or crayons and name tags. Each person should write his or her name in large, clear letters. The color the person chooses should tell something about him- or herself.

People should then talk to several people they don't know very well and find out why they chose the colors they did. In these early moments, you want to establish communication between the older and younger group.

*Tour Through the Crafts (Optional)*

I like this option because it gives each teen three minutes with every woman and man at the party and exposes each student to all the crafts represented.

Position the teachers at different spots throughout the house where they will be working for the evening. Give each teacher a number which he or she sets by a station. Then ask all the kids to go to different spots so there will be at least one teen with each teacher. (If you have more teens than teachers, two may have to go to the same spot.)

Each person spends three minutes with the first crafter. When you blow a whistle, the person will move on to the next number. So the teen at number 1 will go to number 2. The teen who started at number 4 will move on to number 5. If you have only 9 numbers, the kids will move to number 1 after they have been to that last number. During the three minutes people should find out a little about each other: names, where they live, etc. The teacher might have time to show what he or she does.

This is optional. If you have a large group of teachers and middle schoolers, it would take too long to do this. Simply go from the colored name activity to the actual teaching experience.

*Learning a Craft*

Each teen should go to the adult to whom he or she has been assigned. You may want to tell each person before the party which adult he or she will be working with. Some adults will be more popular and outgoing than others and the teens who get the people who seem less exciting might groan out loud if they don't know ahead of time who their teacher will be. That would definitely dampen the evening. Also if decisions are made ahead of time, the teens may have some choice in what they will be learning.

As the couples work around the house, visit the little groups. Give encouragement and praise. If necessary, sit for awhile and enter into the conversation. Tell the workers that they will show what they have completed—obviously not much, but it will allow for group cheering, clapping, and a sense of achievement on the parts of the teacher and student.

I remember how I felt when a woman in my neighborhood taught me to color black and white studio portraits with transparent oils. I took my pictures to our neighborhood meeting, and the women were absolutely amazed at how beautifully I had done. I found those pictures in my attic recently, and they weren't so hot. But that affirmation, I believe, was real. I wasn't good at it yet, but I was doing something they didn't do and they were pleased with my effort.

## GRANDPARENT'S KITCHEN

There are any number of options here. I've suggested just three. But food will be a fun part of this evening no matter which option you choose. Rumor has it that middle schoolers and grandparent-aged people love to eat. Pay special attention to the concept behind "grandparent-aged." A single woman in her forties or a childless widow in her sixties will make as effective a stand-in grandmother as a woman with twelve grandchildren of her own.

*Option 1*

Have each grandparent bring along a favorite dessert. Put the creator's name beside each dessert. You might also want to have recipe cards beside the desserts so the young person can take home the how-to and reproduce something he or she thought was delicious.

*Option 2*

Grandparents cookie jar. Ask each guest to bring along six or seven of his or her favorite cookies. You supply the milk, hot chocolate, and decaf.

*Option 3*

Plan an old-fashioned meal—the type that great-grandparents

Mix the cold milk and gelatin. In double boiler, scald. Add sugar and slightly beaten egg yolks.

Return to double boiler and cook until mixture coats a spoon. Stir constantly. Remove from heat, add salt, vanilla, egg whites. Turn into mold. Chill.

Garnish Spanish Cream with orange marmalade.

You may want to make individual molds. If so, use only 1 Tablespoon gelatin. One mold will serve 8. Make as many molds as you'll need for your entire group.

## MOTHER'S MEAT LOAF

*1 1/3 cups dry bread crumbs*
*2 cups milk*
*2 pounds ground beef*
*1 pound ground pork*
*4 eggs unbeaten*
*1/2 cup minced onion*
*2 teaspoons salt*
*2 teaspoons Worcestershire sauce*
*1 teaspoon sage*
*1 teaspoon garlic powder*
*1/4 teaspoon pepper*

### Sauce:

*1/2 cup catsup*
*1/3 cup brown sugar*
*2 teaspoons dry mustard*
*1/2 teaspoon nutmeg*
*1/2 teaspoon oregano*

Combine bread crumbs with milk; let stand for 5 minutes. Add remaining ingredients; mix thoroughly. Shape mixture into loaf on a 13" x 9" x 2" pan. Mix catsup, brown sugar, mustard, nutmeg, and oregano; spread over meat. Bake at 350° for 1-1/2 hours. Serves 16.

## CHICKEN CASSEROLE

*4 chickens, cooked and deboned*
*4 packages frozen broccoli*
*4 cans condensed chicken soup*
*2 cups mayonnaise*
*2 teaspoons lemon juice*
*2 teaspoons curry powder*
*2 cups bread crumbs*
*2 cups cheddar cheese, shredded*
*4 Tablespoons melted butter*

Cook broccoli. Line buttered casserole dishes with broccoli. Cover with sauce made of soup, mayonnaise, lemon juice, and curry powder. Place chicken pieces on top. Cover with bread crumbs, shredded cheese, and top with melted butter. Bake 25 minutes in a 350° oven. Serves 16.

### CRACKER PUDDING

This old Pennsylvania Dutch recipe is one of my favorites, and I'm not alone. When the company I work for had its hundredth birthday, this Cracker Pudding recipe won first prize in its Early American Foods Contest. On the other hand, it can be tricky. I took it to my boss's house as my contribution to dinner and it never set. There was my milky offering with a few crackers floating in it. I've been invited back, but he never fails to warn me, "Bring something other than that cracker stuff."

*4 quarts milk*
*3 cups rolled saltine crackers*
  *(not so fine)*
*4 scant cups of sugar*
*2 cups coconut*
*8 eggs (whites separate)*

Blend sugar and egg yolks thoroughly. Pour scalded milk over them and add crackers. Cook but don't boil. When mixture nears the boiling point, add coconut. Heat again to near boiling. Remove from stove and fold in stiffly beaten whites. Cool. Serves 16.

### OATMEAL CAKE

*1 cup oatmeal*
*1-1/4 cups boiling water*
*1/4 pound butter*
*1 cup brown sugar*
*1 cup granulated sugar*
*2 eggs*
*1-1/3 cups flour*
*1 teaspoon soda*
*1 teaspoon vanilla*
*1/2 teaspoon cinnamon*
*1/2 teaspoon nutmeg*
*1 teaspoon salt*

Pour boiling water over 1 cup oatmeal. Set aside and do not stir. Cream butter, brown sugar, and granulated sugar. Add 2 whole eggs one at a time, beating well after each. Beat oatmeal mixture with a spoon and add to creamed mixture. Fold in flour, soda, vanilla, cinnamon, nutmeg, salt. Bake in a long pan at 350° for 25-30 minutes.

### Topping

*1/4 pound butter*
*1 cup brown sugar*
*1 cup coconut*
*1 cup chopped nuts*
*2 egg whites, beaten stiff*

Mix the butter and brown sugar over low heat until it comes to a full boil. Remove from heat and add coconut, nuts, egg whites. Spread over the cake; return it to oven and bake 15 minutes longer.

It's a good idea to wait until the cake is almost done to make the topping so you can add it to the cake while it's still very hot.

## PRAYER TIME

No matter which refreshment direction you go, plan a prayer time before the food. Ask two older people and two younger ones to pray. The older ones should thank God for young teens and the kids should thank God for what the older Christians in their church can teach them. The prayers might go something like this:

*Woman Teacher:* "It's been an exciting evening, Lord. I'm extremely happy with the young people who are part of our church. Thank you for them, and especially thank you for (name of the girl she worked with), and her potential for serving you. It was fun working with her. I believe I speak for all the adults here when I say, Thank you, Lord, for our young people."

*Middle School Girl:* "Dear Heavenly Father, I learned a lot tonight and perhaps most important, I gained an appreciation for some of the older people in our church. Thank you for their trust in you. I want to grow toward you, as they have. Thank you for giving them to me as examples and as friends."

# 7

# Project Parties

*Preach the Gospel at all times;*
*if necessary, use words.*

—*St. Francis of Assisi*

These three hospitality ideas are directed toward people who attend the morning worship hour or other all-church functions, but have not been part of the planning. At one party the guests will make banners. At another, they will develop a Scripture and slide presentation, and at the third they will encourage missions awareness at a party to plan a party.

These ideas have special appeal to teenagers and young singles in the church. They encourage them to get excited about ideas, and when ideas arrive, not to just entertain them, but to put them to work!

When an event is structured around a project, it's easy to determine if the goals were met. If the project got planned, you made it! But with these three ideas, go a step further by aiming at these results:

- People of different age groups will work together harmoniously. Each will contribute his or her best and be willing to assume the roles of leader or follower in order to most effectively complete the project.

- Each person in the project will understand the project's greater purpose and accept prayer responsibility for those at whom the project is aimed.

- The total church will benefit from these projects and through them be inspired to greater service.

- Teens and young singles will accept additional responsibilities for the ongoing work of their church. Each person will have the opportunity of working with church leaders in brainstorming and creating these ideas.

## Raise The Banners High

### A Party to Make Special Church Banners

*Objective:* People of different ages will brainstorm, plan, and develop banners for the church. (Until recently, most churches displayed banners only at holiday seasons. An Easter service, a youth day program, or the Christmas Sunday school program all provided excellent banner opportunities. This limitation is no longer true. Think broadly. Create banners for the church year, a special series of sermons, even events that encourage Christians to get involved in the church community.)

Participants will come to know each other better and, by working on this project, feel more a part of the ongoing activities of the church.

**Basic idea:** Church people will create original banners to be hung in the church sanctuary or fellowship hall.

I remember my first exposure to making banners. For weeks my pastor had been preaching about God's giving of his law to the children of Israel. He carefully went over each commandment and its implications for Christians today. Finally the law had been explained, and he suggested that we plan a celebration as a conclusion to the series. We would be praising God for His loving understanding in setting perfect rules for us to follow. The pastor encouraged us to use our creativity and come with praise banners to decorate the church the following Sunday. It was great. The place was filled with homemade banners, many of them attached to broomsticks. Each celebrated our commitment to His Word. "Praise Our Lawgiver!" "Obey—Yes!" "Wave Our Praises High." What a variety of phrases and designs. Yes, there was an amateur aspect to the banners, a

little like "happy hands at home." So what? The church was our home and it was beautiful in a new way. Its uniqueness was an excellent stimulus to worship.

## INVITATION IDEA

Plan a word-of-mouth invitation. Select the number of people you want. Let's suppose you think nine people could develop the three banners you are planning. Begin by sharing the idea with the pastor. If he's enthusiastic, continue by asking him to attend the party and explain what direction he is planning for the worship on the Sunday when the banners will be flown. Ask him to start the invitation chain by calling one other person he thinks might enjoy this type of activity. That person is to be a different gender and different age than he is. That person's number is 1. After that person accepts, the pastor should explain that the person is to call one other person of a different age and gender and invite that person, and give him or her the number 2. And so on until nine people have agreed to come. In this way, you'll get an unusual mix of people, and probably each person will have at least two other friends as part of the group. Make certain, however, that everyone invites another person who in turn accepts. You might want to follow the chain through a second time a few days before the party.

Work hard to get different ages involved. A middle-school child brings a lot to an adult group. Wouldn't you like a church like the one Dean Merrill describes in "Not Married, With Children" (*Christianity Today*, July 14, 1997)? It's called the Church by the Side of the Road, Seattle. Their senior pastor explained, "We pay as little attention to age as possible. If you come to our church on a Wednesday night, you'll see 60 young people, ages 2–17, all in one group! Working with them will be 30 adults—a 1:2 ratio—guiding a wide range of learning experiences. The other night I stopped by, and there was this wonderful Kodak moment: a cluster of four or five energetic little kids gathered around two adult workers: a lady who's in a wheelchair—she's probably in her early seventies—and a 24-year-old single guy."

## MATERIALS EACH GROUP WILL NEED

*scissors that are sharp enough to cut material*
*white glue, such as Elmer's Glue*
*marking pens*
*needle and thread*
*banner fabric*

Heavy fabrics work best because they cut easiest. Felt is most common, but burlap, canvas, and suede cloth will also work.

Trimming material: Here you are limited only by your supplies and imagination. Consider ribbons, fringe, artificial flowers, and pictures large enough to be seen throughout the church.

*Optional:* Patterns for letters. Everything else works well drawn freehand, but your people may prefer stencils for letters. The larger the better. Check your local artist supply store. If you're operating on a huge budget, you might consider professional letters that can be stuck directly to all the materials mentioned.

Decide how the banners will be hung before the guests start working on them. Depending on the size of the banners and the room in which they will be displayed, different methods will work. Some can be hung by attaching string to the banner's top and dangling the banner from a nail. To hang the banner more freely, use a board or broom handle at the top of the banner. Wrap the material around the board or handle and staple it to itself. Then attach wire or cord to each end of the handle and hang it from the ceiling.

My brother Jim enjoys welding and has all the equipment in his garage. He would never accept an invitation to a banner party, but he would enjoy making banner holders—a task every bit as creative as developing the banner itself. Encourage men like Jim to get involved in ways that use their skill sets.

It's important that you make hanging decisions before work begins, because in some cases, this will limit working space. For example, if you're going to wrap the top of the banner around a broom handle, people need to work down about six inches from the top of their banner. Otherwise words or symbols will be lost.

## PLAN FOR
## THE EVENING

### *The Banners' Purpose*

The pastor should share the purpose behind the banners. This is not just busywork for happy partygoers. Hopefully the banners will help focus people's attention on Christ and play a part in their determining to be more dedicated to Him. The pastor gives an informational and pep talk.

### *Working Units*

Divide the group into working units—one unit for each banner. Try to put one leader-type in each group, although that person won't be a designated leader. Leadership should fall naturally as the plans for each unit's banner progresses.

Go over the process each unit should follow. Begin by making sure everyone knows everyone else. The group should then brainstorm ideas for their banner. This means they will be suggesting words, shapes, and decorations that will go into developing the best possible banner. Remind everyone to keep a brainstorming mind-set in the first part of this discussion. Everyone should throw in every idea he or she can think of—even if it doesn't sound so great at first. Perhaps someone else will take it and refine it into the best idea ever.

When all ideas are presented, the unit should pick the best idea and begin planning how the banner will look. It's usually best to sketch a rough of the proposed idea.

The unit should then assign work tasks. Someone could be in charge of cutting the letters. Another person could fringe the material. A third could work to make the symbolic picture.

Encourage the people in the unit to talk as they work. This is, after all, a party. The job has to get done, but if people don't have a good time doing it, half the party's purpose is lost.

Here are some sample banners. The first is an all-symbolic banner which would be perfect for either Christmas or Easter. It was developed by Rich Nickel, a designer, as a page decoration in a Sunday school curriculum. Later it became a church banner. A manager of a large Chicago restaurant saw it and decided it would make a great Christian conversation starter for his office, so he had Rich do an airbrush of the design. "When people ask what the design means," said the manager, "I can explain the truths of John 3:16." For people who are picture literate, this visual representation of what Christ has done for us can be the starting point for conversion.

Choose colors which would add to people's understanding of the symbolism. For example, in the illustration both circles could be yellow.

The line could be gray, and the half circle which represents earth could be green—or perhaps gray. The background could be tan or light blue.

Of course, these aren't the only workable colors, but plan your poster as a total unit—colors, symbols, and words should all blend and all contribute to the message.

The next banner incorporates words with simple art. Encourage your people to keep all illustrations extremely simple; then they will be easier to execute on the banner background, and more easily understood by people who see them at a distance. This poster might be perfect for Easter. Hands could be black and white felt, and the lettering could be any bright color that will shine out from the background color. Yellow words on a red background would work.

It is also possible to plan a whole banner using words only. Usually people would want to hand letter an all-word banner so they can mold the words into a pleasing pattern.

A Thanksgiving banner built around Psalm 30:12 might look something like this:

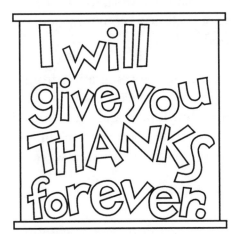

The color on an all-word banner could be used to emphasize the most important words. The unit might choose *you* and *forever*. Or since it's Thanksgiving, it might pick *thanks forever* as the focus.

*After the Banners*

Each unit has already seen what the others are doing, but encourage a formal showing. Each group might tell why it chose the direction it did and what some of its other close-running options were.

The laborers are worthy of some good food. Since your house is probably covered with pins and paste and material scraps, don't get too fancy with the food. Why not plan something that can be taken out of the refrigerator and served? And don't forget the paper plates.

## SANDY'S NO-CRUST PIE

In the blender, combine:
  *4 eggs*
  *1/2 cup flour*
  *2 cups milk*
  *4 teaspoons soft butter*
  *1/2 cup sugar*
  *1 teaspoon vanilla*
Stir in by hand 1 cup of coconut. Pour into a greased and floured pie pan. Bake for 40 minutes at 350° or until an inserted knife comes out clean.

## GERMAN SWEET CHOCOLATE CAKE

  *1 package German chocolate*
  *1/2 cup boiling water*
  *1 cup butter*
  *2 cups sugar*
  *4 egg yolks, unbeaten*

1 teaspoon vanilla

1/2 teaspoon salt

1 teaspoon soda

2-1/2 cups sifted cake flour

1 cup buttermilk

4 egg whites

Melt chocolate in boiling water. Cool. Cream butter and sugar until light and fluffy. Add egg yolks one at a time, beating after each. Add chocolate and vanilla. Sift together salt, soda, and flour. Add alternately with buttermilk to chocolate mixture, beating well after each addition. Beat until smooth. Beat egg whites until stiff peaks form. Fold into batter.

Bake at 350° for 30 to 40 minutes.

### Coconut Pecan Frosting

1 cup evaporated milk

1 cup sugar

1/4 pound butter

3 egg yolks

1 teaspoon vanilla

Combine in a saucepan and cook over medium heat until mixture thickens (about 12 minutes). Add about 1-1/3 cups coconut and 1 cup chopped pecans. Beat until frosting is cool and thick enough to spread.

### RICE PUDDING

1 cup water

1/2 cup rice

Cook for seven minutes. Add 1 quart milk and 1/2 stick of butter. Cover and cook 1-1/4 hours on low heat.

Beat 2 eggs. Add to them 1/2 cup sugar, 1/2 cup raisins, and 1/2 teaspoon vanilla.

Mix together. Sprinkle with cinnamon and sugar. Serve hot or cold.

## Sight and Sound Scripture Alive!

*Objectives:* Christians will gain a new appreciation for God's Word as they plan and present a scriptural choral reading. Christians will work together as a vocal choir to communicate God's Word.

*Basic idea:* Representatives from different age levels in the church will plan and carry out an illustrated Scripture reading for the morning worship service.

### THE PASTOR

He's the key. If he doesn't think a scriptural choral reading is a good idea, don't plan this project party. If he is in favor, ask him to be at the planning event and share with those who will participate what the theme of his morning service will be and which Scriptures he has chosen to use. This choral reading is illustrated with slides. As the slides can take several weeks to develop, he will have to have this information at least a week before the presentation Sunday. (If someone in your group can make large color prints, you can transfer them to overheads for an overnight presentation.)

## WHY CHORAL READING?

How long has it been since you've been excited by Scripture reading? The children of Israel used to listen for hours to God's Word being read aloud to them. I can't believe that the reader was unexcited about sharing the stories of Abraham and the trials of the prophets and the beautiful language of the psalmist.

But today, am I unfair in saying that most adults read children's fairy tales with more enthusiasm and expression than they do God's Word? God gave us our voices with which to praise Him. Choral reading will help people who have never stood before the congregation and praised God to get involved. In this scriptural choral reading, people will be challenged to make the most of God's gift of voice.

I remember the times I've heard my friend Karen read the Bible. I've been amazed! She makes it come alive. She took me along with the Apostle Paul as he spoke to his churches. She made me feel the terror of the disciples on a wind-wild sea. She helped me feel some of the love that went into God's gift of Jesus Christ. I come from a background of well over three decades of Sunday Bible readings. I have heard God's Word stumbled over, droned through, and even shouted. But Karen's reading was something different. She paused where pauses made sense. She let her voice race excitedly through the material that was so special it left the listener breathless. She stopped dead when she came to the mention of sin and its awful consequences. She read with expression about the Christian's responsibility, and I was excited about hearing God's Word read.

Today's project party is designed to put renewed enthusiasm and understanding into the Bible reading at your church.

Choral reading involves talking, using the same vocal grouping and getting much the same effect as a singing choir. I enjoy it so much because I come from a Mennonite background where it seemed everyone could sing— without a piano and in perfect four-part harmony. Not me. I hit a fifth part. I quip that for years I thought I was adopted because I didn't fit the Mennonite singing pattern. I don't have an awful singing voice, but the closest I've ever come to using it to present special music to the Lord was at a Sunday evening youth group meeting where my brother and I whistled a duet.

But speaking! I can talk, and talk with expression. Choral readings allow me to praise God in a special way and I love it. I think there are many people who don't belong in church choirs who would feel the same way I do about choral reading.

The first church in which I heard choral reading used as part of the morning worship had a large international university population. One Sunday when the worship centered around the greatness of God, students from lands around the world participated in an unusual choral reading. It began with each person reading the Scripture in his or her native tongue and concluded with everyone reading the verses together in English, each in a different accent. What a beautiful around-the-globe reading it was.

## WHO TO INVITE

Why not pick an equal number of people from each Sunday school class, starting with the upper elementary class (fourth and fifth graders) and moving up through the adult classes? For example, if you planned for ten people in the choral reading, two would come from the elementary class, two from middle school, two from senior high, two from college singles class, and two from the adult class. You might want to do all the inviting by phone or in person. This is a work session, and in order for it to be successful you have to have five or more attend.

## BEFORE THE PARTY

You've got what appears to be a big job, but stick with me. It's really quite simple. You, with perhaps the help of the pastor and your choir director, should develop the basic scriptural choral reading. This will allow you to have copies duplicated before project party time. Each person participating should have a personal script.

Remember, this is a scriptural choral reading. You will not be writing a single original word. Every word will come directly from Scripture. A word or phrase may be repeated, but it's against the rules to change words.

Follow these simple steps:

1. Read the passage several times. Really get to know it. Ask yourself which words are most important. Which phrases jump out at you and emphasize what the pastor will be saying the Sunday this reading is read? In order to get to know the passage better, you could do an inductive study of it. For directions on simple inductive Bible study, see pages 93 to 98.

2. Begin to write the script, using the words of the passage. Repeat the sections that you wish to emphasize. Never take away or add words. As you write you should leave a two inch margin on the left-hand side of the paper, or double space. This will allow those participating to write in the names of the people who will be saying each line and to underline or circle words they feel should be given special expression.

Here's a starter sample from John 3:16, 17.

*Carrie:* For God loved the
world so much

*Carrie and Brad:*
For God loved
the world so much

*Everyone:* For God loved the
world so much that He
gave His only Son so
that anyone who
believes in Him shall
not perish but have
eternal life.

*Carrie:* For God loved the world

*Elvan:* God did not send His Son
into the world
to condemn it,

*Brad:*  but to save it.

*Thomas:* Condemn

*Carrie:* Save

*Thomas:* Condemn

*Carrie:* Save

*Everyone:* Save, save, save.

*Brad:*  For God loved the world
so much that He gave.

Of course, your passage may be longer than two verses. What I've provided is just a sample.

Look at what I've done. I've started with phrases. Then I built a comparison between two very different words—condemn and save. The participants will have to decide how best to communicate the difference between the two. Perhaps a strong male voice will throw out the word, "Condemn." The group will respond with a loud, joyful, "Save." The fact that God loved is emphasized in the repetition of the phrase. This phrase could be said matter-of-factly the first time and could build in expression and excitement as people catch the implications—the God of the universe loves everyone—even me!

## WHEN GUESTS ARRIVE

Explain the plan of the evening. The pastor may share what text will be made into a choral reading and how he plans to use that text in his sermon. You give a little background on the value of choral reading. Explain that guests will be preparing the reading and then talking about slides which would illustrate the reading.

Slides may actually be taken at the party or scheduled for some later time. The final part of the work session will be spent practicing the reading.

Remember that this event must take place at least three weeks before its results are shared with the congregation. You'll need that time to practice the reading several times, take the pictures, get them developed, and coordinate the speaking with the illustrative slides.

## INTO THE READING

Pick two people to read the Scripture directly as it is written in the Bible. This will give everyone a feeling for the whole text.

Then divide into two task forces.

Each force is to consider the meaning of the text and how the voices in its group can best portray that meaning. Remind people that every singing combination is a possible speaking combination—whole group together, solo, duet, trio. Give the groups time to experiment, to have fun planning the best way to share.

When parts have been assigned, each group should begin practicing and refining what it has done. Refining would include picking the correct expression, deciding on volume levels, and picking special words to emphasize.

Set a time limit on this planning. Go from group to group in the early planning stages to answer any questions, and to make certain the group is headed in the right direction. When there are about five minutes left, give groups a warning so they can put on the final touches.

After the planning is finished, have each group present what has been done for the other.

From the best in both groups, develop the final script. Use everyone in the reading. Those who don't have special parts will be important when the group reads in unison.

A final script might look something like this:

**Alice**
For God loved the world so much (softly)

**Alice & Jane**
For God loved the world so much (louder)

**All**
For God loved the world so much that He gave His only Son so that anyone who believes in Him shall not perish (build to a trumpet finish)

**Bob**
But have eternal life. (joyfully)

**Alice**
For God loved the world so much. (softly)

**All**
God did not send His son into the world to condemn it, but to save it. (Start softly and slowly. Build to a finish.)

**Jack**
Condemn (angry, loud)

**Alice**
Save (soft)

**Jack**
Condemn (loud, anger)

**Alice**
Save (louder)

**All**
Save, save, save. (very loud, joyful)

**Jack & Alice**
For God **LOVED** the **WORLD** so much that He **GAVE**. (Emphasize key words)

## SOME HINTS FOR BETTER CHORAL READINGS

A choral group should pick a speaking leader, someone with an expressive voice. Others will copy that person's expression in all of the group reading parts. This will keep the group from sounding like the waves that wash in an endless rhythm upon the sand. That predictable pattern can be boring. At best, an expressionless choir communicates only words, not the meaning or emotion of those words. A leader is also responsible for starting each total group part. This eliminates the awful false starts when everyone knows it's time to talk, but no one is willing to jump in first.

The most difficult parts of the choral reading will be those sections in which everyone speaks in unison.

*Overlap:* After your group has gotten the hang of choral

reading, you might want to try some more creative things. For example, it is interesting to have someone begin speaking just before the last person is done speaking—especially if he or she is repeating the same phrase.

Diagrammed, the reading would look like this:

*Person 1:*
> For God loved the world
>> so much

*Person 2:*
>> For God loved the world
>>> so much

Person 1's words "so much" and Person 2's words "For God" overlap. This takes a lot of practice because people have a natural tendency to wait until the other person has stopped speaking before you start. If you do use this technique, you might want to use it several times so people in the congregation realize that the group planned this; they didn't just make a mistake.

*Positioning:* Have the voice chorale stand in groupings that help present the message. In this choral reading, you will be illustrating with slides. So the group might stand in the back of the church.

In readings without slides, it might be appropriate to have the groups divide into two and speak back and forth to each other across the church.

In one missions choral reading, the leader stood in the center of the congregation, and the rest of the group divided into four and stood in the four corners of the church—representing the four corners of the world. The leader gave the message of salvation, and the groups responded with Scripture that shared their responses.

*Expressive faces:* If the choral group stands where the rest of the congregation can see it, people's faces must show the type of expression their voices are using. John 3:16 is filled with excitement and drama. The faces of those who accept the "saved" message must show their feelings or the message is dimmed. The people who play the "condemned" lines should use their vocal and facial expressions to communicate the awfulness of that decision.

*Eye contact:* When the readers can be seen by the congregation, they should establish eye contact with people. The speakers have practiced their parts. They will know many of their lines by heart from the repetition. At many points in the reading, they can look up from their papers and at the congregation. Eye contact says, "We're doing this because we care about you.

Please listen." And in response, the congregation just might!

Some people may fear that if they look up for the parts they know, they will lose their place on the sheets when they need to read again. I use the thumb of my left hand as a line mark. I move it down the page as the reading progresses. I can look up at any time and get my place again in a second just by checking the line above my thumb.

### THE SLIDES

Take a break in your choral reading practice to discuss what slides might best illustrate the passage. Should the pictures be literal, or should they convey a mood or an idea?

List everyone's ideas. Then as a group pick those that are best. Either take the pictures now, or assign someone to be in charge of taking them. If you have a senior high or college student who enjoys photography, this would be an excellent way to use that person's talents for Christ.

Here are a few ideas that might work with John 3:16 (*The Living Bible*).

| | |
|---|---|
| For God loved the world so much | Round-the-world shots, flashed at 5 second intervals. |
| For God loved the world so much | Pictures of people from our congregation. Pictures flashed quickly. Many of these are probably available from people who have attended the church for a while. |
| For God loved the world so much that He gave His only Son so that anyone who believes in Him shall not perish | Several sunrise pictures, or plant pictures to symbolize new beginnings. Hands of a child in different positions will convey the same message. |
| But have eternal life | Picture of smiling children. |

| | |
|---|---|
| For God loved the world so much | More church pictures. |
| God did not send His Son into the world to condemn it, but to save it. | Picture or symbol of Christ—perhaps a statue in the church or a painting in the Sunday school room. |
| Condemn | Match lighted. |
| Save | Match blown out—smoke still rising. |
| Condemn | Match lighted. |
| Save | Match blown out—smoke still rising. |
| Save, save, save | Bright colors—yellow, red, green. These could be materials with lights behind them. |
| For God loved the world so much that He gave. | Several quick pictures of people clapping—maybe just their hands. |

Take more pictures than you'll need. Shoot from different angles and change the settings for each shot. This will give you an opportunity for choice, and raise your chances of having a very professional final project.

**PRAYER TIME**

People have been involved in Bible study. First, they read the Bible. Then they studied it to see how they could best communicate it to others. Some may have memorized short portions as they practiced. Finally, they visually interpreted what they had learned. The slides became a picture paraphrase. Prayer naturally follows this study.

Guide the prayer by suggesting topics. Ask people to limit

themselves to sentence prayers on the topic. They may pray as often as they wish.

Allow people to stay on one topic as long as they are continuing to contribute. When you feel everyone has finished with that topic, suggest the next.

I like this type of guided sentence prayers. When I was a child learning to pray in public, it took me most of the prayer meeting to gather up courage. I would mentally list the things I might talk about and go over them in my mind. By the time I prayed my recited sentences, I had lost most of my enthusiasm. But in prayer like this, the topic is chosen for me. People who pray easily in public won't pray about absolutely everything, leaving me nothing to share aloud with God and His people. And since it's fine just to pray a few words or a single sentence, those who are newcomers to shared prayers may dare to try.

Topics of prayer will vary, of course, with your situation. If I were giving this party right now, I might use a list like this:

Thank God for what His Word means to me—perhaps singling out a special verse.

Praise to God for our church leaders who regularly share God's Word with me.

Request for excellence in the choral reading project so His name will be glorified; people might mention their individual fears about participating in the choral reading.

Prayer for people who will be hearing the reading. Perhaps some might mention those who need this message.

Host or hostess should close, thanking God for the food.

## FOOD

Speaking can make people very hungry! Why not provide the makings for great sandwiches, and let people put their own original creations together! Then each person should cut the sandwich in half and exchange a half with someone else. Suggest people give the half to someone they have enjoyed getting to know better.

Or, you could get several long leaves of French bread, fill them with sandwich goodies, and slice off a sandwich for everyone. You might include luncheon meats, cheese, shredded lettuce, tomatoes, egg salad, tuna salad, or the following sandwich spreads.

## MINCED CORNED BEEF

Minced corned beef combined with pickle relish and moistened with mayonnaise between slices of cracked whole wheat bread is great. Add lettuce leaf for freshness.

## CREAM CHEESE SPREAD

Blend two packages of cream cheese, 2 Tablespoons of cream, 1/2 small (grated) cucumber, and 1 Tablespoon grated onion. When blended smooth, spread on wheat bread.

For novelty, add cake coloring to make the spread bright green.

## KID'S SPECIAL

Try peanut butter with sliced banana on top. Or peanut butter and grape jelly, a junior all-time favorite.

## HAM BROILER KID'S SPECIAL

Mix 1 cup ground boiled ham, 1 cup grated cheese, 1/2 cup condensed tomato soup, 1/2 teaspoon mustard, and 1/2 teaspoon horse radish. Toast bread and spread with this mixture. Toast again under broiler.

## DRIED BEEF

Try dried beef between dark bread that has been spread with butter and cream cheese.

## WALNUT-CHEESE SPECIAL

Soften one package of sharp-flavored cheese spread. Add two Tablespoons catsup, pinch of salt. Add onion juice to taste. Add 1/2 cup chopped walnut meats, and spread on rye bread.

## CORN BREAD SANDWICH

Make corn bread. Let it cool. Put 1 cup milk in double boiler with 1 pound of cheese cut into small squares. Leave until melted and blended. Slice corn bread and cover with a slice of fried ham. Top with second slice of corn bread. Pour melted cheese sauce over sandwich. Top with a slice of crisp bacon and serve hot.

## WAYS TO EXPAND THE CHORAL READING IDEA

*Paraphrases*

Young people often enjoy making their own paraphrases of Scripture—setting the biblical situations into their own twentieth century world.

An example of a paraphrase of the twenty-third Psalm will help you see what I mean. You might also read this example to young people just to give them an idea of what to try. This one was written by 19-year-old Bob Cook from Monmouth, Illinois. In it he uses slang that would be perfectly understandable to most younger Generation X and Generation Next people.

The Lord is my right-hand man;
    I won't trip.
  He always makes sure I'm
    gonna get mine even
    when other fools are
    steppin'.
He won't let them fade me.
Your blade and your nine help
    me keep my head up.
He gives me my props even
    though the Bloods are
    rolling up into my set.
The world is mine.
Without a doubt, I'll survive the
    struggles
because with Him after every
    dark night you find the
    brighter day.

*Dictionary:*
  —Right-hand man =
    the one you can trust
  —trip = panic; fear
    (not a drug-induced
    state)
  —fools = not part of your
    group; enemies
  —steppin' = in your face;
    confronting; coming to
    hurt or get you
  —fade = hurt; remove your
    strength or intensity
  —nine = 9 mm gun
  —props = respect; good
    things
  —Bloods = familiar gang

  —rolling up = approaching;
    infringing upon;
    confronting
  —my set = clique; my gang;
    my friends

This may not be the way you would write this psalm in your neighborhood, but is there any doubt that Bob knows what David felt and feels the security of God's protection and love?

*Scripture Collages*
    Sometimes the message we want to share is found in various passages all through the Bible. Encourage people to research the best verses to get across their message and develop a choral reading collage. What a great way to learn what's in the Bible. Can't you just hear a new Christian saying, "There's this great verse about having a thankful attitude somewhere in this Book, and I'm going to keep looking until I find it"?

*Scripture Songs*
    Real singing here! Try an original praise and worship song using the words directly from the Bible. It's an excellent way to learn Bible verses. If you have talented musicians in your church, encourage them to write their own. Artistic friends could illustrate the songs with slides.

*151*

*Sight and Sound and Sound*

In addition to the choral reading and the slides, try a musical background. What a great multimedia way to praise God. Careful—this will take a lot of work. Make certain the final product reflects the message of God's Word and that all people involved realize that the purpose of the reading is to glorify God, not to glorify the people who participate.

In all areas, as we work to serve God, we should strive for excellence. Not many people would say aloud, "God will accept a lot less than total excellence from us, so why work so hard?" Yet often that seems to be the attitude toward much we offer to Him in the name of praise and worship. Aim high. Aim at excellence. Let your choral readings—and other responses to God—speak loudly to the fact that our God deserves nothing less.

# Project:
# Mission Awareness

### A Party to Plan an
### All-Church Party

*Objective:* Church members who are interested in missions will plan an all-church mission awareness event.

*Basic idea:* This is a pre-event to plan an event. People will meet and plan a complete mission awareness evening for the church, perhaps scheduling a Sunday evening for the event. At the planning session, people will learn methods of structuring a good party, and they will have the positive experience of sharing their ideas and seeing them become part of an all-church event.

I've been part of four mission awareness events. They can be great fun; they can also be great learning experiences.

At the first party, I was one of three adult guests. The whole evening had been planned by a group of sixth grade girls who were members of a church sponsored weekly club. That evening they shared a little of what they had learned about God's work in China, the country they had chosen to study. Included in the evening were tapes from Christians who shared Jesus while teaching English, a few cultural games, a report from encyclopedia sources, and a meal that was typically Chinese. I left absolutely certain that there wasn't a girl in that room who wouldn't remember to pray for China.

At the second party, my friend Dee and I worked together to plan an evening of cross-cultural experiences for people who were part of our church's missions task force. At the time I had just returned from three years as a missionary teacher in Japan and she was thinking about becoming a missionary in Japan. About forty people participated in the games and Japanese meal. A great learning experience, and yes, Dee is now on the mission field full time.

While Jack and I were dating we planned a third missions party. Gladys, our good friend, had just returned from Russia where she had traveled for several weeks with Russian-speaking Christians. What stories she had to tell! Jack and I invited about thirty people to a Russian supper followed by Gladys' slides and stories. We learned how much we enjoyed exercising hospitality and our friends got a unique glimpse into missions. Our fourth party was patterned after the Russian one. Only this time Gladys had just returned from China. The Chinese food was a lot easier to come by than the Russian food!

All the missions parties worked! People are interested in missions when they can connect them with people they know.

This hospitality event allows them to freshen that interest by coming at the subject in a unique way.

## WHO TO INVITE

First, clear the whole idea with the pastor, and decide with him when the party should be held. Include him in the planning for the party. Beforehand, invite ten to fifteen people who are already interested in missions and sharing their interest with others in the church. Since this is a work party, you may want to invite everyone in person. Let them know that this will also be a fun evening, but it is basically a party to plan a party. Encourage them to come with ideas for a missions party that would benefit the whole church family.

## THE EVENING'S AGENDA

Here's one way to structure your evening. I'll be following it as I give ideas that might spark others in your group.

Pick a featured country.
Set goals for the all-church mission party.
Brainstorm ideas for the all-church mission party.
Brainstorm food ideas.
Assign all task and prayer groups.

*Pick a featured country.*

Any one will do. You might want to encourage people to pick one on which they have some information. For example, I've done mission work in Venezuela, Columbia, Mexico, Philippines, and Japan. Those would be logical countries for me to suggest. I also know missionaries in France and Greece and could get information from those countries.

It makes sense to pick a country where the church is supporting a missionary. When all countries are suggested, take a vote to decide which country will be the focal point of the Mission Awareness evening for the whole church.

*Set objectives for the all-church mission party.*

Without them, you really don't know what you want to accomplish, and you certainly won't be able to evaluate what you accomplished when the party is over. Setting these objectives as a group will help people feel the importance of what they will be doing.

Everyone should brainstorm objectives, and the group should pick those it wishes to see met. These should be written, and each person at this planning session should receive a copy.

People should keep these in mind as they plan and pray for the coming event.

*Here are some sample objectives:*
- Our church will gain a greater understanding of God's work in (the country).
- (Missionary or national worker) will get prayer and financial support.
- Our church young people will get a greater burden for our global community.

*Brainstorm ideas for the all-church mission party.*

Now it's time to talk about what will happen on the evening of the all-church event. Encourage everyone to throw out ideas. Ask planners to think "participation." Many people have never really participated in a missions evening. They have come and sat and listened. How could that pattern be livened up a bit by getting everyone actively involved?

I'll share some of the ideas I've had. You might want to share one or two of the better ones with the group just to get the juices flowing.

- Write to the missionary we know in our chosen country and ask him or her to send us a five-minute tape talking about what happens on a typical day. Ask the missionary to include one or two specific prayer requests.

- Plan a playlet on life in the chosen country. Perhaps some people in the congregation have visited the country and could help. This might also be an area in which the older elementary children could get involved.
- Show a video of the country.
- E-mail the missionary or a national Christian worker during the planning and get ideas directly from him or her.
- Plan a project offering. Make copies of a map of this country and give each person a copy. Explain the project and ask people to write on the map the amount of money they are able to give toward the project. (You might ask people to sign their pledges and write in the date by which they will give the promised amount.) Anyone, even those unable to give, who also wants to play a most important part should write the word prayer on the map, along with the length of time that prayer will remain on his or her daily prayer list. All should be placed in the offering. It would be excellent if

the time and money pledges could be counted during the evening so people will know immediately if their project will be completed.

Be creative in your choice of projects. For example, I know one church that earned enough money to send builders to Mexico to build irrigation ditches alongside Mexican Christians. Mexicans were so pleased with their willing partners that the group accomplished twice as much as its stated goal. Non-Christians shared with their neighbors that these Christians lived what they talked.

Another church raised money to send a high school teen to the mission field for several weeks to get a firsthand feel for what God was doing in other cultures.

- Plan games. Does the country have any special ones that could be played in the available space? Check an encyclopedia and resource people. Or you could use things from these countries to spark original games ideas that contain the flavor of that land.

For example, you could have a chopsticks relay if your country were Taiwan. People in

Taiwan probably don't have chopsticks relays, but this game will give your church people an understanding of how difficult it is to use chopsticks. They will gain an appreciation of this cultural skill that they may not have had before. In a chopsticks relay, the group would be divided into teams, and a bowl of grapes would be placed at the far end of the room from each line. At the starting bell, the first person in each line would take the chopsticks, run to the bowl, pick up a grape with the chopsticks, eat it, dash back to his line, and give the chopsticks to the second person, who would repeat the procedure. The first line finished wins.

I've played a game very much like this one with young teens in Japan. As the newest missionary teacher, I was assigned the young teen boys lunch table—an assignment few adults would covet. The game at that table was to see who could eat the most Jell-O with chopsticks without breaking the tiny cubes. I got pretty good at it, and I suspect it was that game, and not my teacher status, that gained me the respect of those special kids.

Another game idea. If your country is Colombia, divide into teams for a rhythm band con-test. Teams have ten minutes to collect their instruments (combs, wastepaper cans, etc.) and practice a song using a South American beat.

Plan a postcard blitz. Supply postcards to people at the all-church party and ask them to write immediately to the missionaries they know in that country. One person would be in charge of sending the postcards two or three at a time over the next month or so. Use commemorative stamps.

A variation of this would be to start a round-robin letter, with each person at the all-church party adding a few paragraphs. Or easier, talking a few minutes on a tape.

Plan several roleplay situations in which people at the planning meeting would demonstrate some of the missionary's typical experiences.

Talk about decorations. How could the room reflect the country? Perhaps a curio display, travel posters, or a mural done by the high school department could be considered.

Consider news reports from this country. Cover the secular as well as the Christian events. This might even be done as a newscast with an anchorman saying, "And now we take you to the country of _____ for an update." Other reporters could read their items. Again, this is a good project for middle school and senior high young people.

Now obviously, you'll be developing ideas that are best suited to your situation. Use my list to get a start, but never forget that you are planning an evening that is unique to your situation.

*Brainstorm food ideas*

You might want to plan an entire meal that will be much like the meals served in this country.

Or you might want to plan a rice meal, to give the church people an idea of the poverty meals eaten by many people in third and fourth world nations.

Or you could supply snacks from around the world. Each snack should be labeled by name and country. Many of these are now available in the specialty food sections of grocery stores.

Here are the recipes from my second mission awareness party. If you choose an oriental country, you might want to copy it. Otherwise, it can serve as a sample of the type of thing that is possible.

This meal will cost about $5.00 per person. Invite those who are able to help defray the costs.

## ORIENTAL SALAD

Serves 24

*6 heads lettuce*

*12 small green onions with stems, chopped fine*

*3 large cans mandarin oranges*

*healthy sprinkling of parsley flakes*

*Dressing:*

*1/4 cup wine vinegar*

*1/4 cup lemon juice*

*1 cup sugar*

*healthy dash of pepper*

*6 cups salad oil*

Shake well and pour over salad just before serving. Top with carameled almonds.

### Carameled Almonds:

*2 cups slivered, blanched almonds*

*1 cup sugar*

Combine in skillet over very low heat. Push almonds around until the sugar melts and covers them. Let cool; break apart.

## FLANK STEAK TERIYAKI

*6 pounds flank steak cut into 1-inch strips.*

Have butcher cut with the grain of the meat. Roll into pinwheels. Fasten with toothpicks, and set aside in a shallow pan.

### Marinade:

*3 teaspoons ground ginger*

*3 Tablespoons cooking oil*

*1/4 cup cooking sherry*

*1-1/2 cup soy sauce*

*3/4 cup sugar*

*2 cloves garlic, mashed*

Mix together marinade ingredients and pour over meat. Cover and let stand in refrigerator for three days. If marinade doesn't completely cover the pinwheels. turn them over after about a day and a half.

Shortly before serving time, place flank steak pinwheels on broiler. Brush with marinade once and broil 5 to 7 inches from the heat for another 7 minutes. Turn; brush again with marinade and broil about 7 minutes longer, or until done.

Serve teriyaki with pineapple rings and rice.

If you want to add a vegetable dish, mix canned bean sprouts with French style green beans.

### DESSERT

Sherbet is appropriate. You might want to add a few rice crackers, now available in many foreign food sections of the grocery store as well as at specialty stores such as Pier 1. These crackers have various names, but *O Sembi* is usually written on the packet somewhere.

Or if you really want to have an unusual dessert, try Kaki Pudding (persimmon).

### KAKI PUDDING
*Serves 24*
*6 cups persimmon pulp*

*3 cups milk*
*6 cups sugar*
*6 cups flour*
*1/2 teaspoon salt*
*6 Tablespoons butter*
*1/4 cup soda*
*1-1/2 teaspoons vanilla*
*4 cups nuts*

Mix ingredients together. Bake in a greased 8-inch pan for 1 hour in a 300-350° oven.

### A WORD ABOUT PLANNING MEETING SNACKS

You might want to try some finger foods from different countries, perhaps purchasing everything from the foreign food section of the food store. Lots of things are available. Throughout the evening you could announce what you are serving and pass things around as people are working. Here are some things I know my store carries:

*marshmallow chocolates from Israel*
*O Sembi rice crackers*
*dry roasted peanuts*
*guacamole dip and taco chips*
*mandarin oranges (serve with toothpicks)*
*fortune cookies*
*rice puffs*

*Assign all task and prayer groups*
Now it's time to assign task groups. Involve everyone. One

or two people cannot pull off this event.

### A Parable

*Once upon a time there was a little red hen who owned a wheat field.*

*"Who will help me harvest the wheat?" she asked.*

*"Not I," said the pig. "I don't know how."*

*"Not I," said the cow. "I'm too clumsy."*

*"Not I," said the dog. "I'm too busy with other things."*

*So the little red hen did it herself.*

*"Who will help me grind the wheat into flour?" she asked.*

*"Not I," said the pig. "I never did it before."*

*"Not I," said the cow. "You can do it better."*

*"Not I," said the dog. "Some other time, perhaps."*

*So the hen did it herself.*

*"Who will help me make some bread?" asked the little red hen.*

*"Not I," said the pig. "No one ever taught me how."*

*"Not I," said the cow. "You've never trusted me to do anything before."*

*"Not I," said the dog. "You did it. You're the top dog around here."*

*So the hen did it herself.*

*That night, the guests arrived for a dinner party at the little red hen's house but she had nothing to serve them except bread. She was so busy that she hadn't had time to plan the rest of the menu, to shop, to cook the meal, or even put out the silverware. The whole affair was a disaster, and the little red hen lived unhappily ever after.*

*Moral: A good leader will train and involve others to the extent of their ability. The hen, or anyone who tries to do everything herself, will lay an egg.*

(Used with permission from *Leadership with a Human Touch*, edited by Arthur F. Lenehan)

What you have decided to do in the missions event will determine what groups you need to assign. Here are some possible groups:

- Prayer groups—meeting weekly until the party

- Advertisement group— perhaps contacting each person from the church personally

- Food committee—this doesn't mean that they will do all the food work. But they will decide what needs to be done and head up the process.

- Mission awareness program committee

### A MISSIONS SIMULATION

After the task group has completed its work, you may want to play a missions simulation to give people the feeling of what happens to missionaries when they go to a new and unfamiliar culture. It's a fun and silly game, but it's designed to help participants empathize with those God calls to serve Him in this unique, difficult way. One thing is for sure. If your people take this simulation game seriously, the new missionaries from your church will be upheld in prayer like never before.

In simulation games, there is no winner or loser. It's an experience game rather than a competition game like checkers. In a simulation, people are involved in a simulated or pretend reality. A new cultural experience is reduced in size so that people can participate in it for a few minutes and gain a bit of an understanding of what culture shock is. In this mission simulation, you won't make people feel all the frustration of learning a new language and new customs, but you can let them feel for a few minutes some of the frustrations of being different, of not fitting in, of being lonely and ineffective.

Careful! Simulations can change people's attitudes. This simulation could turn people on to missions in a new way because for a half hour or so, they were there!

I've chosen to develop a simulation about cultural differences because this is an area in which I have faced frustration. I think others who have lived in different cultures would agree.

I remember being in Venezuela as a short-term missionary. I thought it would be dandy if I organized the little boys at the vacation Bible school into baseball teams. We used our arms as bats and hard lemons that had dropped from the trees as balls. It was great fun until the mission leader explained that baseball was a no-no! In Venezuela people bet on baseball games in the same way Americans do on the horses or dogs. So as a testimony to nonbelievers, those Christians didn't play baseball.

The same thing happens, of course, to people who come into our Western culture. One missionary kid who had spent all his teen years in Japan came back to the States for college. He was thrown out of a shoe store the first week back when he repeatedly told the manager that he wore size twenty-eight. The manager thought he was just another smarting off, rude kid. The boy had a terrible time getting up enough nerve to go to another store.

## CULTURE SHOCK

*A Missionary
Simulation Experience*

*Explanation*

When missionaries go into a new culture, they try to conform to the habits and customs of the people, as long as they don't violate the principles taught in the Bible. This can be terribly hard, because we are so used to our old cultural habits. Add the pressures of learning a new language, new living and eating situations, and removal from former close friends and familiar places. It's only through God's help that missionaries survive the first year.

Today we're going to go through a culture shock as we pretend to be missionaries entering the unusual country of Flockland.

In this simulation, our language will remain English, of course, but we will make the experience difficult by setting up a crazy set of cultural imperatives. These are things newcomers must do if they expect to communicate effectively with the people in Flockland.

The list is silly, of course, but then who's to say that these cultural rules are any stranger than our own—we're just more used to our own.

*Cultural Rules*

Here you can make your own list or use mine. Or combine both. You might want to place these on a chalkboard or large sheet of paper so they remain in front of everyone during this first part of the simulation.

- In Flockland, a cultured person never uses pronouns—only complete names.
- In Flockland, when people meet, they jump up and down twice and clap once. When they part, they rub noses.
- In conversation, it is considered very poor manners to laugh or show your teeth. Pleasure is shown by rubbing the tongue quickly back and forth across the lower lip.
- Conversations in Flockland are limited to two minutes. Longer conversations indicate the person is lazy, making poor use of time and vocabulary.
- No one sits with his or her legs touching.
- People snap fingers in a regular rhythm when they are talking with someone of the opposite sex, even a spouse, if they are in public.
- A refined person never covers more than ten inches with each step.

- A sign of friendship is to pull a hair from your head and present it to the person to whom you're talking. This can also be a sign that you're telling the truth.
- Upon leaving a person, you should bestow a wish upon him. For example, "Marlene LeFever wishes Margaret Jones rain for Margaret Jones' potatoes."
- When a Flockland person sits, it is improper for him or her to lean back. Instead the person perches on the edge of the chair.

*Practice:* Tell the group to spend five minutes getting used to the rules. Interact as people of Flockland. At the end of this time, the list of cultural rules will be taken down and players will be asked to act on them without seeing them.

Note mistakes others make and correct them. This is not the main part of the simulation; it's more a practice for it.

It will be impossible for most people to get through the five minutes without making many errors in the etiquette of Flockland. Of course, the rules are ridiculous, but in many lands, such as Japan, Zaire, and France, if missionaries disobey cultural rules their credibility

will be lessened, fewer people will listen to their message, and in some primitive cultures, their very lives may be in danger.

At the end of the five minutes, allow time for people to share some of their feelings and their experiences. If necessary, get conversation going with a few questions:

- How did you feel after the five minutes? Silly? Tired? A failure?

- To us these things are silly. But consider a foreign student coming to our country. What things in our culture might he or she consider funny or strange?

*The Simulation:*

Divide the participants into two equal groups. One group will be the native Flockland people. They are 100 percent at ease with themselves and their culture. In order to illustrate this, they should act normally. Players will all assume that they are doing the list of things that are culturally right in Flockland.

The burden lies with the second group. They will be the missionaries, and they must remember all the rules of Flockland. (Take the posted rules down.)

It is the responsibility of the

second group of people to try to build friendships with Flockland people while remembering all the cultural rules and trying to obey them.

Whenever the missionary makes a mistake, the national should simply walk away. Nationals and missionaries should interact for about five to eight minutes.

Remember, the one group acts perfectly normal and all players assume it is obeying all the rules. The other group represents the culturally struggling missionary.

If you have time, you might want to switch groups. After the end of the simulation, debrief. These questions will help:

- How many of you feel you laid a friendship base? Did you concentrate more on making friends or on your cultural correctness?

- How realistic do you think it is to assume that nationals will turn off the message of Christ if the missionary violates cultural rules?

- What part does the Holy Spirit play in the communication of Christ in a real cross-cultural experience?

- What have you learned from this experience?

This game was designed for a group that is already interested in missions. It is not recommended for the total missions awareness party.

However, you may want to choose four people to demonstrate the final part of the game for the whole church and then discuss what they felt and what this taught them about new missionaries and the need for supporting missionaries with consistent, back-up prayer.

# CHAPTER

# 8

# *God Bless My Home*

*Bring your balloons and your butterflies,
your bouquets of flowers . . . bring the torches
and hold them high! Paint your feelings, sing
your songs, whistle, laugh. Life is a celebration,
an affirmation of God's love.*

—Ann Weems

CELEBRATE THE FAMILY—that wonderfully diverse group of people who live together under one roof! Ideas for bringing the church family together would not be complete without a few directed at the immediate family.

These events are appropriate for anyone—single and living alone, single and living with roommates, married—building a home where God is glorified. They'll work for the single- or two-parent family, or for a couple who has no children. *Home* remains a special word to everyone, even for those people who have never experienced it. Celebrate the Christ-centered home!

## A House Dedication

### This Home, Lord, Is Yours!

**Objective:** A home will be dedicated to God in the presence of special friends.

**Basic idea:** People will plan a dedication of their home, inviting their close friends as witnesses and participants. In this dedication they will be saying that this house, the things that are in it, and the people who live in it are God's, and He is in control.

House dedications are usually for people who have just moved into a new home, but that's certainly no absolute. If you like the idea and you've never dedicated your home, why not plan your own celebration? Better several years late than not at all!

You might also want to share the idea with people in your congregation who have moved—each year more than 18 people in every 100 change homes.

House dedications make a lot of sense. At the beginning of marriage, Christians plan a special ceremony asking God to be a third partner in the relationship. That commitment in front of friends makes the whole event more special. The imprint of God's presence in the life of the bride and groom is not easily erased. In the house dedication, the home is treated with somewhat the same seriousness. It forces those who will live in it to be more aware of the presence of God. They have erected a caution against using the house and those it houses incorrectly. And just as the Christian marriage ceremony is a witness to the world of our determination to be different, so is a Christian home dedication.

I'm going to share Jack's and my house dedication ideas with you. Use parts from it in your own dedication, but add your own ideas. Make your home dedication truly unique—just as you are.

## GUESTS

We kept the guest list small, limiting it to people we thought would enjoy participating in this type of celebration. Our list, just like our social life, was pretty equally divided between singles and marrieds.

To each single and couple, we gave an assignment. We wanted our friends to feel a little responsibility for the event—for the success of our witness and our home. We wanted them to pray for us, and if they thought we were headed for trouble, we wanted them to feel close enough to us to tell us.

Our invitations were handwritten, and each included the special assignment.

Individual assignments included:

Please pray a prayer of dedication for our living room. (Or the kitchen, or the bedroom.)

Please bring a verbal gift that you would like us to use in our new home. This should be something you would wish for us.

(To the pastor) We would like

you to share what God expects of us in our new home.

These different assignments allowed for a variety of serious and lighter interaction. Our dedication followed this format (approximately 45 minutes):

1. Welcome to our home (5 minutes).
2. An explanation of a house dedication (2–3 minutes).
3. A walk through the house. Prayers of dedication for the assigned rooms (15 minutes).
4. Verbal gifts in the living room (10 minutes).
5. Brief words from the pastor (5 minutes).
6. (Optional) Prayer of exorcism (1 minute).
7. Our vows (3–4 minutes).
8. Brunch.

## A CLOSER LOOK AT OUR DEDICATION

### 1. WELCOME TO OUR HOME.

This might be the place for a little history of the house, especially if it is not new. Ours had been built in 1907, and our neighbors have shared several interesting, if conflicting, stories about the people who have lived there before us. The son of the first owner, or so the story goes, was an illustrator for hot dog commercials!

## 2. AN EXPLANATION OF A HOUSE DEDICATION.

Jack and I wrote what we wanted to say:

*Jack:* Sometimes we feel like misplaced apartment people, but deep down we are beginning to belong to this house. Living here has been a day-by-day educational process.

*Marlene:* I'm forever noticing noises I can't identify and rushing off to the basement to put my ear to the furnace or water heater to determine just where the shake, rattle, or roar is coming from. It beats me what I intend to do when I find it!

*Jack:* More than anything, we want our house to be a home where God is glorified. So we've asked you to participate in our giving of our house to the Lord. You are very, very welcome.

## 3. A WALK THROUGH THE HOUSE.

Prayers of dedication for the assigned rooms.

The prayers people offered for our rooms were beautiful. Most of our friends wrote what they wanted to say so we had a lasting record of their words.

*Living room*

"God and Father, may this doorway welcome friends and strangers into a room filled with Your love and watched by Your Spirit. May these walls keep the confidences of heartfelt conversations and reverberate with fellowship and laughter. May these floors uphold weary feet, bringing comfort to those in need. May these chairs become symbols of the encircling of Your love by those who partake of the hospitality of this household."

*Kitchen*

When we were dating, Jack and I were invited to a house dedication. Our own event was patterned in part after that first one. We were assigned a prayer for the kitchen that I've reproduced below. I think Jack's love for cooking and his excitement about what can happen between friends around food led to that assignment. It's been several years since we prayed our kitchen prayer. Unfortunately, the couple that it was offered for has gone through a difficult divorce. Events like this dedication and the prayers of friends don't keep marriages from falling apart. Only God and the determination of the couple will do that. Yes, I look back with sadness on a marriage that didn't last, but I also know that those of us who attended this long-ago dedication left it with a stronger will to build Christ-centered homes.

Jack and I did our kitchen prayer as a choral reading.

*Both:* Father, we dedicate this kitchen to your service.

*Jack:* We dedicate the food that will be prepared here. Keep the family thankful and aware that many whom You love have never tasted so bountifully of Your gifts. Thank you, Lord, for the creative possibilities You have left open to us cooks—all the many foods and colors and tastes—to mix or spice or eat raw. Thank You for the opportunity to exercise this talent daily in love for the family and for those You bring to eat in this home.

*Marlene:* We dedicate the hours this family will spend in this small area working together—planning, cooking, cleaning up. Keep those times free from frustration and complaining. Use this space and the tasks done here to bind the family into a working, loving, sharing unit.

*Jack:* We dedicate the hours that this couple will spend in this small area alone—planning, cooking, cleaning up. Often the jobs done here allow the workers mind-drifting time. Guide this drifting toward thoughts of You. While the potatoes are being peeled or dishes are being wiped, this room can become a "closet of prayer." Lord, we dedicate these free moments to You.

*Both:* Father, for this couple and their family, we dedicate this kitchen to Your service. Amen.

*Bedroom*

Carol and Robert had just gotten married after several very difficult years that followed their divorces. As a rather happy joke, Jack and I asked them to dedicate our bedroom. When they finished their reading, there was hardly a dry eye in the room. And Jack leaned over to me and said, "I'm glad we're married."

*Robert:* Lord, this is a room of rest.

*Carol:* And love. Two of the most delightful gifts that come from you.

*Robert:* Rest, sleep, slumber. "Now I lay me down to sleep. I pray You, Lord my soul to keep."

*Carol:* Sleep that knits up the raveled sleeve of care.

*Both:* How incredibly good it feels to ease your aching bones down, stretching your length uncramped. To lie folded in your darling's arms, to kiss, embrace, enjoy.

*Robert:* And then to sleep, peace attending, all through the night.

*Carol:* Waking to a bright, new sunlit morning, you see each other's faces. And true, plain hearts do in those faces rest.

*Robert:* Mellow is the feeling in the morning when you rise.

*Both:* Lord, in this room, two share your love; as one they do recline.

*Carol:* In rest be here.

*Robert:* In love be here.

*Carol:* Refresh them in the quiet nights.

*Robert:* And at those touching times.

*Both:* Hold them near You from dusk 'til dawn. Amen.

## 4. VERBAL GIFTS IN THE LIVING ROOM.

After our walk through the rooms and their dedication, we all returned to the living room for the presentation of verbal gifts from some of our friends.

This was from Rita and Bob, two singles who were dating.

"We wish you a personality blender. This unique appliance works something like a food blender. Instead of combining different food ingredients, the personality blender helps you mix different people into enriching friendships.

"Our personality blender does not work with rotary beaters, nor is it powered by electricity. Instead, personality blending is accomplished by your word of welcome, by your thoughtful introductions and conversation starters, by the comfortable and pleasant surroundings your home provides, by the fun activities you plan.

"Your blender gets its power from your love for Christ and your concern for other people. Use it with Christ's help to share your home and your friendship."

Monette and Bob decided to be totally humorous with their gift, and they sang it to the tune of "We Wish You a Merry Christmas." Here are several verses.

*We wish you no faulty furnace*
*We wish you no leaking rooftops*
*We wish you no cracking plaster*
*And no need to call cops.*

*We wish you lots of green plants*
*And flowers blooming year 'round*
*And in your home much music*
*And from neighbors no sound!*

*We wish you cash for mortgage*
*We wish you cash for taxes*
*We wish you bread for table*
*With sugar and molasses!*

Not great poetry, you say? Well, you're wrong. It was one of the loveliest gifts we received.

## 5. BRIEF WORDS FROM THE PASTOR.

How very special it was to hear from our pastor what our responsibilities before God were. At the end of his five-minute talk, he presented Jack and me with a little handmade sand and cement castle. "This will remind you," he said, "that this shingled 'castle' that you are buying should be a reflection of your inner spiritual castle." Then he led the group in singing "Joy is

the flag flown from the castle of my heart when the king is in residence there."

## 6. (OPTIONAL) PRAYER OF EXORCISM.

We asked Karen to pray a prayer of exorcism for our house. Here is her prayer:

*Now, Holy Spirit, come*
*And fill this house with Your*
*   presence.*
*Permeate the atmosphere, the density,*
*   the concreteness of this place.*
*Breathe here.*

*Breathe spiritual breath.*
*   Begone any choking adversary,*
*   any evil breath-taker,*
*   any life-robbing,*
*   stealing dark thing.*

*Let this be a hallowed place,*
*Consecrated to the Lord, the*
*   Life-Breather, the Breath-Giver.*

*Cover this house with the blood of*
*   Christ.*
*Mark it as sacred,*
*   filled with Him and none other.*
*Begone any who are not under this*
*   mercy.*
*And come Breath.*
*Come from the four winds,*
*   O Breath.*
*Breathe upon all who dwell*
*   within here,*
*That they may live.*
*   Come Breath.*

## 7. VOWS OF THE FAMILY

At one home dedication we attended, the father included his two daughters in this part of the dedication. The father asked each girl simple questions which allowed her to share her child-like faith that Jesus was indeed part of their family. His questions to his preschool and young elementary daughters were:

What room in the house do you like best?

Who are your new playmates?

What do you do together?

Why do you think Jesus gave us this special house?

What would you like to thank Jesus for?

How do you know that Jesus is part of our family?

The children's responses dedicated that house to God as completely as the father's.

Vows are very special things. Let me share what Jack and I said, but use it only as a pattern. When you write your own, ask yourselves why you are dedicating the house to God and what you mean by the phrase—House Dedication. Everything you speak should be your intention. These are not just pretty words. They are promises made before God for which He will hold you accountable.

*Our Vows*

*Jack:* I vow before God and you, our friends, to work hard on our marriage—the real structure of this house. I will love Marlene and share her excitements and disappointments. I will remember that she is my home, and this building is just the shingled structure where that home resides.

*Marlene:* I vow before God, and you, our friends, to work hard on our marriage. I will respect Jack as my husband and my best friend. I will build him up and support him. I know that this house loses its heart when he's not here.

*Jack:* Through the home that Marlene and I are creating, we vow to remain aware and sensitive to our Creator and to acknowledge ourselves as servants to whom He has given this very special assignment—to live, grow, and serve on North Spring Street.

*Marlene:* I want this house to be a place where people feel comfortable and welcome. I vow to do my part to make *hospitality* a key word in our partnership with God. I want those who walk through the door to know that God is here, and that He's as pleased as we are that guests have come.

*Jack:* God, thank you for this house and what you are going to do with it and with us. Thank you for the laughter that has already been a part of our two months here. For the little things, thanks—for the furnace man and for discovering how to fix the garbage disposal.

*Marlene:* Thank you for the laughter that will come. Give us the strength we will need to go through the difficult times and the times when we fail each other and you.

*Jack:* Give us the wisdom to continue building this home—not with bricks and shingles but with love and understanding and excitement.

*Marlene:* Thank you for your creation of our first home.

*Jack:* We dedicate ourselves and this home to you.

You may want to end your vows with a song in which the words and music say exactly what you want them to say. If you can't find one that fits well, then pick a song that everyone knows and write words that allow you to glorify and praise God for the house He has given to you.

This example of original words to a familiar melody is built around "Come Ye Thankful People, Come."

*God, your thankful people come*
*Raising songs of this new home.*
*For the roof and for the floor*
*Praise for space and so much more.*
*For the neighbors we will meet*
*For the food we here will eat.*
*Praise you, Father, Praise you, Son.*
*Praise you Spirit, for our home.*

*God, your thankful people come*
*Giving you this special home.*
*Take the title that we bring.*
*Let our honest praises ring.*
*This is also your new home,*
*Welcome, Lord, to all we own.*
*Praise you, Father, Praise you, Son.*
*Spirit, come, dwell in our home.*

## 8. BRUNCH

### FRUIT BASKETS

Select large oranges or grapefruit with not-too-thin skin. Cut fruit in half, and remove segments. Save shells.

Section all the fruit, removing seeds and pulp. Mix with other fresh or canned fruits, and place fruit back into the basket shells. Chill. Just before serving sprinkle each shell with ginger ale and top with nuts; garnish with washed mint leaves.

### SANDWICH LOAF
*Serves 10-12*
*1 loaf unsliced bread*
*butter*
*2 large packets of cream cheese*
*3 Tablespoons milk*
*ripe olives*
*pimento*
*parsley*
*watercress*

Remove crusts from bread and cut into 4 slices lengthwise about 3/4 inch thick. Spread 3 slices with butter. Place one slice on platter or board. Top with tuna spread. Spread two of the remaining slices, one with ham spread and the other with cheddar cheese spread. Reassemble loaf, cover with a damp towel, and chill.

Before serving, frost with cheese frosting. Beat cream cheese and milk until it reaches a frosting-like consistency. Spread on sides and top of chilled sandwich loaf. Decorate with olives, pimento, parsley, and watercress. You might make a little flower design using the pimento as the petals. Chill until serving.

### TUNA SPREAD
*1 large can of water-packed tuna*
*mayonnaise*
*5 green olives*

Cut olives into little pieces. Mix all ingredients, adding mayonnaise until a good spreading consistency is reached.

### HAM SPREAD
*1/2 cup shredded Swiss cheese*
*1 small can of deviled ham*
*1 teaspoon minced onion*
*1 Tablespoon sweet pickle relish*
*1 Tablespoon finely chopped*
*  green pepper*
*1/2 teaspoon nutmeg*

When Swiss cheese has come to room temperature, add ham spread, onion, pickle relish, and green pepper. Beat.

### CHEDDAR CHEESE SPREAD
*1-1/2 cups shredded cheddar cheese*
*1/4 cup milk*
*1/4 teaspoon Worcestershire sauce*
*1/2 teaspoon curry*
*2 Tablespoons chopped ripe olives*

Allow cheddar cheese to come

to room temperature. Add milk and Worcestershire sauce; beat until smooth. Stir in olives.

If you have a large number of children, you may want to age-grade the food! For example, corn puppies might be a lot more popular than a sandwich loaf.

## CORN PUPPIES

*1 pound frankfurters*
*1/2 cup catsup*
*1/2 cup crushed cornflakes*

Cut the frankfurters into bite-sized pieces and roll them in catsup and cornflake crumbs. Bake in 350° oven for 15 minutes.

Or use mustard instead of catsup.

## SPAM SPECIAL

*Spam, sliced*
*brown sugar*
*ginger ale*

Sprinkle Spam slices with a small amount of brown sugar, nutmeg, cinnamon, and ginger ale. Place in a 350° oven and bake until brown. Serve on buttered whole wheat toast.

## CHOCOLATE SCOTCHAROOS

*1 cup granulated sugar*
*1 cup light corn syrup*
*1 cup peanut butter*
*6 cups Rice Krispies*
*1 cup chocolate drops*
  *(or butterscotch drops)*

Combine sugar and corn syrup. Place over moderate heat until they boil. Stir constantly. Remove from heat and add peanut butter. Stir. Pour mixture over Rice Krispies. Pat into buttered pan approximately 3/4 inch deep. Cool. Melt chocolate drops (or butterscotch drops) and spread on the top.

## SOME ADDITIONAL HOUSE DEDICATION IDEAS

*Choral Reading*

Why not develop a Scripture choral reading that will involve both the person or couple whose home is being dedicated and the guests? (See pages 140 to 149 for some more ideas on how to write a choral reading.)

This could be an extension of section 7—Vows of The Family. Here are a few lines to show you what your finished reading might look like. All quoted references are taken from *The Living Bible*. I changed the pronouns from "I" to "we" when the group was speaking. The references should not be read as part of the reading. (If non-Christians are part of the dedication, rewrite anything that will be said by them or by the total group so you will not be asking them to speak a lie.)

*All:* "We will sing about your loving-kindness and your justice, Lord. We will sing your praises!"

*Family:* "We will try to walk a blameless path, but how we need your help, especially in our own home, where we long to act as we should" (from Psalm 101:1-2).

*Father:* "Decide today whom you will obey."

*Family:* "But as for us and our family, we will serve the Lord."

*All:* "Yes, we choose the Lord, for he alone is our God."

*Pastor:* "You have heard yourselves say it. You have chosen to obey the Lord."

*All:* "Yes. We are witnesses."

*Family:* "Yes, we will worship and obey the Lord alone." (from Joshua 24)

*Guest 1:* Build a house known for its love. "Don't forget to be kind to strangers, for some who have done this have entertained angels without realizing it."

*Guest 2:* "Honor God, and be pure."

*Guest 3:* "Share the sorrow of those being mistreated, for you know what they are going through" (from Hebrews 13:1-4).

*Guest 1:* "God has given each of us the ability to do certain things well . . . If your gift is that of serving others, serve them well . . . If God has given you money, be generous in helping others."

*Guest 2:* "Don't just pretend that you love others; really love them." Love with brotherly affection and take delight in honoring others who are part of your life.

*Guest 3:* "Be glad for all God is planning for you" (from Romans 12:6-12).

*Family:* But as for us in this home, we will serve the Lord.

*All:* But as for us and the homes represented here, we will serve the Lord.

*Symbolic Gifts*

In a home where there are children, a symbolic gift can

take on great significance. For example, as a mother and her child prepare a gift before their house dedication and then share with the guests what it means, they are affirming together that this house does indeed belong to God. For the child who understands, the symbol can make a lasting impact. The symbol should remain on display in the home—daily bringing to the child's and parent's minds the vows they took.

Here are some symbol possibilities.

*Rocks*—these can symbolize both the home's stability and the fact that the home is founded on Christ Jesus, our Rock. Imagine what this symbol could mean to an eleven-year-old boy whose parents have just gotten divorced. He may have heard that he's safe and he's loved and he's not the cause of what has happened. The visual reminder helps that reality become part of him.

*Homemade wooden cross*—a reminder of the sacrifice Christ made for us and how little the sacrifice of our home is by comparison.

*A collage of items belonging to each member of the family*—perhaps arranged in the shape of your house. The center could be a picture of Christ. Baby could contribute a rattle. The school age child might give a well-done school paper. The toddler might add a crayoned picture. Mother might add something important to her. For example, I would add a toy mouse since I spend most of my free time writing on my computer. All these could be glued inside a house frame to make an "US" picture.

*The family could make a family flag*—Use the coat of arms and add some special indication of the King to whom the family belongs. The family might actually want to fly the flag on special days: birthdays, holidays, and the yearly anniversary of the home dedication.

### A Gift from the Guests

It might also be appropriate for the guests to present the home with a symbolic gift.

At one house dedication, I brought a small tree to plant in my friend's first yard. I told her that I wanted her home to grow in all the special personal ways a living home can grow. As she watches the growth of the little tree from year to year, she will be reminded of how good God has been to provide for her needs and how much she has grown in her love for Him.

## OTHER SYMBOLIC GIFT IDEAS:

*A lovely picture frame, probably 8" x 10".* Specify that the frame should be refilled each year with a picture that shows one way the house was used for Jesus in the past year.

*A jar or can of fruit from each person present.* This is a symbolic picture of the fruit that this new owner can potentially bear as he or she lives for Christ in this community.

*A large, homemade card on which everyone present has written a prayer.* Greeting cards that are homemade are always special.

## Family Communion

### "Remember Me Until I Return."

*Objective:* A group of two or three families will remember Christ's death and resurrection by holding a communion service.

*Basic idea:* A celebration of communion will be held in the home. This event can be especially poignant for single parents and their children. Consider including a few singles without children who are close to the children. This event allows parents to talk with children about what the elements mean, and allows the children to ask questions. It also provides an opportunity for a meal together, followed by some family praise games.

This communion service is designed to take place in the home with one head of a household taking the lead. Some people are uncomfortable celebrating communion without the pastor leading. If you are, invite the pastor to share the experience with you. Let him offer the elements while you take responsibility for the rest of the evening.

What you do will depend on the ages of your children. But this outline could serve as a starting point:

1. Preparation—the night before
2. Sing resurrection songs
3. Share a Christlike action
4. Talk about the purpose of the Lord's Supper
5. Spend time in private prayer
6. Participate in taking the elements
7. Serve someone else a meal
8. Play a praise game
9. Again, sing resurrection songs

If you allow 45 minutes for the meal, the entire communion evening will run about two hours for two family units of three people each.

*1. Preparation—the night before*

Explain what will be happening. Make certain everyone has cleared his or her schedule. Encourage young people to approach this evening with anticipation. If you have junior or older aged children in your home, involve them in all the planning, including the preparation of the meal. Each person should come to communion time with some special personal offering—something that expresses that person's love and thankfulness to Jesus. Parents will need to help younger children. A simple scribbled picture from the four-year-old boy to Jesus might be just as meaningful at his stage of development as an original song would be to you or your teenager.

**THE EVENING**

*2. Sing resurrection songs*

In communion we are remembering Christ's death—that horrible, painful expression of His total love for us. And we are also remembering that He is coming again. Begin by singing songs that focus on the joy that lies in our understanding of communion. These could be favorites suggested right now or the choices could be made at the planning the night before. Songs could include the old hymn "Christ the Lord Is Risen Today" or the praise song, "Celebrate Jesus, Celebrate."

*3. Share a Christlike action*

Christ has made some differences in our lives, and if we are growing to be more like Him, those differences between us and non-Christians are growing daily too. Ask each person to share some positive thing which emphasizes to him or her personally, and perhaps to others, that growth is taking place.

You may need to help young children with a few leading questions like, "How did Jesus help you today?"

An elementary child might answer, "I didn't cry today when I was scared. Instead I remembered that Jesus is with me."

An adult might say, "I actually witnessed today. This guy at the office asked if church was just a social deal for me or if I really believed what they were peddling. I honestly opened my mouth and told him what God meant to me."

*4. Talk about the purpose of the Lord's Supper*

In this section, involve everyone in questions and answers. Here's where you have the opportunity to train your young people, to guide them toward a greater understanding of this ordinance than they could ever get in an all-church explanation of the Lord's Supper.

Read 1 Corinthians 11:23-31 aloud. You may want to use a modern version or a paraphrase of this familiar text. (I'm fond of the paragraph in *The Message* by Eugene Peterson.) Allow your voice to pick up the expression you think the early church leaders might have used when they read these commands.

Here are some questions about communion that have been arranged by age levels. Pick those which seem best for you and your group. Don't use all the preschool questions at one time and then go on to another age level. Intersperse them so everyone will be participating together.

*Preschool children:*

How do you know that Jesus loves you?

What is a story about Jesus that you want to remember forever?

Would you lead us in singing "Jesus Loves Me"?

Who else in this room do you think Jesus loves?

Note that none of these questions calls for any symbolic understanding on the part of the child. If young Cheryl has grown up in a Christian home, she knows in her heart that Jesus loves her.

Of course, Cheryl won't understand all the ramifications of what is happening, but she can feel safe in Jesus' love and in the love of other adults and children who love her and Jesus. She is included, and as she matures, this very special event will take on deeper significance.

*Younger elementary children:*

Are you sure that Jesus still loves you even when you're bad?

How do you know?

Will you tell us the story of Jesus' dying on the cross?

You may have to help the children, but allow them to share as much as possible. Probe to remind them of more details. For example, you might say, "Jesus and His disciples were in a garden. Jesus was praying when all of a sudden . . . what happened?"

Can you tell us why Jesus had to die on the cross?

What do we mean when we say we are going to have communion?

Tell a reason why you love Jesus.

If you are certain the child understands what Jesus has done for him or her, ask the child to share why it's important to have Jesus as a forever friend. If a child affirmed his or her faith in a public setting, you may ask the child to share the significance of that occasion.

*Middle school children:*

Usually when we have communion in church we just have a swallow of juice or wine and a small piece of bread. So why do we call communion "The Lord's Supper"?

Tell us the story of Jesus eating his last supper with his disciples, the night he gave them the communion service as a way of remembering him.

Ask a good reader to read Matthew 26:26-29 and Mark 14:22-25.

How do you define sin for a teenager who has never been to church?

Suppose we had a visitor at our church and she asked you if she should participate in this part of the service. What would you say?

*All Others:*

What is a symbol? What does communion symbolize? Or, what do the bread and wine become

when we participate in communion? What makes this important to us?

If you were going to explain communion to a very young Christian, what would you say?

This will recap what others have said. The question forces people to think what they believe and state it without the clichés that so often limit our conversation with non-Christians or new Christians.

What areas in your life are you interested in giving more fully to Christ? (Do not assign this question. Allow volunteers to answer.)

Share how you felt the first time you took communion.

What are some of the things that often make communion less special to you now than it was the first time? How can we bring new life into our personal participation of this living ordinance?

5. *Spend time in private prayer*

Each person should ask Jesus to clear his or her life of sin. This is an important time, directly commanded by Scripture. To emphasize its importance, you may want to reread 1 Corinthians 11:27.

Pick the version that the children will have the easiest time understanding.

At the end of this time, play a recording of quiet music.

*6. Participate in taking the elements*

There are a number of ways this communion can be served. Here are a few ideas that have been meaningful to me:

a. The pastor will serve the elements to each person. To each, he says something personal: "Marlene, this is Christ's body which he gave for your sins."

b. Bread loaf and juice are placed on the table. As each person finishes the prayer time, he or she rises and breaks off a piece of bread, eats it, and drinks from the cup.

c. Each person comes to the table and takes a piece of bread from the loaf. He or she breaks that piece in two, eats one, and gives half to someone else in the group, saying something like, "I'm glad we can participate in remembering Christ together." Or, "I'm glad we're family members—physically and spiritually."

At a small Sunday evening service at our church, our pastor led this type of service. Three people shared their second piece with me. I have rarely felt as affirmed and accountable for my growth as a Christian.

d. The head of the house where the communion is being held will break off a piece of bread and serve it to the next person, saying, "This is my body, which is given for you." That person will eat and then break off a piece and serve the next person. Each person is symbolizing commitment to Christ and to these family members. The same process can be followed with the passing of the cup.

What about small children who up to this point have been part of the family celebration and who may now feel left out because they are not yet aware of what Christ has done for them?

Within a Christian family, it may be perfectly fine for them to take a piece of bread and a sip of juice. When they are served, the person may say, "This food (drink) is to help you remember that Jesus loves you. Do you love Jesus?" When the children answer, they are allowed to partake. For those who see communion as symbolic, the leader's words have changed the meaning of the symbol for the child into something concrete that he or she can understand and affirm.

Or you may want to have special food for the children, perhaps cookies and milk. Explain that they are to eat and drink slowly, and try to think as they eat of all the reasons why they love Jesus.

### 7. *Serve someone else a meal*

Why not plan a love feast—a meal in which the conversation is structured so that Christ is the focal point? Work to avoid the trap the early Christians fell into. Remember Paul's scolding! "When you come together to eat, it isn't the Lord's Supper you are eating, but your own. For I am told that everyone hastily gobbles all the food he can without waiting to share with the others." Place a simple supper on the table.

Each person should serve the person next to him. This will be difficult for small children, but help them. All but the smallest children should understand that what they are doing is a symbolic picture of what Christ expects them to do all the time—think about others first and show love to them, just like Christ showed love to us.

You may want to set a chair at the table to visually represent Christ's presence at the meal.

After everyone is served, the head of the house should direct conversation. At this meal, everyone is going to talk about things that point to our love for Christ or the things that make us special because we have accepted His love.

I've supplied some topic ideas. In some cases, it will be hard for young children to participate. Make certain that children comment often enough to allow them to feel a part of the conversation.

Be careful, too, not to cut off conversation because it doesn't fit the list of topics you've supplied. Your goal is to have Christ glorified by the conversation at the table. If that goal is being met, don't worry about your topics.

*Topic ideas:*

Talk about the special things God has done for your family this year. (If this has been a year of hurt, this question can be especially meaningful.)

Talk about some of the good things that have happened at church.

Share some of the dreams you have for the growth of the children around the table.

(Be careful not to embarrass anyone. For example, a woman might share with her third-grade nephew David, "David, this year I hope you'll learn to read so well that you'll be able to read some of the stories about Jesus directly from your Bible. Wouldn't that be exciting?")

What are some of the things that make us different because we are Christians? What are some of the things we should work on so it will be more obvious to others that we belong to Christ?

Talk about some of the problems that worry family members. Perhaps Mother could share her frustration with her job or a teen might share that he really needs prayer that he'll stick with algebra. Encourage everyone to accept these as "family" problems, not just the problem of the one member directly involved. Everyone should be aware of problems and provide prayer and personal support. (This is not the time to talk about discipline problems.)

You might want to end the meal with the family singing a few of its favorite praise choruses or the first verse of several favorite hymns.

*8. Play a praise game*

Why not? Keep the games fun and encourage everyone to participate.

### BIBLE CHARACTERS' PRAISE

Before the evening begins, cut out at least twenty-five paper blocks that are big enough for people to stand on. Number them in order—1, 2, 3, and so on. Color two or three of the blocks.

Place the blocks in a line around the room. As people answer questions, they will move along the line, standing on the correct block.

You will need a spinner or a penny to tell each person how far to move on each turn. For example, if the spinner goes to three, the person will move three blocks. Or heads could be two moves and tails one.

I've gotten you started by writing ten praise questions, but you'll need many more.

The object of the game is to be the first person to get through the twenty-five blocks.

If that doesn't seem like a long enough game, make the winner the first person to go through the blocks twice.

People are to stand on their blocks. If they answer their questions correctly they are to move ahead the number indicated on the spinner. If they miss, they move back the same number as the spinner indicated. When a person lands on a colored block, ask a personal question rather than a Bible praise question. I've given you several personal questions, but you will need to develop others. When you have prepared this game, it will truly be your original!

*Praise questions*

The head of the house will ask questions and not participate in the game.

(All these questions are built around people in the Bible who had reason to praise God.)

1. What woman praised God for her new baby and later gave the baby to serve God in the temple? (Hannah)
2. Peter was walking on the water. Suddenly he began to sink. Minutes later he was safe. What reason did he have for praising Jesus? (Jesus lifted him from the water.)
3. A very smart sister saved her baby brother's life. Years later when the baby was grown he became a great leader. What was the baby's name? (Moses)
4. An angel told a woman she would have a special baby who would grow into a man who would save people from their sins. What was the

woman's name? (Mary)
5. What a terrible rain! But the man in the boat and his family could praise God that they were safe. What was the man's name? (Noah)
6. The disciples praised God because His Son had chosen them to be fishers of men. Name these disciples. (Adjust the number of disciples to the capabilities of the person who gets this question.)
7. A lady was very old and she still hadn't a baby. Then she had Isaac. What was the name of this lady who praised God for her miracle baby? (Sarah)
8. What special reason did Cornelius have for praising God? (His family wasn't Jewish, yet God made it clear that everyone would be included in his new family.)
9. What prophet didn't praise God when God saved a whole city through his preaching? (Jonah)
10. What book of the Bible is filled with songs of praise to God? (Psalms)

Now you're on your own. Write some more praise questions. They're fun and easy— and also a great way to involve your young people in the planning for this evening.

*Colored blocks*

When a person hits a colored block, he or she has to answer a personal praise question, or say, "Pass," and miss the next turn.

Here are some personal praise questions. You will need to write more. Keep them fun and light.

Name one thing you should
    praise God for this week.
Spell the word praise backwards.
Tell why praise is such an impor-
    tant part of the life of Christ.
What does the word praise mean
    to you?
What happens when a Christian
    neglects to praise God?

*9. Again, sing resurrection songs*
    Re-sing some of the songs you

sang earlier. Between songs, each member could present to Jesus in front of the group the special offering that was prepared the night before.

*Optional:* If most of the people participating are ten years old and older, you might want to end this family communion evening by writing and reading acrostic prayers. In an acrostic, you start with a key word. In this case you would want to pick the word PRAISE that has been key throughout the evening. Each person writes a praise-prayer sentence or phrase for each letter in the word.

Here's my example. You might want to do one for your family to give them an idea of

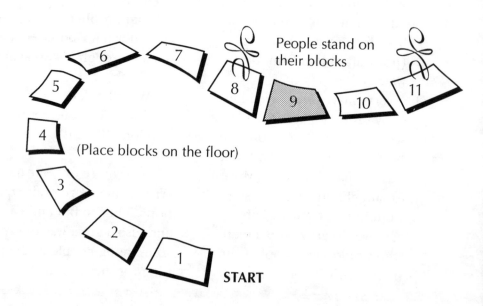

(Place blocks on the floor)

People stand on their blocks

START

what you mean. This is a special poem to God. If someone can't think of something to say about one letter, he or she should just move on to the next one. No one has to finish. When a few minutes of writing have passed, each person who wishes should pray aloud what has been written.

**P**— Praise you, God, because You love me,

**R**—Really love me enough to send Jesus to die.

**A**—Am I thankful to You?

**I**—I sometimes forget to say it, but I am.

**S**—So hear my poem of praise tonight.

**E**—Each day I'll remember to tell You I love You.

This whole service is aimed at the Christian church family. However, many families have members who are not committed to Christ. Should they be left out of this family time? My opinion is that they should be told exactly what will happen and be warmly invited to participate as fully as they can without violating the meaning of communion.

For example, they might enjoy the resurrection songs. They might answer some of the communion questions that do not require personal answers. They would enjoy the meal and perhaps the game. Do what you can to help these people not feel like they're the odd-people-out.

Head of house
asks questions

If a non-Christian comes, don't adjust any of your responses to fit what you think that person needs to hear. This evening is for Christians. Don't feel obligated to present the entire plan of salvation complete with invitation. That not only limits the effectiveness of the communion time for the Christians, but it may offend the non-Christian family member who has agreed to take part.

## Progressive Housewarming

*Objective:* The church will "warm" the homes of families who have just moved to new houses or recently joined the church.

Adaptation: Welcome non-churched new neighbors with the church's version of Welcome Wagon. Planning this event to include the new home of someone who is not part of the church can be tricky. Ask the person ahead of time if seven or eight people from the church can show up on the front lawn around 6 P.M. with supper (or dessert). Explain that this is a welcome from your church and requires nothing of the new homeowner or apartment dweller. You may not be invited into the home, and that's fine.

Ask permission to pray for God's blessing on the newcomer's life in this community. One person could be designated to invite the person to a church service or to a home Bible study. Keep the time short, fun, and "unchurchy." Some non-Christians will reject a gift like this. Others will consider it weird but fun. For others, it will be the perfect first step into a new life.

*Basic idea:* Church members will visit at least three homes of people who are in new homes, and eat one course of a meal in each home. Church members will supply the food.

Several years ago, our home was the middle part of a three-house warming.

- House one: a newly married couple
- House two: Jack and I in our first house
- House three: A single woman and her teenage daughter

Each of us in the three houses had recently made our purchases and were still in the process of moving in. Our guests were Christian friends who wanted to see our homes and welcome us into our new surroundings.

People signed up to bring an appetizer, main course, or

**INVITATION IDEA**

# A PROGRESSIVE HOUSEWARMING

**Appetizers at** _____
**Main Course at** _____
**Dessert at** _____
R.S.V.P. with the dish you will bring.

TIME:

DATE:

**Optional warming ideas:**
A homemade warming card for each house
A warming plant for each house
A warming can of soup for each house

dessert to one of the three houses. This took care of the food and left the new home-owners free to take care of unpacking and housecleaning!

Under no circumstances try to make this type of housewarming a surprise for the families.

When people came to our house, I was ready. There was still a hole in the front porch step, the bottom pane in the storm door was missing, and there were no lights in two of the upstairs rooms. I didn't mind; those just happened to be areas we hadn't gotten to yet.

But because I knew people were coming, I had time to clean the place—sort of—and put the unpacked boxes into neater piles. There were so many people that they had to sit on the rug. It was comforting to know that no one would have to be dry-cleaned after the party!

Because I knew about the warming, I also had time to buy a mum and put it in the rather empty family room. I don't think too many people noticed or cared that it was there, but it was good for me. That flower said that the evening was special. I didn't have to apologize for what wasn't done yet. The flower announced, "Look folks. I'm blooming. Have a good time at the housewarming, because

we're prepared!"

There was one room that had become a huge junk pile. I hadn't done anything there at all. I put a big purple note on the closed door begging people not to enter that room. The note was laughed at and a lot of people threatened to peek, but as far as I know, no one did!

We started our Progressive Housewarming at the condominium of two young people who had a great time showing us through empty rooms and dreaming along with us about what the place would look like when it was actually filled with furniture.

The main course was at Jack's and my home. It was fun to greet all the people who came— thirty or forty, I think.

It was a warm feeling to know that they had cared enough about us and the others on the new house list to take a whole evening from their busy schedules to help us celebrate. This may have been the first evening I really felt at home in our new house. It was so much bigger than our apartment and so unfinished. I had longed to go back home—back to the apartment. But this occasion, along with our house dedication, made the place mine. I decided we'd stay!

At each home a friend of the host couple had been asked to pray. Gladys wanted to pray for our home and I was delighted. I'd been single for over 30 years before I met Jack and married. The last few months before the wedding, she suggested that I live with her instead of living at my apartment. "I've been single for over fifty years," she said. "I can't even imagine what it would be like to suddenly add someone to my life. I suspect you're going to have some problems, too. You need to get used to sharing the bathroom and having someone else around most of the time." When she offered her guest room to me she said, "Consider our housemating as practice for the hard parts of being married!"

She prayed for our home:

"Peace be to this house and to those who dwell in it. Peace be to those who enter, and to those who go out from it.

"Almighty God, bless and hallow this house, this home, so that by your power and love, it may be for Marlene and Jack a pure and happy place of shelter from the storms of life, and of provision for their needs of body, mind, and soul.

"O God, whose Son for thirty years made His home with us, enable Marlene and Jack, taught by Him, to live together in loving-kindness, peace, and prayerfulness. May their home always be a dwelling fit for Your presence.

"Protect them from disease and privation, from calamity and accident, from fire, flood, and all perils of the elements and from the violence of men.

"Let this household, O Lord, be ever linked with the household of faith, ever receiving the inspiration of Christian fellowship, and always open to those in need. Let others come here freely for love and understanding, and let Your love radiate joy and peace from within its walls. Come into this house, Lord Jesus. Dwell here, our Savior and Lord, forever and ever. Amen."

The warmers of the new homes may want to leave a personal note at each place. A homemade card is an excellent idea. A can of soup, a symbol of warm hospitality, is also a good idea. Or how about a plant, a symbol of growth!

The dessert in our housewarming was at the home of a single parent and her daughter. It was great to see how Cathy, the twelve-year-old, became part of the whole celebration. She'd been very young when her parents divorced, and had most recently spent several years in a shared housing situation where there were other kids around all the time. But this house, in a new way, was all hers. She gave tours, spending lots of time showing her new pink bedroom.

I think that during dessert she was feeling what I had felt during the main course—warm feelings that occur when a person knows her house is becoming a home.

# 9

## *Special Holiday Celebrations*

*The business of Christ is not about
chicken-noodle dinners and bazaars.
The business of Christ is about winning
the lost and setting the oppressed free.*

—Michael Slaughter

## New Year's Eve Dinner and Worship

*Objective:* A few adult members of the church family will meet in a home to have dinner together. After dinner, they will divide into task groups to plan a worship service. Over the midnight hour they will all participate in praising God through the service they planned.

*Basic idea:* A group of from ten to twelve people will plan their own worship service around the theme: Father, we praise you for our years—those past, this year, and the years to come.

I've thoroughly enjoyed our New Year's Eve worship celebrations. They had just the mix of worship and participation that I had been looking for.

I grew up attending watch night services at my church. I dreaded them. They included several Christian films, the annual report, a short punch and cookie break, and a long prayer time as we brought the new year in. It was a sitting marathon. I had no feeling of personal participation, of being involved in praising God for the new year. The quiet, and the people hedging my right, left, front, and back boxed me in.

Of course, many of my friends celebrated New Year's in a totally secular way. Jack and I were in Mexico City on our honeymoon. New Year's Eve fell on our fourth day together—a perfect opportunity to join in the world's festivities. We made 10 P.M. reservations at a French restaurant. The evening was awful. People were loud, slightly drunk, pathetically determined to have a good time. Everything seemed forced and phony. We finished our meal quickly and went back to the hotel. The secular celebration was no option for me if I wanted to start the new year in a God-directed way.

After a lot of thinking, Jack and I came up with this party idea. It worked for us and the people in our church family. Would it work for you?

We invited thirteen people to our home for a late supper, followed by a planning time in which each of us contributed ideas on how we might praise God for the past, the present, or the future. When the worship planning was done—what songs we would sing, who would give testimony, etc.—we worshiped God together. Everyone was involved; everyone was praising God.

When our friend Ken called to let us know he would be

**INVITATION IDEA**

# New Year's Eve Dinner & Worship

---

## NEW YEAR'S EVE DINNER AND WORSHIP
### Dinner: 9 p.m.

Where:

*After dinner, help plan a celebration honoring God's work in our lives and world. Over the New Year's Hour, we will present our worship to Him.*

### Worship Planning Groups (choose one):

*1. Praise to God for years past*

*2. Praise to God for this year*

*3. Praise to God for years to come*

coming, he said, "I've had three other invitations, but this one sounds different. I've had it with New Year's, and your party just might revive my enthusiasm."

He and his wife, Carol, came loaded with ideas to contribute to the worship planning. She had brought her guitar and copies of new songs she had written especially for praising God for the future. Looking back on this detail is bittersweet. This was Carol's last New Year's Eve. Before the next year's celebration she died from a brain tumor. I've got this fanciful notion that God and a small strolling choir met her in Heaven to welcome her and sing her praise songs the way only heavenly choir members can.

At 12:30 after our worship service ended in a song of praise, we all clapped. We had found a personal and Christian way to celebrate the New Year.

*A caution:* Make sure everyone knows this is not a couples' event. People will be participating as individuals. Married couples will not necessarily be on the same worship planning committee.

## OUR PLANNING OUTLINE

Use our outline as a guide. Change it to fit your own personal New Year's celebration.

*Invitations*

Send them by November 1. Limit the number of guests to the number you can serve in a single room. (If you have a very small kitchen and no dining room, line up card tables across the living room.) It's nice to have everyone eating the late supper around the same table. For us it added to our growing feeling of oneness as we worked together on our worship service. For our celebration, we invited only people who were dedicated Christians.

*New Year's Eve*
- 8 P.M. People start arriving. Hors d'oeuvres and punch time.
- 9 P.M. Sit-down dinner.
- 10:30 P.M. One hour of planning for the worship celebration.
- 11:30 P.M.—through the coming of the new year. The worship celebration.

Now let's look at the evening a little more closely.

*8 P.M. People start arriving. Hors d'oeuvres and punch time.*

## HOT APPLE CIDER PUNCH
*1 gallon apple cider*
*2 teaspoons whole cloves*
*3 cinnamon sticks*
*2/3 cup sugar*

Heat all ingredients until boiling. Reduce heat and simmer until serving time—at least a half hour. Optional idea: Float whole oranges studded with cloves in the punch bowl.

### RUMAKI

*chicken livers (each liver will make 2 appetizers)*
*water chestnuts (each chestnut will make 4 appetizers)*
*bacon (each slice will make 2 appetizers)*
*teriyaki sauce (see page 157 for recipe)*
*toothpicks*

Cut chicken livers in half and quarter water chestnuts. Pour teriyaki sauce over them and allow them to soak in refrigerator for at least 6 hours. Drain.

Cut bacon slices in half and wrap a piece of liver and water chestnut in the bacon slice. Secure with the toothpick. Place in the broiler until bacon is crisp, about 6 minutes.

### STUFFED CAPS

*mushrooms (each mushroom cap will be one appetizer; recipe adjusted to 1 pound of mushroom—about 25 caps)*
*3 Tablespoons butter*
*1/4 cup chopped green pepper*
*1/4 cup chopped onion*
*1-1/2 cups soft bread crumbs*
*1/4 cup grated Parmesan cheese*
*1/2 teaspoon salt*
*1/2 teaspoon thyme*
*1/4 teaspoon pepper*
*1/2 cup chopped black olives*

Wash mushrooms. Remove stems and chop them to add to the mushroom cap filling. Melt 3 Tablespoons butter in skillet. Cook and stir chopped mushroom stems, pepper, and onions until tender, about 5 minutes. Remove from heat and stir in remaining ingredients.

Fill caps with mixture. Place mushrooms filled side up in a buttered baking dish and bake for 15 minutes. Then broil for about 2 minutes.

*9 P.M. Sit-Down Dinner*

This is a perfect occasion to get dressed up and eat a dinner that's a little more special than usual. You may want to do the entire dinner yourself, or ask others to bring certain dishes that will add to the festivities and participation. We chose to ask people to help. It was less money and work for us, and everyone seemed to enjoy preparing something for this evening.

### JELLIED SALMON SALAD

*3 cups canned salmon (water packed)*
*1 Tablespoon unflavored gelatin*
*2 cups hot water (use water from salmon pack)*

197

1 Tablespoon finely chopped
  green pepper or parsley
1 teaspoon scraped onion
1 hard boiled egg, chopped
1 cup finely cut celery
  shredded lettuce

Soak gelatin in two Tablespoons cold water for ten minutes; then dissolve it in the hot cups of water. When cool, add the rest of the ingredients.

Rinse individual molds in cold water and fill 3/4 full of the mixture. Set in refrigerator until firm.

Turn out on shredded lettuce and garnish with olives cut in rings. Put a dash of mayonnaise on each mold. Serves 6 to 8.

## SUNFLOWER HAM CHICKEN

*(12 servings)*
16 skinned, boned chicken
  breast halves
16 slices of ham (thin)
1 cup salted sunflower seeds
4 cups herb seasoned stuffing mix
2/3 cup undiluted evaporated milk
2/3 cup melted butter
  toothpicks

Flatten chicken breasts until 1/4 inch thick. Place each on a piece of ham. Combine sunflower seeds, stuffing mix, and evaporated milk. Mix well. Place equal amounts of the mixture on each breast. Roll and secure with toothpicks.

Place chicken and ham rolls seam side down in buttered baking dish; brush tops with butter. Bake at 350° for 50 minutes. Brush several times with additional butter. Remove picks.

## GOLDEN HEART CROQUETTES

*(12 servings)*
12 small carrots
2-1/2 cups cooked beef or veal
1 large can drained peas
1 medium onion
1/2 teaspoon salt
1/4 teaspoon nutmeg
1/4 teaspoon pepper
1 teaspoon Worcestershire sauce
2 eggs
2 Tablespoons water
1 cup fine dry crumbs
  vegetable oil for deep frying

Cook carrots in salt water until tender. Drain.

Put meat, peas, and onion through the fine cutter of a food grinder. Add seasonings and 1 egg, lightly beaten. Mix. Cover each carrot with this mixture. Form into croquettes.

Beat second egg with water. Dip croquettes into the mixture. Then roll in crumbs.

Fill flat-bottomed saucepan 2/3 full with melted vegetable oil. Heat it slowly. When it will brown a bread crumb in 50 seconds, it has reached the correct heat (375°). Slide in croquettes. Raise heat for a minute to prevent cooling.

Fry until rich brown. Drain on absorbent paper. Serve with white sauce or tomato sauce.

## Cinnamon Sweet Potatoes

*(12 servings)*
*4-1/2 pounds pared, diced*
  *sweet potatoes*
*2-1/2 cups boiling water*
*3 teaspoons salt*

Cover and boil slowly for 12 minutes or until tender. Do not drain.

Add:

*8 Tablespoons brown sugar*
*1-1/2 teaspoons cinnamon*
*2 cups evaporated milk*
*4 Tablespoons butter*

Cook slowly, uncovered until sauce is thickened, about 5 minutes. Serve at once.

## Bananas Foster

*6 firm bananas sliced in half*
  *lengthwise*
*3/4 cup butter*
*2 cups brown sugar*
*1 cup chopped nuts*
*dash cinnamon and nutmeg*
*French vanilla ice cream*

Sauté banana halves in butter. Sprinkle brown sugar over them. If sauce is too thick, add a couple of Tablespoons of orange juice. Add nuts, cinnamon, nutmeg. Broil in oven for two minutes.

Place bananas and sauce over ice cream.

*10:30 P.M. One hour of planning for the worship service.*

## HOST COUPLE'S PREPARATION

Read through the following material and decide what you want to use, change, or adapt. As people call to say they will be coming, explain a little of what you have in mind. Each person will choose if he or she wants to praise God for the past, the present, or the future. In fact, as people call, they may want to decide immediately what group they will be part of. In this way, they could be thinking about some songs or praise ideas that would fit with their group.

For example, a woman may choose to be on the team to praise God for the present—this year. This is the year the educational wing of her church has been completed and she has pictures showing the progress. She brings along the pictures, and then with her group composes a praise prayer to read to God while the pictures are passed around.

You will also want to have some supplies on hand that all groups can use: pad of paper, pencil, large sheets of paper, magic markers, overhead, computer and printer.

## WORSHIP PLANNING

What does the phrase *worship planning* mean? Simply, that each of the three groups will go through the process church leaders go through each week. They will pick songs that fit their aim. They will think of ways to involve the people. They will spend time praying about their part in the worship service.

I've suggested some ideas that would be helpful for each group. If groups are doing just fine without any outside help, great. Don't interject these ideas. But it's always good to have a few examples ready just in case the worship planning groups draw a blank.

*Group 1:* Praise God for the years that are past.

*Theme:* Father, we praise You for Your direction over the years that are now past.

Get started by discussing how you could lead the other two groups in praising God for the years past.

What songs would be helpful? How about "God of Our Fathers"; "Rock of Ages"; and "A Mighty Fortress Is Our God"? Add some of the newer praise songs. You might want to write the words on large sheets of paper or print them off the computer so everyone will be

able to participate in the singing.

Ask, "How can we involve others in the worship?" Perhaps you could ask for praise testimonies for specific things God has done in the past. Or you could ask people to share verses that have been meaningful to them in years past.

Could you develop a choral reading based on Scripture that would allow you to praise God for His past care?

Does the group have a sense of the dramatic? Perhaps two members could begin with a roleplay between a Christian and a non-Christian. The Christian is telling the non-Christian why it's exciting to have God as a guide through his or her personal history.

*Group 2:* Praise for this year.

*Theme:* Father, we praise You for this year.

Get started by discussing how you can lead others in praising God for things He has done this year.

Could each person in the group give a three sentence overview of how God has guided this year?

Could the group develop a current events reading? One person would act as a newscaster reporting some of the key events of the year. Other people from the group would respond with Scripture verses showing God's control, or testify with personal affirmations that God has His hand on all of history and will control the eventual outcome.

Could the group write some words to a hymn or chorus that would praise Him for this year?

For example, sung to *America*, the New Year's words might be:

*Events that shocked us all*
*The crime, the pain we saw,*
*We ask God why.*
*The graft in government,*
*The way the dollar went,*
*The bullets on killing spent:*
*Is life worthwhile?*

*We feel Your presence near*
*Dissolving doubt and fear.*
*Help us to cope.*
*When evil seems to win,*
*Where God's love might have been,*
*We raise a banner over sin,*
*And claim God's hope.*

Could you supply questions for discussion and ask the whole group to participate in grappling with the issues of the past year? For example:

In what ways are we Christians responsible for the government we have? In what ways can we have influence as "salt of the earth"?

Secular sources report on groups that offer "family" to those who join them—something the joiners can get nowhere else. How do you think God wanted us, the church, to "family" our world this past year?

What do you think was the event that most shook people's faith this year? How do we know God is really in control?

What about a prayer time in which people bring their current praises and concerns before God and the group?

Could the group plan a mini-sermon, giving illustrations from the lives of biblical people who praised God in the middle of terrible circumstances? For example, Abraham had his arm raised to kill his only son. Puah, the midwife, agreed to stand against Pharaoh and not kill male Hebrew babies. Peter stood alone in the crowd after denying Christ. John was exiled. None of these people knew at the moment of crisis how God would use their terrible experience for His glory. But He did! Can we have that same assurance?

*Group 3*: Praise for the years to come.

*Theme:* Father, we praise You for the future.

Get started by talking about what the world will probably be like in the next few years. How can Christians have total assurance that God is really in charge? Select a few songs that talk about the return of Christ. Consider playing some traditional Negro spirituals. Many of these songs were filled with despair for the present, but beyond today's pain, people had the assurance that Jesus and heaven awaited.

Could you lead a sentence round? The first person will start something about personal faith in God as controller of the future and others will add to that.

How about sharing a little about people who pointed you to Christ? Pick people who are now enjoying their futures forever with Christ.

In the worship, give everyone a sheet of paper. Ask people to tear a symbol of their feeling as a Christian thinking about the future. Everyone should share what his or her symbol means.

*11:30 P.M. through the coming of the new year*

*The Worship Celebration*

Each group will lead the other groups in its part of the worship service. Have a wonderful, Happy New Year!

At the end of our worship service, people immediately began talking about the next

year. We decided that we would not get together in the same group again. Instead we would use what we had done in other New Year's Eve home celebrations and enlarge our circle of people who could participate.

This idea worked perfectly in the church we were attending because the church had decided not to plan a watch night service. A caution: The church is of primary importance in the growth of the Christian community. Don't run competition with it even if you think your idea will reach people the church's traditional service is missing. Why not present this home celebration to your pastor and suggest that the whole church break up in homes across the community for smaller, less formal services? Divide the membership and regular attendees among the host families, and have a wonderful time praising God for the past, the present, and the security of our futures in Him.

## Passover

### An Easter Freedom Celebration

*Objective:* The church family will celebrate a Christian Passover. This celebration begins with the story of God's salvation for His people in Egypt and ends with our praise to Him for our salvation through Jesus Christ.

*Basic idea:* Members of the church family will follow some of the Jewish traditions associated with Passover, the most important Jewish festival of all. Christ's followers will discuss the Exodus Passover, celebrate a Passover meal, and conclude with a communion service. This should be a meaningful occasion for everyone, and a special teaching opportunity for parents with young children.

## WHO TO INVITE:

Why not divide the congregation into house groups? Hosts will be responsible for inviting their assigned group to their homes. Portions of the meal should be assigned to each guest. Our church did this for several years, and it became one of our most meaningful traditions.

This is a unique enough event to raise the curiosity of people who are investigating Christianity. It would be very appropriate to invite several to attend as participants in much of what is done, excluding the Eucharist. Some would simply enjoy learning more about an historical holiday. Others would be interested in the Jewish/Christian

connection. Work hard not to allow the seeker to change the tone of the evening. This is "church family" time, not a time to argue polemics. It is a teaching celebration, not an evangelistic outreach. (This does not for a moment mean that God will not use what a visitor sees and feels during this event to encourage his or her "pass over" into new life.)

Peggy Wehmeyer, the religion correspondent for ABC News, said what many in our communities believe: "I'm definitely on a spiritual journey, but my church is not the focal point" (from "Why Bother with the Church?" *Christian Century*, Jan. 24, 1996). For some, an evening like this can redefine the direction on their journey.

## GETTING READY

If the host families have small children, the meaning of the Passover can begin with the housecleaning for the event. Years ago, Jewish families combined housecleaning and the special cleaning for the festival which they called Pesach (Passover). Walls were washed, furniture was scrubbed, and even clothes were given a good airing. All this was in preparation for remembering what God had done for His people.

## WELCOME

The head of the home where the celebration is held should be in charge of the order of the service. Everyone is seated in the same room. Keep the seating arrangements comfortable, informal—no rows of chairs. In fact, it's appropriate for the small children to be seated on the floor.

The leader welcomes everyone: "Welcome to all who have no celebration at their home. Welcome to all who are hungry. Come and feast with us. Welcome to all who wish to join. Welcome as we look forward to the future and remember the past."

The host will fill a glass with juice or wine for each guest. Each one should take one sip. Then the host takes three matzos (unleavened bread available in most large grocery stores). Originally Jewish families took great pains to make this special bread from flour that had been harvested and milled under the watchful eye of the rabbi. The host should put these, one on top of the other, on a large plate and cover them with a napkin.

He or she then explains: "Matzo stands for unity. For Jewish people, the top matzo represents the priest. The middle one represents the Levite.

The third one is known as the Israelites. One on top of the other, this bread symbolizes that all Jews are brothers.

"Can you tell me what the three pieces of unleavened bread might mean to us Christians here tonight?"

A young person could suggest that for Christians they might also stand for unity. All people who believe in Christ as their Savior are brothers and sisters in Christ.

The leader should then take the top piece and pass it around the group. Each person should break a bite-sized portion from the piece and eat it. Then he or she should hand it to the next person saying, "I'm glad we're together in the family of God."

## THE STORY OF THE EXODUS

A good reader, chosen ahead of the Passover service, should read the story of the Israelites in Egypt. If there are a lot of children present, the reader may want to read the story from a Bible storybook. The story may be summarized from Scripture by reading Exodus 1:8-14; 2:1-10; 3:4, 7-10; 11:1-6; 12:1-14.

After the story has been read, the children participate in answering questions asked by the host. Here are some questions that might be helpful:

- Why did the Israelites want to leave Egypt?
- Why didn't the Egyptians want them to leave?
- How did God help His people, the Israelites?
- Why did God tell the people to celebrate the way they left Egypt for the rest of their life as a nation?
- What are some special days Christians celebrate?
- What does each mean?
- What is the most important Christian holiday? (Easter) What happened on Easter?
- On the Passover, we remember that God saved His people from slavery to the Egyptians. What did God save His people from on Easter?

## THE SYMBOLS OF EXODUS

The host should now explain that the group is going to participate in a remembering celebration much like the celebration the Jews will be having on Passover. Each thing the group will eat points to something that they don't want to forget—and they don't want their children or children's children to forget.

### Morar (horseradish)

The host should take the second piece of matzo and pass it with some ground horseradish. Each person should scoop a bit of the horseradish onto a piece of the matzo and eat it. He should explain that bitter horseradish is a part of the ceremony to help the people remember the bitterness of slavery and life in Egypt. The Talmud says, "In every generation, every Jew should see himself as if it were he who was redeemed from slavery in Egypt."

The leader should draw a parallel between the bitterness of physical slavery and the spiritual slavery to sin.

### Haroseth (mixture of chopped nuts, apples, and fruit juice or wine)

The leader should point out that this mixture looks a little like clay. Perhaps the leader could ask a child what the Hebrew people were to remember when they saw the food that looked like clay. (It symbolizes the bricks the Israelites made for the Egyptians when they were slaves.) The mixture is passed and each person takes a bite.

### Cooked egg

The egg is broken into pieces and passed. As each person takes and eats a bit of the egg, he or she is to remember the sacrifices that were offered for sins in the temple. The host should ask why Christians no longer offer sacrifices for sins.

*Salt water and parsley*

The salt water represents the bitter tears shed by the Jews when they were slaves under the oppression of Egypt, and the parsley represents the new life that God promises His people. Each person should take a bit of parsley, dip it in the salt water and eat.

*Prayers and Singing*

In the Jewish Passover celebration, the people sing thanksgiving songs to God. The Christians at this Passover should sing songs now about the joy of being Christians and having new life in Christ. People can suggest a few favorite hymns or choruses.

Then the host should pray, thanking God for His great gift of freedom from sin.

*Wine (or juice)*

Now everyone takes another sip of the juice (wine). In the Jewish festival, four sips of wine are taken. No one knows why just four, but some people think that each sip represents a promise that was made to the Israelites when they were freed from Egypt. "I will take you out of the land of bondage." "And I will save you." "And I will free you from slavery." "And I will take you to be a chosen people."

*The Meal*

In a Jewish home, this meal is traditionally the best the family can afford. Depending on your enthusiasm for Jewish cooking you may want to try some of the traditional foods like egg soup and matzo balls. You might want to have roast chicken or lamb as a main dish. Other traditional touches that you can pick up at most grocery stores include figs, marinated herring, kosher pickles, bananas, honey (for dipping apples), and kumquats.

In a Jewish home, one of the young children hides the dessert. The father turns to the child and begs him or her to find the dessert. The child will finally agree but only if there is a reward involved. The father and child banter back and forth and finally the father agrees—for the sake of dessert. The host family may want to play out this special drama to add some fun to the evening for the children.

The meal is concluded with everyone thanking God. You might want to write a prayer that everyone will read in unison.

"Lord, we praise You for the way you took care of Your people. The stories in the Old Testament are exciting and filled with examples of Your power. But our favorite story is in the New Testament. It's the story of the Resurrection! You gave up Your life to pay for our sins. But you conquered death and rose to life. You, Son of God, are our Messiah. We praise You. Amen."

*Coins for Wheat*

You may want to take an offering for people who need special help this Easter time. Young people should be encouraged to participate on their own in this part of Passover.

*Open Door Ceremony*

Explain that Jewish tradition says that Elijah visits the homes of Jews on this night. He opens the door and announces that the Messiah will come, the one who will lead the people to their homeland.

On this night more than any other, the Jewish people who do not believe the Messiah has come continue to pray that God will send him soon.

You may want to change this ceremony and invite the small children to participate. Explain that in several days, Christians will celebrate the raising of Jesus from the dead. Sing a celebration Easter hymn. Then ask the children to open the door and shout in a loud voice, "You are welcome in this house, Jesus."

## COMMUNION

For the Jew who has not accepted Christ as Messiah, the celebration has ended. But for the Christian who knows that Jesus is the Messiah, the most important part of the celebration is still ahead. Communion! Through celebrating communion, Christians remember what Christ did for them, and they are reminded that He is coming again. They are looking forward to the Messiah's second return.

Before you serve the elements, make certain elementary children understand this transition. You might explain it once and ask them to answer these questions which will require them to state their understanding of what you have said.

Why are we ending our Passover with the celebration of communion?

Why don't Jewish people who haven't accepted Jesus as Messiah celebrate communion?

What does Passover help us remember? What does communion help us remember?

What does the Passover look forward to? What does communion look forward to?

For communion, there should be one piece of bread left for Christians to break and pass.

The final bit of juice in the glasses should be used. For unique ways of passing communion, see page 182.

## LEAVING

Ask people to leave in silence (or the children to silently go to bed). In this way their thoughts can remain more completely on what has happened at this Passover. They have been reminded of the things that God has done in the past, the sorrow of Christ's death for us, and the joy we can have because we know He will return for us.

## Recycled Christmas Party

*Objective:* Each Christian will invite an unchurched person to a home to sing Christmas carols and enlarge the potential for friendship evangelism.

In preparation for this evening, a group of prayer warriors should meet to ask God to guide Christians as they send out "second" invitations and to take away any fear of following through with God talk when a natural opportunity opens.

*Basic idea:* Each person is to bring an ornament that has been made out of recycled material to trim the tree. Everyone will judge all the ornaments, play a recycled game, sing Christmas carols, and get to know each other better, perhaps removing fears and stereotypes the unchurched guests may have about Christians.

## INVITATION IDEA

Send two invitations to each Christian. The invitations should be made of recycled paper—old Christmas cards, backs of bread wrappers, soup labels—be creative. The recipient keeps one and sends the other along to a friend who needs to know that Christianity is not dull and gray.

## AS GUESTS ARRIVE

Take people's recycled ornaments at the door. Put a number on each and hang it on the tree. Try to keep guests from knowing who brought which ornament.

You'll be amazed at the creativity some people will exhibit. At the recycled party where I was a guest, people made doves from soap bottles, geometric balls from old Christmas cards and last year's wrapping paper, and a hanging pants pocket starched and filled with straw flowers. Quite often all people need is the starter idea. You've given them that with the recycled theme; don't be surprised if this party turns into a lot of fun.

## INVITATION IDEA

# RECYCLED CHRISTMAS PARTY

**Why WASTE December (party date)?**
Put your WASTE together in an artistic form.
Add a hook and come hang it on our Christmas tree.
RECYCLE your junk!

JUNK IDEAS: *8 used paper cups,*
*painted and strung together.*
*Christmas bells made from*
*old juice cans.*
*Soda tab wreath*

**R.S.V.P.**
**You just might win a RECYCLED prize.**

At this party, like most others at which people may not all know each other, plan on using name tags. Make them before the guests arrive out of all sorts of recycled material—similar to the materials you used for the invitations! Each tag should be original and different. This will add a festive start. For example, you could take the Styrofoam base under some vegetables you buy in a grocery store and write a guest's name on it. Decorate the base with last year's Christmas cards, colorful cellophane from around candy and gum, and who knows what else! I'd start my collection of *potential recycling material* (a nifty phrase for *junk*) about three weeks before the party. It's not hard to put together dubious works of art when you have all the materials in front of you.

After all guests have arrived, give each a ballot and ask each to vote on the ornaments now on the tree.

---

- The most creatively recycled ornament _____
- The most amazing recycled ornament _____
- The ornament that rids the world of the most junk ____

---

Prizes should be fun. As you award them, explain why the prize qualifies as a recycled goodie. For example, I'm recycling a half-burned candle I've had setting around for years. It just drops and drips all over the place. I've burned it as long as I could stand all its ugliness, and I would be happy to recycle it into someone else's home.

A better idea for me would be to recycle a packet of ten of Jack's favorite recipes. Actually, that is a pretty nice gift.

There are magazines on recycled paper and writing paper made from recycled materials. If you want to spend money on prizes, these are possibilities.

## CAROLS

Do you ever get tired of singing Christmas carols? I don't. I love to sing them, and I watch for their first appearance with as much enthusiasm as I do my first spring robin.

So gather everyone around a piano or a guitar (or just someone who can sing on tune) and sing away. Supply books, if possible. This way you can sing more than the most familiar verses.

Intersperse the singing with readings. People might bring a funny or serious article to share with the group. *Reader's Digest* is often a good source. Limit readings to three or four minutes. What you are doing here is recycling stories that others have enjoyed—passing along enthusiasm about Christmas.

A grab bag might also help break up the singing time. Before everyone arrives put each name into a bag. About every four songs, blow a whistle, stop everything, reach into the bag, and pull out a name. That person should then answer a recycled question. Here are some questions that would be great for recycling:

Recycle the story about the best Christmas gift you've ever gotten.

Tell about something you've gotten secondhand that you just love.

If you could recycle an event that happened this past year, living it again this coming year, what would it be?

Recycle the first verse of a carol we've already sung this evening.

Tell about something in your house that you really do recycle.

If you could recycle one year of your life, which year would you choose? Why?

## RECYCLED GAMES

Both of these games grow from the same basic idea, so use just one of them.

*New Clothes for Santa*

Save several weeks' newspapers.

Divide the party into recycling groups. Explain that Mr. and Mrs. Santa need new outfits, and each group will be recycling the newspaper to make these special costumes.

Each group should pick two people to dress. Provide no scissors. With only the newspaper, tape, pins, and perhaps some construction paper, the group must come up with a nifty outfit for the pair.

Why not award the winning group a pack of gum? Explain that the gum is new, but it can be easily recycled by sticking it on the bedpost every night.

*Recycled Christmas Music*

Divide the party into recycling groups—recycling objects into musical instruments. Explain that each group is to roam through the house picking up unique musical instruments. They are to use their voices and their homemade instruments to present a Christmas carol.

Ideas for the musical instruments abound. For example, someone might fill glasses with different amounts of water, and try to get a tune by hitting the glasses with a pencil. Or someone could put waxed paper over a comb and hum through it. Or how about just getting a pan and a spoon and banging away? Again, the award could be new gum—just perfect for recycling!

I like these games because they force people to create something out of nothing. Nearly everyone enjoys participating in this type of foolishness, and is amazed by what a group produces—not always pleased, but always amazed!

*Food*

Christmas cookies. You could ask each guest to bring eight cookies or you could supply them yourself.

### FRUIT JUMBLES

*1-1/2 cups sugar*
*1/2 cup shortening*
*3 eggs*
*3 cups flour*
*1 teaspoon vanilla*
*1 pound chopped dates*
*1/4 pound chopped walnuts*
*1 teaspoon soda dissolved in*
*  hot water*

Mix sugar, shortening, eggs, flour, and vanilla. Batter will be stiff. Add dates and nuts. Mix. Add soda last.

Drop by teaspoons on greased cookie sheet and bake in a (moderate) 350° oven for 12 to 15 minutes. Makes 2 dozen or more cookies.

### OATMEAL MACAROONS

*1 cup shortening*
*1 cup brown sugar*
*1 cup white sugar*
*1/2 teaspoon vanilla*
*2 eggs*
*1 1/4 cups flour*
*1/2 teaspoon salt*
*1 teaspoon baking soda*
*1/2 teaspoon cinnamon*
*3 cups uncooked oatmeal*
*1/2 cup chopped nuts*

Mix shortening, sugars, vanilla, and eggs thoroughly. Add sifted dry ingredients. Fold in oats and nuts.

Drop by teaspoon onto ungreased sheets. Bake 12-15 minutes in 350° oven. Cool for 2 minutes before removing from baking sheets. Makes about 4 dozen.

On a second mix, why not add a package of milk chocolate chips?

### ORANGE COCONUT CRISPS

*1/2 cup butter*
*1 cup sugar*
*2 eggs*
*1 teaspoon vanilla*
*1 Tablespoon grated orange rind*
*2-1/2 cups sifted all-purpose flour*
*1/4 teaspoon soda*
*1 teaspoon baking powder*
*1/2 teaspoon salt*
*1/4 teaspoon cinnamon*
*1/4 cup orange juice*
*8 ounces shredded coconut*

Cream butter and sugar until fluffy. Beat in eggs, vanilla, and orange rind. Sift flour with soda, baking powder, salt, and cinnamon. Add half the flour mixture, blending well. Add orange juice. Blend in remaining flour.

Spread coconut on wax paper or in shallow pan. Drop cookie dough (it will be soft) by teaspoonfuls on coconut. Roll in coconut, coating generously. Place cookies 1-1/2 inches apart on greased cookie sheets. Bake at 375° for 15 minutes.

### NEVER-FAIL FUDGE
*12-ounce can of evaporated milk*
*1/4 pound butter*
*4 cups sugar*
*12 ounces chocolate, melted*
*4 heaping Tablespoons of*
   *marshmallow cream*
*chopped nuts (optional)*
Place milk, butter, sugar in saucepan. Bring to a full rolling boil. Stir constantly. Boil for 5 minutes.

Remove from heat and fold in chocolate and marshmallow cream. Stir until blended. Add chopped nuts, if desired. Pour into greased 8" x 13" pan. Cool and cut into squares.

### CHOCOLATE SANDWICHES
*4 cups flour*
*1-1/2 cups butter*
*1/2 cup fine sugar*

Mix and roll into five long rolls—about 1 inch in diameter. Wrap in wax paper and chill.

When chilled, slice into 50-cent-sized circles (1/4 inch thick), and bake for 10 minutes at 400°.

Spread half the pieces with chocolate filling and top with the other half to create chocolate sandwiches.

**Filling:**
*4 squares chocolate*
*3 Tablespoons butter*
*3 cups powdered sugar*
*1/8 teaspoon salt*
*5 Tablespoons cream*
*1 teaspoon vanilla*
Melt chocolate and mix all ingredients together.

### ORANGE NUT BARS
*2 cups flour*
*1/3 cup sugar*
*1/2 teaspoon salt*
*2/3 cup butter*
Sift dry ingredients together. Cut in butter until size of small peas.

Combine:
*1 slightly beaten egg*
*1 teaspoon vanilla*
Add to flour mixture, stirring with fork until dough is moist enough to hold together. Roll out half of the dough on 9" x 13" piece of wax paper.

Roll to the edge of the paper. Invert into a 9" x 13" greased pan. Remove paper.

Roll out remainder of dough on waxed paper to a 9" x 13" rectangle; set aside.

**Filling:**
*2 cups chopped nuts*
*2/3 cup sugar*
*1 Tablespoon grated orange rind*
*1 cup orange juice*
*1 Tablespoon lemon juice*
Combine all ingredients. Spread over dough in the pan.

Place remaining dough over filling. Remove paper. Prick generously with fork. Bake at 375° for 25 to 30 minutes. Frost immediately after taking out of oven.

**Frosting:**
*1-1/2 cups sifted powdered sugar*
*1 teaspoon grated orange rind*
*2-1/2 Tablespoons orange juice*

## Christmas

### Ideas to Add to Your Home Celebrations

*Objective:* To start you thinking about the importance of starting meaningful traditions in your own home at Christmas time (and the year round).

Traditions are very important in a Christian home and the family, no matter how you define that unit. They tie us to our past and help us remember events and emotions that might otherwise be forgotten. They say, "We always do this together. We are a family."

Think about the days when you were a child. What family traditions did you have—the things your family always did together? You could count on these things happening.

I think about Friday nights and lemon ice cream sodas. I'll never drink a lemon soda without remembering the nineteen-cent ones at Garvin's Department Store and my mother. Every Friday night, we would go to town, often with only fifty cents between us.

We would wander through the stores and talk. During those adolescent years it was easier to tell her what I was feeling and what had happened at school while we window shopped. She would share things that happened to her at work and what her dreams for my brother and me were. We would never have talked like that if we had just sat down and said, "Now, we'll talk." That would have been too threatening for me. Those two hours on Friday nights were tradition for us. She's dead now, but I can still look back on our

Friday night outings and remember some of the wonderful ways she mothered and guided me.

*Family traditions.* What helps you remember those years gone by? More important, what will help the children in your life remember?

Christmas is the easiest time of the year to start or improve traditions—but don't stop there. Traditions fitted anywhere into your year highlight positive feelings and help the people involved feel that they belong.

Here are some traditions celebrated by people I know. They don't fit into the holiday seasons, but they're great for pulling people together.

*First robin tradition.* When someone in the family sights the first robin of spring, the rest of the family is alerted. The next free day is robin-picnic day—even if there is still snow on the ground. This family will have their picnic anyway—don their coats and off they go. Spring is just around the corner.

*Family flag traditions.* Each person in the home has a flag. On birthdays and special achievement days (a daughter scores the winning point at the basketball game), the person's flag is flown. Flags can be purchased, but it will be more fun if everyone makes an original flag

that says something about himself or herself.

*Doll tradition.* One mother with five daughters makes each girl a birthday dress and an identical dress for each girl's doll.

*Cleaning bird tradition.* To make housecleaning a little more fun, a mother hides a cloth bird. The small children clean until they find it. Then it is break time for milk and cookies before finishing their jobs.

*Save-it-up tradition.* One grandmother on a limited budget sends her grandchildren cards on special occasions. The cards act as bank cards telling the child how much money is in the account. So for Christmas, Adam's account may be $27, and for birthday, it may go up to $37. Grandma keeps the money and when the child has saved enough, Adam gets a plane ticket to visit Grandma.

*Postcard tradition.* A woman who travels a lot collects names and addresses of children who need the affirmation of an adult. She sends cards from different places where she travels. She may never have children of her own, but she has built a caring tradition with over 30 children.

Little traditions woven into the fabric of our lives! Begin to build traditions into your year. And start at Christmas. It may make a difference in the enthusiasm of those who participate, and more important, it may make a difference in your children's appreciation for family.

When they were children, our three nephews, David, Danny, and Douglas, added a lot of life to the celebration, especially when we wanted to settle down and listen to the Bible story of the first Christmas before we opened presents. Chairs squeaked, wrapping paper crinkled as little hands squeezed.

We'd hear whispers of, "When can we open the presents? How much longer?"

"What can we do to make them as interested in the true meaning of Christmas as they are in their gifts?" Jack asked. And then laughingly he answered his own question. "Nothing!"

He's right; they were just young children. But we could do a lot to increase their interest in the Bible story and at the same time begin to grow their understanding of the Christmas message.

So we decided to make them part of the Christmas story, instead of just listeners. These next two ideas were our answer to a meaningful Christmas tradition. Each year through their childhood, we worked together to make the story of Christmas live for the adults and children in our family. The birth of a tradition is exciting. People hardly realize it's been born until they look back and know how much it means to them and look forward to next year with new anticipation.

Try our ideas, and add to them, making them your own.

## CHRISTMAS STORY ENVELOPES

*Objective:* To involve each person in the extended family at his or her own age level in the retelling of the first Christmas story.

*Basic idea:* Before the family meets for Christmas present opening, write one question for each person who will be attending. Put that question into an envelope with the person's name on it. Match the questions to the abilities of the person. For the non-reader, draw a little stick figure picture that will illustrate a part of the Christmas story. When you're all together, read the Bible story and stop at appropriate places to ask the questions.

The child will tell the part of the story that the picture represents.

Here's what we did in our extended family Christmas. Since we have a wide age span, this script will give you an idea of how you might develop your own.

*Bible Reader:* Luke 2:1-7. Encourage the person who reads to use a lot of expression. After reader has finished the verses indicated, he or she should call on the person who will answer the questions.

*Envelope 1 for David, a third grader:* If Joseph and Mary had come to your door and asked for a room, what would you have said?

*Bible Reader:* Luke 2:8-14
*Envelope 2 for David's daddy:* Suppose you had been one of the shepherds. How do you think you would have felt when the angels came?

*Bible Reader:* Let's sing a Christmas carol. David, which one would you like to sing? (Again, involve the youngsters.)
*Envelope 3 for Danny;* he's four years old and doesn't read yet. In his envelope was this picture. The Bible reader asked him to explain the story.

*Bible Reader:* Luke 2:15-19
*Envelope 4 for Grandma:* Pretend you are a shepherd on your way back from seeing baby Jesus. You meet a good friend. What do you tell her?

*Bible Reader:* Matthew 2:1-12
*Envelope 5 for Auntie:* God gave us a wonderful gift when He sent us His Son, Jesus. What gifts can we give to Jesus?
*Envelope 6 for Uncle Marc:* What makes Christmas so special for Christians?

Christmas Story Envelopes are fun and they involve everyone. Even the opening of the envelopes is part of the fun. No one really knows what part of the story will be inside.

These envelope questions were designed to make the story clearer to small children and to hold their interest—if only for a few minutes—even in a room full of wrapped presents.

What if your family is older? The same idea will work but you'll need to age grade the questions.

For example, in a family of teenagers you might use questions like these:

*Bible Reader:* Luke 2:1-7
*Envelope 1:* You meet someone on the bus who is just about toppling over with Christmas presents. You start talking about the real meaning of Christmas, and he says he can swallow everything but the virgin birth. How do you reply? Explain why the virgin birth is absolutely essential to the story of Christmas.

*Bible Reader:* Luke 2:8-14
*Envelope 2:* If God were sending His Son into our world today, to whom do you think He would send his special announcements? Why?
*Envelope 3:* What do God's birth announcements tell you about Him?

*Bible Reader:* Luke 2:15-19
*Envelope 4:* Next to your salvation, what would you say is the most exciting gift God has given you? Lead us in prayer, thanking Him for His most important gift, and all the others He gives.

## THE CHRISTMAS STORY: A FAMILY PLAY

An easy way to involve the whole family in the reading of the Christmas story is to script it and assign parts.

CHARACTERS:
JOSEPH—Father
MARY—Aunt
SHEPHERDS—youngsters
ANGEL—Grandmother
INNKEEPER—Uncle

We adjusted the parts to the people at our Christmas celebration. You'll have to do the same. If you have a very small group, there is no problem with someone being assigned two roles.

When we did this in our family, we gave the younger child a picture to read. Note that the following sample has been written at the children's level. They should be totally involved with the tradition of sharing the true story of Christmas.

*Daddy:* I got an order from Caesar Augustus, the Roman Emperor. I was to return to the town where my family used to live in order to put my name on a tax list. I am a member of the royal line, so I had to go to Bethlehem in Judea, King David's ancient home. I had to travel all the way from Nazareth in Galilee.

*Aunt:* I am Mary, and I went with Joseph. It was a hard trip because I was going to have a baby. When we got to Bethlehem, I knew that the baby was coming soon. Joseph and I looked everywhere for a room where we could stay.

*Uncle:* When Mary and Joseph asked me if they could stay in my hotel, I said no. I didn't have any more rooms. But I did let them sleep in my barn.

*Aunt:* There my baby boy was born.

(If there is a small baby in the group, Mother could invite the younger children to wrap a blanket around the baby just as Mary did with her little newborn son.)

*Shepherd (child who can read):* I was a shepherd in a field outside the village, and I took care of sheep. It was a long, hard job.

*Shepherd (child who is too young "reads" this picture):* (An adult may have to ask the non-reader to explain the picture and prod the child until he or she shares the correct answer. Most children who live in Christian homes or attend Sunday school will know immediately what the next part of the story is.)

*Child (divide the shepherd roles among the children who can read):* Suddenly the one angel was joined by many, many others, and they all praised God.

*Child:* Come on! Let's go to Bethlehem! Let's see this wonderful thing that has happened which the Lord has told us about.

*Aunt:* The shepherds came and worshiped the baby. It was wonderful of God to send them a special birth announcement for His Son.

*Daddy:* What a wonderful Heavenly Father we have. Let's sing a Christmas carol now to thank Him for sending Jesus to earth.

## CHRISTMAS TIC-TAC-TOE
*A Family Bible Game*

You'll need at least twelve people to play Christmas Tic-Tac-Toe, a game involving review of the Christmas story and praise to our Savior.

Arrange your chairs like a Tic-Tac-Toe game—three rows of three chairs in each row. One person should sit in each chair.

Two players should stand in front of the chairs. Each player has six construction paper blocks in his or her hands. One person's blocks should be red and the other's green.

Players should take turns

A WIN

*Reader with questions*

*Reader with colored cards*

calling on the people in the chairs to answer questions. They must call on someone before the twelfth person reads the question. If the person called on knows the right answer, the player gives that person one of his or her cards to hold up. If that person doesn't know the answer, the next player takes a turn. The object, as in Tic-Tac-Toe, is to get three red or three green cards in a row.

Of course, children can play this game with adults. The person reading each question might adjust the difficulty of some questions for the younger children.

Make up your own questions for the game and build them all around the Christmas story. Here are a few to give you an idea. When all your questions are answered correctly, your family will have had an excellent review of the Christmas story.

- Why did Joseph go to Bethlehem?
- Who was the ruler at the time of Jesus' birth?
- Why didn't the innkeeper take Mary and Joseph into his inn?
- How many shepherds came to the manger to see Jesus? (Trick question. The Bible doesn't tell us.)
- What did the shepherds do after they left the barn?

## GOD GIFTS

Both children and adults can participate in this worship experience. Before the family opens its gifts, each person is given a colorful square of construction paper and asked to write or draw a gift on that square that he or she would like to give to Jesus this year.

Encourage adults to share what they are giving with another adult and ask that adult to hold them accountable to follow through on their gift. For example, I might draw a dollar sign and explain to my sister-in-law that I promise to give God five percent more money this year than I did last. She would check with me every once in a while to make sure that I was really doing what I had said I would do. Or she might write, "I will give my children to God by making a daily effort to teach them more about Him." I, in turn, would check with her to see how daily devotions are coming and in what ways she is seeing their understanding of Jesus grow.

A young child's gift will have to be more immediate, something that can be done right now. For example, Caleb might draw a picture of himself talking to a friend and explain that later today when he goes over to visit Rodney, he will tell him about the true meaning of Christmas. Or he might write, "I won't fight with Lee today."

These gifts should be something you can measure. If the child doesn't fight with Lee all day, he has given Jesus the gift he said he would. On the adult level, I can measure the amount of money I give to God.

## CHRISTMAS LIGHTS

After all the gifts are opened, each person takes a candle. The head of the home lights a large candle and places it in the middle of the room.

The leader explains that the large candle is a symbol of Christ, the light of the world. Our smaller candles represent us. Each person should take the unlit candle to the larger one and light it. In this way the person is saying how important it is for Christ to shine through his or her life; each wants to share a Christian light with others who are in darkness.

As Sara lights her candle, for example, she should share one way she has grown in her reflection of Christ this past year. Or, she could share one way she has shared her light with others.

After all candles are lit, the family might sing the doxology together.

This simple ceremony takes

only a few minutes. It can be an excellent reminder to the whole family that this household is set apart by God.

## GIFTS OF TIME

Each person will present a gift of time to other family members. What a difficult gift! It's not the type that can be purchased, given, and forgotten. This gift requires something of ourselves.

These gifts may be written or presented in the form of stick figure pictures. If the family is large, you might draw names and have each person give a gift of time to the person whose name he has drawn. This is an excellent tradition to start. If you do, stress creativity.

The first year, people may need some ideas. After that, they should do great on their own. Here are some gifts of time.

I promise to vacuum the whole house every Tuesday after school throughout January and February.

I'm going to take you out to dinner with the money I make baby-sitting. Please save January 12 for the big event.

I promise to read you a story for fifteen minutes every night I possibly can for the next two weeks.

I will paint the kitchen and have it done by January 17.

I will save fifteen minutes talk-time just for you every evening right after supper.

I will help you with geometry until you bring your grade up to a B—even if it takes the rest of the year.

See? These are hard gifts, and I like them. Christmas is so much dumping of gifts all at once. Gifts of time compel a family to think about what the other people would like to do. They stretch Christmas into the month of January. Gifts of time make me feel loved.

This parable might encourage your young people to try gifts of time:

## TWO TREES
*A Parable on Giving*

The two trees winked at each other through the windows of their two houses. "You should see the stack of presents under me," bragged Spruce. "A red box, a huge green box, an enormous blue box, and a little silver box that looks very expensive."

Pine smiled. "I've got envelopes under me," he said.

"What!"

"Yep!" Pine quivered his needles lightly. "I've got a white envelope, a tan one, and one that has little roses printed on it."

"How mortifying," Spruce sympathized. "Your family must be very poor. I feel sorry for you."

But Pine Tree only smiled.

Days passed and each day Spruce would report on the fine and wonderful additions under him. "Why, I'll bet it's going to take hours just to open all these gifts. And the wrappings. Why, they cost a fortune! I'm really impressed with Christmas in this house."

From his house across the street, Pine would share the growing number of envelopes, and Spruce couldn't help but hear the happiness in his voice as he reported.

"He's just hiding his embarrassment," Spruce thought. "Every Christmas tree's dream is to be filled to the boughs with presents."

The big day came. Spruce watched with pride as the children at his house whooped and hollered over their wonderful presents. One after another after another was opened. The beautiful paper was crumpled and thrown into a corner. And finally each person sat beside his huge stack of gifts. "They must be very happy," Spruce thought.

Then to his surprise he heard the girl say, "Is that all?"

"Yeah," the boy said. "Where's my bicycle? I wanted a bicycle. You never get me the stuff I want."

The girl grabbed a puzzle. "I'm going to put this together," she said.

"That's mine," screeched the boy and grabbed for the puzzle box.

"That's enough," the father shouted. "You ungrateful kids just get up to your rooms, and . . ."

More wails.

Spruce was flabbergasted! His branches dipped in sorrow, and one glass ball slipped off and crashed to the floor. "Isn't it awful," he said to Pine when the noise had cleared. But Pine was grinning. "Isn't your family screaming and hollering and fighting!" Spruce asked.

"No," Pine said. "First, they hugged. Then the mother and the oldest boy had happy tears running down their faces. Now they're eating dinner and talking about their gifts."

"What gifts?" asked Spruce. "You just had envelopes."

"Yes, but in each envelope," Pine explained, "was a gift of time. Each person promised to do something nice for the other. Janet promised her parents she would make their bed every day in January. Robert promised Janet a trip to the aquarium and pizza afterward. The father promised the mother he would make window boxes by spring and plant them with flowers. It was great fun opening the envelopes."

Spruce wiped the sap from his eyes. "I would give up all my tinsel if I could teach my family what your family knows."

## CHRISTMAS PROJECT

September is the time to start. Decide on a Christmas Project to be completed by the holiday. Why not make it a big one—one that you couldn't possibly complete by yourselves? Then the household will have to depend on God's help, a very healthy dependence to build.

What is a Christmas Project? For you, I have no idea. It will be something done for the Lord. Usually it will involve money. Make it a rule that the money must be made for this project—no dipping into the bank account at the last minute to come up with promised dollars. Every member must contribute a fair share—a little for the young children and more for people who have more to give and more understanding of God's gift to us. No one should make up the part that another

has promised to contribute. For example, if four-year-old Danny has offered to contribute one dollar, he will have to think of ways to earn it. If he doesn't, the project will be one dollar short; no one else can make up the difference. Make sure the choice of the project is a family decision. Talk about what's involved and why the project makes sense. For example, here are some projects I've been involved in, or that I have considered.

Buying a mule for Ed, a missionary friend in Mexico. Yes, the mule was purchased. Ed wrote a thank-you note and explained how much he had needed that mule. He added, "If you are looking for a project for next year, think about getting me a computer. Next to a mule, that's what I need most."

Sending Marian a $100 Christmas check to help with her work at the Japanese orphanage.

Donating a Mr. Coffee to the Community Center the church supports, and including enough money to pay for the first three months of coffee.

Sending Christian magazine subscriptions to fifteen retired people in our church.

All these projects are large and would take time and energy.

What a perfect way to keep the truth about God's Christmas gift alive in our most commercial season.

How does a household earn money? Again, I have no idea. Each person will have different ideas, but the key word is *creativity*.

Have a garage sale, and tell everyone who shops where the money will be going. This sets the garage sale off as a type of mission project, too.

Use baby-sitting money to buy cake-making materials. Then have a cake sale in the neighborhood. Again, let everyone know where the money will be going.

Parents, make a list of extra chores smaller children could do that will allow them to earn a little money. These should be in addition to their regular responsibilities around the house.

Offer to scrape frost off neighbors' car windows before they leave for work; shovel snow; change spark plugs.

There's no end to the list.

## FAMILY REVIEW

Pick out six family pictures for each of the last five years. Pass them around as a review of each year. Then ask family members to talk about what gifts God gave the family that year.

If possible, each family member should be pictured in each year's collection of photos.

If I were doing this and my pictures were for last year, I'd show the grand old house where I lived for almost 20 years with a "For Sale" sign in the front yard. I'd also show my new home nearly a thousand miles away where deer often come to eat the buds off the plants. There would be Marc with his new rig, smiling because he's working again and truck driving is his favorite job of all. How about a picture of my 90-year-old father who praises God for good health and a growing garden?

Be as specific as you can.

Close the review and praise time with sentence prayers.

## A FAMILY CAROL

Write your own family carol. It's not difficult, and it can be a great way to praise God.

Start with a favorite carol, and then work together to write new words to the familiar music.

It's not difficult for elementary children to help here. Each line should fit with the music, and it doesn't matter if the rhyme and meter aren't perfect. This will be a family song, and that makes even its imperfections perfect.

Years ago, our family's song was sung to "Away in a Manger."

It's affirming to look back and follow the extended family's progress through the growing years. Dougie is now Douglas, and is in college.

Tonight in Oak Park, Lord,
　　we pause before You
To tell you we love You the
　　whole year through.
We thank You for Dougie, new
　　baby this year,
And all of Your gifts that have
　　brought us good cheer.

We thank You for Marc and
　　the new job he got,
For Grandma who's fun and
　　who loves us a lot
For Daddy and Mommy and
　　presents tonight,
For aunts and for uncles to hold
　　us real tight.

## CHRISTMAS PICNIC

A family Christmas picnic is especially for young children. The purpose of the picnic is to capture for the children a little of the feelings Mary and Joseph had. Explain to the children a few days before the picnic that the special day is coming. Pre-arrange with a friend (one the children know and like) to tell you and your children that there is no room in her house for you when you knock on her door.

Pack a picnic lunch. Since much of the world is cold around Christmas, this picnic may be eaten in the car.

Explain that on this picnic, you will be reviewing the wonderful Christmas story. Don't tell the children where they are going—only that it will be fun. Stop the car about a mile from home, and read the portion of Scripture in which the census was ordered (Luke 2:1-5).

Then talk about where the children think they are going. How do they feel about the trip? How would they feel if they were taking the trip out in the cold?

Move on to the friend's house. Together go to the door with your picnic things. Explain that you would like to eat your picnic lunch there. The friend should sadly shake her head and explain that there is no room for you and the children to eat at her house, but they are welcome to go use the garage.

Parents should decide against that and get back in the car. Read Luke 2:6, 7. Ask children to tell how they felt when the friend did not want them in her house. Draw the parallel between their experience and Mary and Joseph's experience. How might Mary have felt? What might she have said to Joseph?

Continue on your trip to a place in the country where there

are fields, and if possible, barns. Stop the car near a field and read the story of the shepherds and the angels. See Luke 2:8-20. Talk about how the shepherds might have felt. Could you all pretend to be shepherds and hold a little conversation such as they might have held as they returned from seeing baby Jesus?

Point to a barn, if there is one nearby. Ask the children how they think Mary felt about having her little baby in a barn. If the youngsters think this is a great idea, guide them in realizing how smelly and dirty it was. Share the reason God allowed His Son to be born on earth — this was His way of telling us that He loved us.

Finally find a nice place to park and eat the picnic lunch. Talk about the rest of this year's Christmas activities and how they glorify Christ. Talk about why we give gifts and how much fun it is to give, as well as get, them.

On the drive home, sing Christmas carols.

## SOME CHRISTMAS GOODIES

### MINCEMEAT CAKE
*1 cup mincemeat*
*1 cup chopped nuts*
*1 Tablespoon rum flavoring*
*1 teaspoon vanilla*
*1 cup mayonnaise*
*1-1/2 cups buttermilk*
*3-1/4 cups flour*
*1 teaspoon salt*
*1-1/2 cups sugar*
*3/4 teaspoon baking soda*
*grated rind of one orange*

Combine mincemeat, nuts, rum flavoring, and vanilla. Blend in mayonnaise and buttermilk. Sift dry ingredients over mayonnaise mixture. Add orange rind and mix well. Stir in mincemeat mixture. Grease a tube pan. Place heavy brown paper on the bottom.

Pour batter into pan. Bake at 325° for two hours. Remove from pan and cool.

### FUDGE CAKE
*2-1/4 cups sifted cake flour*
*1 teaspoon baking soda*
*1/2 teaspoon salt*
*1 cup cocoa mixed*
  *with 1/4 cup water*
*1-1/4 cups milk*
*3/4 cup brown sugar*
*1 teaspoon vanilla*
*2/3 cup butter*
*1 cup sugar*
*3 eggs*

Sift flour, soda, and salt together.

Heat cocoa and milk in saucepan until blended. Add brown sugar and beat until smooth. Mix in vanilla.

227

Cream butter with sugar.

Add eggs one at a time, beating well after each addition.

Add flour and chocolate mixtures alternately in small amounts, beating well after each addition.

Pour into 2, 9-inch cake pans or 3, 8-inch pans. Bake at 350° for 30 to 35 minutes.

### APPLESAUCE SPICE CAKE

*1 package white or yellow cake mix*
*1 package small instant vanilla*
*  pudding*
*1/4 cup vegetable oil*
*1 cup applesauce*
*1/2 cup water or coffee*
*4 eggs*
*1/2 teaspoon nutmeg*
*1/2 teaspoon cinnamon*
*1/4 teaspoon pumpkin pie spice*
*1/2 cup chopped raisins*

Combine all ingredients; mix well. Beat at medium speed for 4 minutes. Pour into 2 greased and floured 4" x 8" loaf pans. Bake at 350° for 50 to 55 minutes, or until inserted toothpick comes out clean and cake pulls away from sides of the pan. Do not underbake. Cook 15 minutes. Remove from pans. Finish cooling on rack.

### APPLE CAKE

*2 cups sugar*
*1 stick butter*
*2 eggs*

*1 teaspoon vanilla*
*2 teaspoons allspice*
*1/2 teaspoon salt*
*2 teaspoons cinnamon*
*1 teaspoon baking soda dissolved*
*  in 1 Tablespoon hot water*
*1 teaspoon baking powder*
*4 cups finely diced apples*
*2 cups sifted flour*

Cream sugar and butter together. Add eggs and beat well. Add the rest of the ingredients. Add flour last, a little at a time. Put into an oblong 13" x 9" x 2" greased pan. Sprinkle with topping before baking. Bake at 350° for about 1 hour.

**Topping:**

*1/2 cup brown sugar and 1 cup*
*chopped nuts, blended together*

### CRUNCH CAKE

*1 cup shortening*
*2 cups sugar*
*4 eggs*
*1 cup milk*
*1-1/2 teaspoons vanilla*
*2-2/3 cups flour*
*1/2 teaspoon salt*
*1-1/2 teaspoons baking powder*

**Topping:**

*1/4 pound butter*
*1/3 cup sugar*
*1-1/4 cup chopped nuts*
*1/4 pound crushed vanilla wafers*

Crumble and mix all topping ingredients. Press them on the bottom and sides of a tube pan or 2 loaf pans.

Cream shortening with sugar. Add eggs and beat well. Add remaining ingredients and mix thoroughly. Pour batter into prepared pans. Bake at 350° for 1 hour. Can be glazed while warm.

### PECAN PIE

*1 Tablespoon butter*
*1 cup brown sugar*
*1 cup light corn syrup*
*3 eggs*
*1 teaspoon vanilla*
*1/4 teaspoon salt*
*1 Tablespoon grated orange rind*
*1 cup pecan halves*

Cream butter and sugar. Add syrup, well-beaten eggs, vanilla, salt, and orange rind. Mix well. Add pecan halves. Pour into a prepared, frozen crust. Bake at 350° for about a half hour or until inserted butter knife comes out clean.

### MINCEMEAT COOKIES

*1-1/2 cups soft butter*
*3/4 cup granulated sugar*
*3/4 cup brown sugar*
*1 egg*
*1/4 cup milk*
*1 Tablespoon rum flavoring*
*4-1/2 cups sifted flour*
*3/4 teaspoon salt*
*3/4 teaspoon baking soda*
*2 cups mincemeat pie filling*
*1/2 cup orange marmalade*

Cream together the butter (or margarine) and sugars until light and fluffy. Add egg, milk, and rum flavoring. Beat well. Sift together flour, salt and soda. Stir into creamed mixture.

Divide dough into half. Wrap and chill thoroughly.

On a well-floured surface, roll half the dough at a time into 1/8-inch thickness. Cut out cookies using a 2-1/2-inch cutter. Using a 3/4-inch cutter, cut a small hole in the center of half of the circles of dough. Combine mincemeat and marmalade. Place two teaspoons of mincemeat mixture on each uncut cookie. Top with the cut-out cookies. Seal edges with a fork.

Bake on ungreased cookie sheet in a 375° oven for 10 minutes or until a light golden color. Remove cookies from the sheet while they are still hot. Makes 3-1/2 dozen cookies.

### FILLED COOKIES

*1/2 cup shortening*
*1/2 cup sugar*
*1 teaspoon vanilla*
*1 egg yolk*
*1 cup flour*
*1 teaspoon baking powder*
*1/4 teaspoon salt*
*red jelly or other filling*

Cream shortening with sugar. Add vanilla and yolk. Blend. Stir in dry ingredients. Blend. Roll into balls. Make depression. Fill with jelly before baking. Bake at 350° for about 10 minutes.

### Soft Gingerbread Cookies

*2 sticks margarine*

*1 cup sugar*

*1 teaspoon ginger*

*1 teaspoon cinnamon*

*1/2 teaspoon salt*

*1 teaspoon baking soda*

*1 cup molasses*

*2 eggs*

*4 level cups of flour*

Cream margarine (or butter) with sugar. Add spices, salt, and soda. Stir in the molasses, and then the eggs. Blend in the flour 1 cup at a time.

Chill well, overnight.

Roll a little at a time. For soft cookies, roll thicker. Bake approximately 12 minutes at 350°. Watch carefully so they won't get too done, or else they won't be soft.

### Macaroons

*2 egg whites*

*1/4 teaspoon salt*

*1 cup sugar*

*3/4 cup ground almonds*

*1/2 teaspoon almond extract*

Cover the bottom of a cookie sheet with unglazed paper.

Beat egg whites and salt until frothy. Add sugar one spoonful at a time, beating thoroughly after each addition. Beat until stiff peaks are formed.

Fold in the ground almonds with almond extract.

Drop by teaspoonfuls about one inch apart. Keep small and uniform. Bake at 350° for 20 minutes or until lightly browned.

## Red and White Party

**Valentine's Day**

*Objective:* Christians and secular friends will take part in activities that encourage interaction, laying the groundwork for friendship evangelism.

*Basic idea:* Everyone will be asked to bring a dessert that is either red or white. The evening's activities are built around the red and white theme. A singles group or adult Sunday school class should come up with the guest list.

If your guests have difficulty thinking of red and white recipes, you might suggest a few, but much of the fun of this party will be deciding for themselves what would work.

### RED AND WHITE RECIPES

### Ice Box Cherry (or strawberry) Pie

*8 ounces cream cheese*

*1 cup powdered sugar*

*1 package Dream Whip*

*1 teaspoon vanilla*
*1 can cherry pie filling*
*baked pie shell*

Beat sugar and cream cheese. Prepare package of Dream Whip according to the directions and flavor with vanilla.

Fold the whip into the cheese mixture and pour into baked shell. Cover with 1 can of cherry pie filling. Add a few drops of red coloring, if you wish. Chill for 1 hour.

Or use frozen strawberries instead of cherries. Thaw and drain off juice. Add 3 Tablespoons sugar to juice; thicken with 2 Tablespoons cornstarch over low heat. Cool, add the strawberries, and pour on top.

## CHERRY RICE PUDDING

*(Serves 40)*
*5-1/2 quarts milk*
*3 cups rice*
*12 Tablespoons sugar*
*8 teaspoons vanilla*
*1/4 pound almonds*
*2 large cans dark pitted cherries,*
  *drained*
*1-1/2 quarts cream, whipped*

Bring milk to boil. Stir in rice and cook under a lid for 45 minutes over very low flame. Take pot from stove and cool. Mix in sugar and vanilla when lukewarm. Stir occasionally. Grind almonds and add. Fold in drained cherries and cream.

An idea: put just one whole almond in the pudding. Announce that the person who gets the whole almond must tell a story from his own life that is appropriate to Valentine's Day.

## RASPBERRY ICE CREAM PIE

*1-1/3 cups crushed*
  *graham crackers*
*1/4 cup sugar*
*1/2 teaspoon cinnamon*
*1/8 teaspoon salt*
*1/3 cup butter, melted*
*1 quart vanilla ice cream*
*1 pint fresh or frozen raspberries*

Mix crumbs with sugar, cinnamon, and salt. Blend in melted butter. Line a 9" pie pan with mixture, pressing firmly over bottom and sides of pan. Chill. Fill shell with a layer of ice cream. Top with raspberries, sweetened to taste. Add another layer of ice cream and top with berries. Serve at once, or keep in freezer until serving time. Serves about 6.

## WHITE VALENTINE'S PIE

*1 prepared pie shell*
*1 cup sugar*
*4 Tablespoons flour*
*1/2 teaspoon salt*
*1-1/2 cup milk*
*1 Tablespoon unflavored gelatin*
  *softened in 1/4 cup cold water*
*3/4 teaspoon vanilla*
*1/4 teaspoon almond extract*

## INVITATION IDEA

You may want to print the invitations on children's valentines.

**RED & WHITE**

**VALENTINE'S**

**PARTY**

### THE COLORS OF VALENTINE'S DAY

*Come dressed in red and white*

*Bring a red or white dessert*

*Be prepared to tell what makes you blush.*

WHEN:

WHERE:

*1/2 cup stiffly whipped cream*
*3 egg whites, beaten*
*1/4 teaspoon cream of tartar*
*1/2 cup sugar*
*1-1/2 cups moist coconut*

Mix 1 cup sugar, flour, salt in saucepan. Gradually stir in milk. Cook over low heat, stirring until it boils. Boil 1 minute. Remove from heat. Stir in softened gelatin. Cool. When partially set, beat with rotary beater until smooth. Blend in vanilla and almond extract.

Gently fold in whipped cream. Carefully fold in egg whites, cream of tartar, and 1/2 cup sugar. Then fold in 1 cup moist coconut.

Pile into cooled pie shell. Sprinkle with moist coconut and chill about two hours until set. Serve cold.

## CHERRY NUT MUFFINS

*2 cups sifted flour*
*1/2 teaspoon salt*
*3 teaspoons baking powder*
*1/2 cup sugar*
*1/2 cup water or cherry juice*
*1/2 cup chopped nuts*
*3 Tablespoons melted shortening*
*1/2 cup evaporated milk*
*1 beaten egg*
*1/3 cup chopped maraschino cherries*

Optional for this party: add a few drops of red food coloring. Sift dry ingredients together. Add nuts. Mix all liquids together. Add cherries. Blend into dry ingredients just until moistened. Bake in greased muffin pans at 350° for about a half hour. Makes 1 dozen muffins.

## PIE CRUST

*1-1/4 cup flour*
*1/4 teaspoon baking powder*
*1/2 teaspoon salt*
*1 stick shortening*
*3 or 4 Tablespoons cold milk or water*

Cut flour into shortening that has been sifted with dry ingredients. Gradually add liquid until rolling consistency.

**For a two-crust pie:**
*2 cups flour*
*1/2 teaspoon baking powder*
*3/4 teaspoon salt*
*1 cup shortening*
*4-6 Tablespoons milk or water*

Follow the instructions above.

## CHERRY JELL-O SALAD

*2 small packages tapioca padding*
*1 package small cherry Jell-O*
*2-3/4 cup water (minus two Tablespoons)*
*1 large container Cool Whip*
*1 large can drained cherries*
*1 small jar applesauce*

Bring to boil the tapioca, Jell-O, and water. Let cool. Mix in Cool Whip. Add cherries and applesauce. Stir together. Chill for several hours.

## PINK PATS

*1 cup butter, softened*
*1 cup butter mints, crushed*
*2 cups all-purpose flour*
*red food coloring*
  *(just for this party!)*
*1 Tablespoon sugar*

In a large mixer bowl, cream butter at medium speed until light. Add crushed mints and flour. Add food coloring. Blend well at low speed. If necessary, chill dough for easier handling. On waxed paper, roll out or pat dough to a 9-inch square. Sprinkle with sugar. Cut into 1-1/2 inch squares. Bake at 300° for 18-20 minutes. Do not overbake.

*Chocolate variety*

(But not for this party!): Add 1 or 2 Tablespoons cocoa with flour.

## PINK PARTY DESSERT

*1 large package strawberry Jell-O*
*2 cups water*
*2 cups small marshmallows*
*1 small can crushed pineapple*
*1 cup chopped nuts*
*1 small container cottage cheese*
  *(1/2 pint)*
*1 large container Cool Whip*

Heat Jell-O, water, and marshmallows until marshmallows are dissolved. Chill until Jell-O begins to set. Fold in pineapple, nuts, cottage cheese, Cool Whip. Refrigerate until set.

## RED AND WHITE QUESTIONS

On your invitation, you asked people to come prepared for red and white questions. In the first few minutes of the evening, ask everyone to find out from at least ten other people what things would be most likely to make them blush or turn ashen.

Name tags will also make the opening minutes of the party easier. Perhaps you could print names on children's valentines.

## RED AND WHITE TAFFY PULL

Divide the group into sets of two. One set makes red taffy and another white. I've been to several taffy pulls. Even when the taffy doesn't pull perfectly, the interaction has been fun.

This recipe for salt water taffy comes from Betty Crocker. One group will add red food coloring to the mixture.

## SALT WATER TAFFY

*1 cup sugar*
*1/2 cup light corn syrup*
*2/3 cup water*
*1 Tablespoon cornstarch*
*2 Tablespoons butter or margarine*
*1 teaspoon salt*
*2 teaspoons vanilla*

Butter square pan, 8" x 8" x 2". In 2-quart saucepan, combine sugar, corn syrup, water, cornstarch, butter, and salt. Cook over medium heat, stirring constantly, to 256° on candy thermometer (or until small amount of mixture dropped into very cold water forms a hard ball). Remove from heat; stir in vanilla (and food coloring). Pour into pan.

When just cool enough to handle, pull taffy until satiny, light in color, and stiff. If taffy becomes sticky, butter hands lightly. Pull into long strips, 1/2-inch wide. With scissors, cut strips into 1-inch pieces. Wrap pieces that aren't eaten immediately in waxed paper. (Candy must be wrapped to hold its shape). Makes about 1 pound.

## RED LETTERS

Give each person a red pencil and white paper, and ask him or her to write a love or appreciation note to someone in the community, city government, someone he or she wishes were a real family member (like a mentor from the past—anyone who deserves a valentine).

Notes should be short. You might want to provide envelopes for sending those valentines that can't be delivered in person.

## ROSES ARE RED

Everyone will have an opportunity to direct ROSES ARE RED valentines to others at the party. Caution people as they develop these to be careful not to hurt anyone's feelings. These should be expressions of real appreciation or fun little ditties that say, "I like you." Remember the original rhyme!

*Roses are red.*
*Violets are blue.*
*Sugar is sweet,*
*And so are you.*

Here's one that might be directed at a pastor who is respected in the community as well as in his own congregation. It's fun and it wouldn't hurt his feelings.

*Roses are red*
*Three words say a lot*
*You're known for preaching*
*But three words it's not!*

Or how about this more genuine message to an elderly widow who never forgets to send your children birthday cards:

*Roses are red.*
*Praises to the sky.*
*My children love you,*
*And so do I.*

## A READ RED STORY

Everyone gets a sheet of paper. The host reads some incomplete sentences and each person fills in the blank. Then that answer is folded under and the sheet is passed to the person on the right.

That person will fill in the next blank in the story without knowing what the first person has written. And so on until the end of the story.

The last person to get the sheet at the end of the story will open the whole sheet to see for the first time what everyone in the group has written. The host will then call on several people to fill in the blanks from their sheets as he rereads the parts.

Here's the story. Lines such as different people may write have been included to give you an idea of how disjointed and fun the final story usually is.

1. Red woke up one morning with the scarlet sun pouring through his window. He walked to his window, looked out, and turned white because there . . .

*One possible answer:* he saw his high school principal arriving with eight suitcases.

(Do not read the possible answers. This is just to give you an idea of what might happen at your party. Pause long enough after each question to allow people to write.)

2. He jumped up, and . . .

*One possible answer:* grabbed the aspirin bottle.

3. This called for some quick action so he . . .

*One possible answer:* had his car waxed.

4. Finally he calmed down. He said, "I think I'll . . . "

*One possible answer:* have a peanut butter sandwich.

5. Unfortunately, that wasn't such a good idea because . . .

*One possible answer:* the golf course was flooded.

6. "What do you think is the matter with me, doctor?" he asked in exasperation. The doctor looked grave and said, ". . . "

*One possible answer:* "I think you've got bunions."

7. Red was amazed, to say the least. He decided to get a second opinion, so he went to . . .

*One possible answer:* the local pet store.

8. Unfortunately the original diagnosis was confirmed. He was told again that . . .

*One possible answer:* He would have to take water pills.

9. His girlfriend's opinion of the whole thing was . . .

*One possible answer:* expressed in great gales of laughter.

10. Red always was one to bounce back, so after his

eventful day, he went back to . . .

*One possible answer:* polishing his shoes.

## A LOOK AT MOTIVES

Let's take a look at our motives—or in other words, how do we handle it when friends don't get as excited about a party as we do?

It happens. And when it does, we've found it can taint our enthusiasm for the whole event.

Kathy helped us. I invited her to an event she didn't think she would enjoy. Instead of coming up with a bogus engagement or begging off with a splitting headache, she came right out with the truth.

"I've had it with groups for a while. I just don't want to come. How about the two of us going out to dinner soon instead?"

Crunch! She was a good friend, and I'd always included her. She fit in so perfectly. Now she had said bluntly that she didn't want to come. I seriously considered canceling the whole event.

Instead, I rethought what an invitation is. It's not an obligation. I wanted people to come— if they wanted to and if they would enjoy the evening. Actually, it was nice of Kathy to be honest with me and to reinforce our friendship by suggest-ing we have dinner soon.

People must have the freedom to say no just as we have the freedom to invite them.

How can we expect good things to happen among us and our guests if our attitude is, "Look at all these people having a wonderful time in our home! Pat our backs!"

The important thing is to put God in control of our parties— not the hostess or the host.

## Thanksgiving

### Making One Big Family Out of Little Ones

*Objective:* Singles, small families, and foreign families without Thanksgiving traditions will combine resources at a Thanksgiving meal. Together everyone will praise God for His bounty this year.

*Basic idea:* Everyone will provide one dish to add to the Thanksgiving meal; the host family will supply the turkey. By combining resources, the meal will not be expensive.

Jack and I decided to go through the church directory and invite all the singles, foreign families, and small families. We figured nearly everyone would have a place to go already, so we

---

## INVITATION IDEA

# Thanksgiving

---

Thanksgiving Invitation

Home—4051 Vance Court

At about 1:30 on Thanksgiving Day

Now don't forget to bring a covered dish

Kids—don't leave home without them

Sure hope you can come

**RSVP**

could safely invite as many as we wanted to.

We were flabbergasted when the calls from those who were coming began to arrive.

"Thanks so much," a woman from Australia said. "We'll all come. We were wondering how Americans did this holiday, but we never thought we'd be able to find out."

"I'll be there with the kids," another woman said. "I didn't have money for the trip to my folks' place in Georgia. It's great to have something special to do close to home."

A guy announced that he'd bring real mashed potatoes. "I was feeling a little family-less," he said.

This Thanksgiving party is the only one we've had where I have no idea how many people actually showed up. It was in the neighborhood of sixty, give or take a dozen kids. When the crowd filled our place, Diana, the neighbor across the hall, opened her doors for the overflow. Then the lady upstairs opened her place. Thank goodness we lived in an apartment building! A house would never have been big enough.

## NAMETAGS

A must! Ours were little drawings of fat pilgrims. Each said,

"In case you've forgotten, I'm _____."

## CHORAL READING

Before the meal, we gave all readers a copy of a Thanksgiving Choral reading. We had contacted a few friends before the meal, and they were ready with short personal statements.

*Host:* Lord, You have poured out amazing blessings on this land! You have poured down your blessings on the land and it yields its bountiful crops.

*All:* Lord, You have poured out amazing blessings on this land! Now bring us back to loving You.

*Friend:* Oh come, let us sing to the Lord! Give a joyous shout in honor of our God!

*All sing:* "Come Ye Thankful People Come."

*Hostess:* God said, "What I want from you is your true thanks."

*Friend:* Father, I thank You because . . . (This person should complete the sentence with a personal reason she has for thanking the Lord this year.)

*All:* Sing your praise accompanied by music from the harp. Let the comets and trumpets shout! Make a joyful symphony before the Lord, our King! Let the sea in all its vastness roar with praise! Let the earth and all those living on it shout, "Glory to the Lord."

*Friend:* Glory to the Lord! Let the waves clap their hands in glee, and the hills sing out their songs of joy before the Lord.

*Friend:* Father, I praise You because . . .

*Friend:* Glory to the Lord.

*Friend:* Father, I praise You because . . .

*All:* Sing the doxology, perhaps to one of the newer melodies, as the Thanksgiving prayer.

And then we ate! There was more than enough for all. Jack had made two turkeys, and their total forty pounds was perfect. Actually, with all the great things others brought, I don't think anyone would have minded if we had run out of turkey.

Some of our neighbors were older women who were spending the holidays with their children. When they heard about our enormous party, four people offered their door keys and ovens even though they wouldn't be able to attend.

Don't skip a little Thanksgiving program and head immediately for the turkey. For four years, I planned a Thanksgiving in September for a group of Christians from developing nations who were in the states for training. The first year, I figured I'd be busy with the food so I suggested a friend handle the Thanksgiving-specific stuff. She prayed and thanked God for the food. For the foreign guests, the meal was just a big American spread. They never heard about its history or its significance to Americans and Canadians, or, most especially, the added significance Christians give to it. They stuffed themselves, following our example, I'm sure. But they never were rewarded spiritually. The next three years, I gave the food to friends to prepare and I handled the program. Thanksgiving is a concept I'd like to share with friends around the world.

## PILGRIM SCAVENGER HUNT

In between the main course and the dessert, we needed to clear dozens of people out of the apartments for a few minutes so we would have space to reorganize. So the entire group was divided into Pilgrim Scavenger Hunt groups. Children were all included. For some adults, especially those without kids, it was the first time they had worked hand in hand with youngsters. It was fun to see these randomly chosen people become competitive, enthusiastic groups. They all left cheering and insisting that their group would be back first with all the items needed to win the Pilgrim Scavenger Hunt.

Here's the Scavenger hunt list we used. It is adapted to the area in which we lived—about two blocks from a railroad track in a suburban community. Change anything you couldn't find in your community.

*Pilgrim Scavenger Hunt*
1. One wild turkey feather or unreasonable facsimile.
2. A Pilgrim's Pet Rock. Be prepared to demonstrate a trick it can do.
3. Ten different types of leaves from the dense forests here abouts.
4. One forked stick that would be perfect for killing snakes.
5. One piece of post-Indian litter.
6. One hat camouflaged to avoid detection in hostile Indian territory.
7. One coin of this kingdom.
8. One Thanksgiving carol sung before a neighbor's house. Have astonished neighbor sign his/her name here (not that Pilgrims are not to be trusted!) _____.
9. One musket ball or one round button.
10. Any tree's berry.
11. Any small weed—roots and all—that grows down by the iron horse's tracks.
12. A four-line poem in rhyming couplet about Thanksgiving.
13. Number of steps around our settlement (this block):

_____.

14. Piece of wood to add to winter's fuel supply.
15. A friendly hello to a Pilgrim stranger on the street. Name of the thrilled person:

_____.

16. Names of all churches within five minutes of our front door.
17. Scalp count—one gray hair, one brown hair, one blond hair, one red hair.
18. Scout around—one thumbprint in a mud ball.
19. Pilgrim panic—something growing outside that you could eat in a pinch.
20. Anything that rhymes with pie—and come back for dessert!

I had the first group back show what they had collected and then I awarded them each chocolate turkeys.

However, people from the losing groups were still complaining months later that they had written wonderful rhyming couplets and developed excellent rock tricks that they hadn't had an opportunity to show off. So if you copy our Thanksgiving party, don't copy our mistake. Wait until all groups are back, and then allow creative people from each group to share what they have done.

## Creative Pumpkin

### Halloween or Autumn Party

*Objective:* To provide an occasion at which people in a specific group (a large Sunday school class, singles group, church neighborhood, or home Bible study group) can have a good time getting to know each other better, and in the process demonstrate some of their creative abilities.

*Basic idea:* Guests are divided into random pairs and given a pumpkin to carve. Prizes for the most creative finished pumpkins add an element of competition.

You'll need one pumpkin for every two guests. Look for the cheapest ones you can find. I got mine at a farm just a few miles outside the city. I bought eight rather large ones for a little more than a dollar each. I think the teenager who helped me load my car with them

thought I had a terrible case of Halloween fever.

The night of the party, I had the pumpkins circling the table.

Because I had an equal number of men and women show up, I had each woman put her name in a bag. After everyone had arrived, the men drew partners. The new couples then rushed to the table to pick the perfect pumpkin that would win them the top prizes.

People had followed the invitation and brought amazing pumpkin decorations. One man, a woodcarver, had come with carved and painted wooden pieces to stick on his pumpkin's face. He created one of the most professional orange men I've ever seen.

I gave each pair a written set of directions.

1. Carve your pumpkin.
2. Name the clever little thing and be ready to give a bit of its family background.
3. Teach it to do one trick and be ready to have it perform the trick for everyone here.

The results were great fun. See if your guests can match what ours did.

One couple carved out the whole inside of the pumpkin and cut a female face on it. They stuck marshmallows over

**INVITATION IDEA**

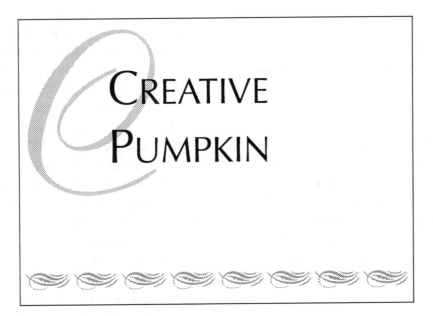

**CREATIVE PUMPKIN**

**COME CARVE WITH US.**
We'll supply the pumpkins . . .
you bring extra materials that will make your
pumpkin a winning wonder (corn cobs, bits of
material, buttons, crepe paper, and . . .)

WHEN:

WHERE:

WHY:   It's high time we laughed together!

the head like little curls. The finishing touch was a candle inside. It was their trick that won them a prize. "This pumpkin," George explained, "is an oven. She invited you to pull off one of her curls, stick it in her mouth, and toast yourself a gooey marshmallow."

Another couple had made a lovely pumpkin face, but the main part of the creation was the arms and legs they made out of construction paper. To each appendage they attached string, and made a moving puppet. The pumpkin's trick was to kick at people who tried to steal him from the patch.

Everyone was asked to vote for pumpkin winners. We used the following ballot:

Pumpkin with the best family tree: _____
Most talented pumpkin:

_____

Most amazing pumpkin face:

_____

Prizes: Come up with your own ideas, but try to keep the prizes as fun and light-hearted as the carving. For example:

Pumpkin with the best family tree—the makers will each get a bag of pumpkin seeds to grow more pumpkins of high quality.

Pumpkin with the most talent —a frozen pie crust for each originator because people who can create a talented pumpkin ought to be able to figure out a way to create a great pie as well.

Pumpkin with the most amazing face—a can of pumpkin pie filling to each carver. The filling might be used on the face each night as a face mask to keep the face in good condition.

One of our guests was a librarian. She was so impressed with the creations that she wanted to put them on display in the children's section of the library. Funny thing—not all those adults would give up their pumpkins. We need to provide more opportunities for wild creativity.

## FOOD

Of course, you'll want to play up the pumpkin idea in the foods. How about one of these?

### PUMPKIN PIE

*1 9-inch pie shell, unbaked*
*1-1/2 cups canned pumpkin*
*1/2 cup brown sugar*
*1/2 cup granulated sugar*
*1 teaspoon cinnamon*
*1/4 teaspoon salt*
*1 tablespoon flour*
*1/4 teaspoon cloves*
*1/4 teaspoon ginger*
*2 eggs, slightly beaten*
*1 cup milk*

Mix. Pour into pie shell. Bake at 425° for 45 to 50 minutes.

## PUMPKIN BREAD

*4 eggs*
*1 cup vegetable oil*
*1 teaspoon nutmeg*
*1 teaspoon cinnamon*
*3 cups sugar*
*1-1/2 teaspoon salt*
*1 cup canned pumpkin*
*2/3 cup water*
*2 teaspoons soda*
*3 cups flour*
*3/4 cup white raisins*

Beat first 6 ingredients together. Add the rest in order, one at a time. It will be easier if you beat the eggs first, then the oil and the spices, before adding the rest of the ingredients. Grease and flour three 1-pound tall coffee cans. Fill 2/3 full and bake 1 hour at 350°. Cool about 10 minutes in can before removing.

You'll have a delicious bread —almost like cake. Spread a little butter on the slices before serving.

## PUMPKIN REFRIGERATOR DESSERT

*2 cups graham cracker, vanilla*
*wafer, or gingersnap crumbs*
*1/3 cup each: sugar, melted butter*
*1 pound marshmallows*
*1/3 cup milk*
*1 pound can pumpkin filling*
*1/3 cup sugar*
*3/4 teaspoon cinnamon*

*1/4 teaspoon each: ginger, salt*
*2 cups whipping cream, whipped*

Combine crumbs, sugar, and butter; press in bottom of 13" x 9" x 2" pan. Melt marshmallows in milk in double boiler. Combine pumpkin, sugar, cinnamon, ginger, and salt. Blend in marshmallows; cool. Fold in whipped cream. Turn mixture into crumb crust. Chill until firm.

## ICE CREAM PUMPKIN SQUARES

*1-1/2 cups graham cracker or*
*gingersnap crumbs*
*1/4 cup melted butter*
*1 cup canned pumpkin*
*1/2 cup brown sugar*
*1/2 teaspoon salt*
*1/2 teaspoon cinnamon*
*1/2 teaspoon ginger*
*1/4 teaspoon nutmeg*
*1 quart vanilla ice cream*
*Optional: whipped cream and*
*chopped nuts*

Mix crumbs and butter. Press into an 8" x 8" x 2" buttered pan. Save some crumbs for top. Combine sugar and spices with pumpkin; fold in soft ice cream. Pour into crumb crust. Freeze. Cut into squares and top with crumbs, whipped cream, nuts.

## PUMPKIN NUT BARS

*1/2 cup shortening*
*1 cup brown sugar*
*2 eggs*
*1 teaspoon vanilla*

1 cup sifted all-purpose flour
1 teaspoon cinnamon
1/2 teaspoon each:
  baking powder; soda
1/2 teaspoon each: ginger, nutmeg
2/3 cup canned pumpkin
1/2 cup chopped walnuts

**Frosting:**
1-1/2 cups confectioners' sugar
2 Tablespoons each, shortening
  orange juice
1 Tablespoon grated orange rind

Cream shortening and sugar until light and fluffy. Add eggs and vanilla; beat thoroughly. Sift together dry ingredients; add to creamed mixture in thirds alternately with pumpkin, beating until smooth after each addition. Fold in nuts. Spread in a greased 13" x 9" x 2" pan. Bake at 350° for 20 minutes. Cool.

To prepare frosting, combine ingredients; beat until smooth. Spread over baked dessert. Cut into bars.

## PUMPKIN COOKIES

2 cups brown sugar
2 cups canned pumpkin
1 cup salad oil
2 teaspoons vanilla
4 cups sifted flour
2 teaspoons soda
2 teaspoons baking powder
1 teaspoon each: salt, cinnamon,
  nutmeg
1/2 teaspoon ginger

2 cups raisins
1 cup chopped nuts

In mixing bowl, beat together: sugar, pumpkin, oil, and vanilla. Sift dry ingredients together; add and stir until smooth. Blend in raisins and nuts. Drop by spoonfuls on oiled baking sheet. Bake at 350° for 12 to 15 minutes. Makes about 7 dozen soft, moist cookies. (No eggs needed.)

If baked in the summer, keep refrigerated.

## SOME ADDITIONAL GAME IDEAS

*Ghost Stories*

If your pumpkin party is around Halloween time, ghost stories can be great fun. They allow guests to be ten years old again. Turn out all the lights and ask people to tell stories from their camping-trip and pajama-party days.

You might come prepared with one. How about "The Headless Horseman"?

*Pass the Glop*

This idea is a throwback to junior high or middle school days. Again, all the lights are turned out and the host couple passes Halloween goodies around the circle of guests for each to touch. Each person whispers to the next person what it is that is being passed.

There is absolutely no point to this activity, except it does bring back the creepy, crawly, giggling sensations that we're usually too adult to enjoy.

Think up your own horrors, but just to get you started: skinned grapes could be passed with the whispered explanation, "eyeballs." Or a piece of liver could be passed as . . . be creative. The more adolescent, the better!

## Creative Snowmen

### An Alternative to the Creative Pumpkin

A "Creative Snowmen" party can break the winter blahs. It follows the same idea as the "Creative Pumpkin" party, but in this party people will be asked to decorate snowmen. Use the same goal as the "Creative Pumpkin." But this time you provide Styrofoam balls which will become the base of snow people. Each person should bring scraps, pins, buttons, whatever to help decorate a snowman.

Divide people in the same way you did the "Creative Pumpkin" party, and make the appropriate changes in your directions. For example:

1. Build and decorate your snowman.

2. Name the clever little thing and be ready to give a bit of his family background.

3. Teach it to do one trick.

Prize suggestions for the following categories:

1. Best name and background— prize would be a snow scene in a cheap frame.
2. Talented snowman—an ice cream scooper for making lots of clever snow or ice cream designs.
3. Most amazing facial features —a gift certificate from an ice cream store.

### SOME ADDITIONAL GAME IDEAS FOR A SNOW PARTY
*Can You Top This?*

Everyone in snow country has a snow story. Start with one of your own, and encourage people to try to top it. Give a prize to the person who has the top-of-the-topped story.

This year I might win this prize. I experienced my first heavy snowfall in southern Colorado on the day before I was to leave to speak at a west coast conference. Jack and I just moved here and weren't prepared for Colorado people's determination not to allow snow to slow them down. With two feet on the ground and more falling, I was certain I should cancel my trip, but decided to wait until the last minute. If the taxi could get through the next day and the plane could take off, I'd go. The next morning, I was out half-heartedly shoveling a path for the taxi. I knew it would never make it. Then, at the other end of the unplowed street, I saw the taxi driver shoveling his way up the hill. We met in the middle and I made the flight. The flight was on time. Can you top that?

*Snow Charades*

Divide the group into teams. A person from each team takes turns pulling a snow related word or phrase from a bag and trying to communicate the word or phrase to the teammates by drawing it. The actor is not allowed to speak or give any signs. He or she just keeps drawing until someone guesses or until the time—60 seconds—runs out. Keep track of seconds, and the team with the fewest seconds wins.

Some snow ideas that you

might place in the bag for this game are:
• tundra
• reindeer
• "Walking in a Winter Wonderland"
• igloo
• "I'll Be Home for Christmas"
• snow removal crews

**FOOD**

Ice cream makes sense. How about ice cream sundaes? Or if you're having this party with a lot of teenagers, you might want to have crushed ice snow cones.

**PEPPERMINT ICE CREAM**
*3/4 cup honey*
*1/2 teaspoon sea salt*
*2 cups milk*
*1 Tablespoon mint extract*
*4 cups thick cream*
Put all but the cream in a pan. Heat just until small bubbles appear around the edges. Cool to lukewarm. Freeze several hours until mushy. Beat smooth. Whip cream until wavy. Blend in the milk and honey mixture until well blended. Freeze until firm, stirring often the first few hours.

## Let There Be Showers

*On an average day,
6,567 couples are married.*

—Thomas H. Heymann

I WAS TWENTY-THREE before it dawned on me that a shower didn't have to be an all-woman activity. All-women showers can be great fun—my own wedding shower was one. But men can have as much fun at a shower as women.

Think about it. Most showers are an affirmation of a couple or family—a wedding shower or a baby shower. In both cases, the woman is only half of the big doings. Why not include the man in the party, and his friends, as well?

When I was in grad school, I attended a church where the singles group was almost entirely made up of students living away from home. So when one of the men in the group set the date with a girl back home, the group discussed the possibility of throwing a shower just for him. We giggled a lot. Somehow it didn't feel right to be honoring the man. But our better sense took over, and we had a great party honoring him and his life-changing decision. He got some excellent gifts—a man's apron, a screwdriver kit, some houseplant tools, and a subscription to *Apartment Living*.

So I'm suggesting that for all these showers, you consider coed participation.

## For The Bride and Groom: Picture Perfect Marriage

**Objective:** To honor the engaged couple and affirm the church's support of their decision to live for Christ together.

### THE GIFT

At a large shower, the process of opening fifteen to twenty gifts can be tedious for everyone, except perhaps the bride and groom. I've found that when everyone contributes to one gift, the interaction time at the shower can be longer and more fun. It also allows the group to make a substantial contribution to the couple, providing them with something they really want. Candy and Joe, for example, asked that we get them zip-together sleeping bags, an expensive gift that was possible because we divided the cost twenty ways.

### PICTURE PERFECT MARRIAGE PREPARATION

*Part One—Slides of the Couple*

The host should try to get representative pictures of the life of the couple, hopefully without them knowing it. Gladys did this for my shower. She got my mother to donate pictures of me diapered, learning to walk,

**INVITATION IDEA**

PICTURE
PERFECT
MARRIAGE

We're honoring _____ and _____
at a **Bride and Groom Shower.**

WHEN:

WHERE:

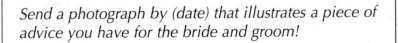

*Send a photograph by (date) that illustrates a piece of advice you have for the bride and groom!*

on my first date(wrong guy), graduating from high school, and early pictures of Jack and me. She had the pictures made into slides. As she showed them she shared bits of our history so that the people attending learned a little more about Jack and me and could participate more fully in the big step we were about to take.

*Part Two—Slides of Guests*

These pictures should also be made into slides and placed into some order in preparation for showing them and having guests share advice the night of the shower.

## SUGGESTED ORDER FOR THE PARTY

*Slides of the Couple*

Work up a little talk about the slides of the couple. For example, "Here's a picture of baby Jack at the seashore with his bucket and shovel. Off to the right are the local bathing beauties. You can see how unimpressed he is. My, how times have changed!" Keep this part of the evening light and fun.

## PRESENTATION OF THE GIFT OR GIFTS

*Guest slides*

Each guest should share the piece of advice that his or her slide illustrates. Hopefully people will get creative with their pictures and advice and this section will be great fun.

*Panel on Marriage*

Place four chairs at the front of the room. Draw the names of four guests out of a hat. Introduce them as great experts on marriage, and explain that you will be interviewing them on the subject of their expertise. Make sure everyone knows this is not a serious activity. The funnier the panel is, the better.

After a panel has answered two or three questions, retire them and pick another group of four.

Use questions like these:

1. One of the biggest decisions young married people have to make is who will take out the garbage. Could you give us some weighty words on how to solve this dilemma?
2. I understand that most men like eggs over easy in the morning. Could you give some directions to the bride on the best way to make them?
3. If you surveyed 1,000 people who have been married for twenty-five years or more,

what do you think would
be the three most common
reasons they would give for
their longevity?

4. Experts say it's important
for a couple to continue to
date each other after they
are married. How about some
crazy, a little off-the-wall date
ideas?

5. Wedding services can be
hard on the groom. What
advice do you have for him?

6. I've heard it said that there
are three or four things
a woman just won't stand
for. The groom ought to
know what they are so he
won't get off to a bad start.
Can you clue him in?

7. Usually one half of the
couple is neater than the
other half. What do you
suggest to the disorderly
part of this marriage team?

8. Finish this sentence: You
will never have trouble with
your in-laws if you . . .

9. Usually the bride and groom
get a lot of suggestions on
places they might go for a
honeymoon. Where would
you suggest and why?

10. Sometimes if people
know what might cause
fights they can avoid them.
Can you tell us the three
things married couples argue
most about?

*Pair on Marriage*

Switch the process around
now, and put the bride- and
groom-to-be in the chairs
in front of the group and allow
the guests to ask the engaged
couple questions. Let the couple
know they have veto power;
they don't have to answer all
questions.

I've done this at several showers and have never had anyone
ask a question that was in poor
taste. Instead people ask questions like, "Where did you
meet?" "What did you think of
Rita the first time you met her?"
"How did you feel the first time
you met your mother-in-law?"
"Who proposed?"

*A Prayer Pact*

A shower is a fun occasion
for Christians to say, "Yes, we
affirm your decision to marry."
A prayer pact can be an important part of that affirmation.
The host will want to have
copies of a pact for people
present, and they should read
it together to the couple and to
God.

Here's a sample. Edit it to
most perfectly fit your situation.

**PRAYER PACT**

*All to the couple:* We, your
Christian church family, are
pleased that you are getting

married. We have watched your relationship grow and smiled with you through your happy days of getting to know each other better.

Marriage is a difficult and totally rewarding vocation. In no other way can two people better share their lives and expand their ministries together. We know, some of us from experience, how difficult the days ahead may be. It will be helpful on those days for you to remember that you are not in this marriage alone. You are loved and cared for by us—your friends, your church family.

In return, you have a responsibility to us, to share with us when you have needs or when you want to be uplifted in special prayer. You are accountable to God and to us to make your marriage work—to make it an example of Christ at work in our community.

*Host:* Father, we bring _____ and _____ before You. Tonight we celebrate their coming marriage. Give them a special love for each other that will continue to grow through the years. Thank You, Lord, for Your wonderful plan of marriage. Thank You for all the gifts that are part of marriage, and for the responsibilities that are part of it as well. Shower your blessings on _____ and _____ as surely as we have showered them tonight with our gifts and celebration. Amen.

*Refreshments*

Anything from a full covered-dish supper to simple dessert will work perfectly. It might also be the time to do some novelty things. Here are some ideas we have collected through the years. They take time to do, but they are fun and seem to fit with the festive mood of wedding showers.

*Pimento Carrot*

Pimento cheese rolled into a shape of a carrot—add a sprig of parsley as the stem.

*Egg Shell Basket*

Hollow egg shells out into the shape of baskets. Fill with candy. Tie with ribbon.

*Candle Holder*

Tie a ribbon around a marshmallow. Attach a Lifesaver as a handle. Stick a tiny candle in the marshmallow.

*Celery Curls*

Cut celery ribs into 3-inch lengths, making parallel slits at one end. Have the slits narrow and reaching almost to the other end of the piece of celery.

Cover with icy-cold water and refrigerate until the cut ends curl.

*Stuffed Radishes*

Hollow out some good-sized radishes and fill with sweet butter or cheese spread.

*Carrot Curls*

Use large, crisp carrots. Peel and cut off lengthwise slices to make flat surfaces. Cut off thin strips with vegetable peeler. Soak in ice water and they will curl.

*Fruit Baskets*

Select large oranges or grapefruits with thick skin. Cut fruit in half, and remove segments. Remove pulp from the shells. Mix grapefruit or oranges with other fruits and refill the shells. Chill in the refrigerator. Just before serving, sprinkle each basket with ginger ale. Top with whipped cream.

## Tangram Shower

*Objective:* To honor the engaged couple and affirm the church's support of their decision to live for Christ together.

A tangram is square piece of paper cut in pieces that you put back together in different, sometimes symbolic shapes. At a Tangram Shower for Amy and Ron, we were flabbergasted at the variety of interesting shapes and advice they got. We put the sheets into a scrapbook for them. We also included tangrams from people who were unable to attend the party.

Remember, you will have to cut pieces for each invitation; include a sample of a finished tangram to get people thinking.

If people tape the pieces on construction paper, make your tangrams from squares no bigger than 4" x 4".

### SUGGESTED ORDER FOR THE PARTY

*Tangram Advice*

Everyone should go around the room and share the tangram and advice with the couple. Encourage everyone to write the advice on the tangram and sign his or her name so the couple will have these fun and serious advice pictures as a treasure of the evening. Make sure everyone tells what the tangram means. Most tangrams are symbolic and won't make a lot of sense until the developer shares what was meant by the arrangement of the pieces.

### FOOD

Why not serve sheet cakes that have been cut into tangram shapes! People would cover

## INVITATION IDEA

*Never go to
sleep without a
goodnight kiss.*

# Tangram Shower

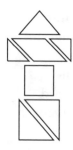

*Marriage is a
growing shiny
trophy as long
as it points
to Christ.*

Tangram
Shower for:
WHEN:
WHERE:

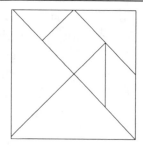

Tangram: a square that has been cut into 7 pieces.

In this invitation, you'll find a cut tangram. Please arrange the pieces on a piece of construction paper to illustrate some advice you would like to give the engaged couple.

Write your advice on your tangram.

their tangram shape with a variety of toppings—whipped cream, fruit, or chocolate sauce.

## STANDARD SHEET CAKE

*1 cup shortening*

*2 cups sugar*

*4 eggs, separated*

*3 cups flour*

*3 teaspoons baking powder*

*1 cup milk*

*1-1/2 teaspoon vanilla*

Cream shortening and sugar, mixing thoroughly. Add beaten egg yolks. Sift flour and measure. Sift with baking powder. Add alternately with milk. Add vanilla and fold in stiffly beaten egg whites. Bake at 375° for 35 to 40 minutes.

## MINI IDEAS

You can build complete parties around the following ideas, or simply add them to whatever other shower ideas you have.

### Around-the-Clock Engagement Gifts

Each person is assigned a time on a twenty-four-hour clock—all time slots don't have to be filled. That person is responsible for selecting a gift for the couple that could be used at the assigned time of day. So if he is assigned (or picks) 7 A.M., he might bring an egg coddler. Gifts are opened in sequence, starting at 1 A.M.

### Fatten the Couple

Each guest brings a favorite dish and a copy of the recipe for that dish. The recipes are collected and put into a newlywed book. This is an excellent idea for a group in which buying a gift would cause difficulty or when gifts are not appropriate.

### Calendar Party

Each guest signs a year's calendar, picking an evening when he or she would like to do something with the newly married couple as guests. This is a good idea, especially if the couple is well acquainted with everyone and the first year of marriage could be a financial struggle.

### Money Tree

Often nothing is more needed or appreciated than money. Ask each person to bring a gift of money in single dollar bills. Fold each dollar in accordion style and tie it tightly around the middle with thread. Then fan the edges to look like leaves. Tie the money to a tree branch and present it to the couple.

## Ma and Pa Initiation

### A Shower for the First Baby

*Objective:* Christian friends will celebrate the coming baby, and pray together for the new family.

For many women who are having babies, "pa" will not be part of the celebration. A single mom who will be keeping her baby will need even more support than a couple who can depend on each other. With a little tweaking, this shower idea will work for the single mom as you celebrate her new baby with her.

Other women will have made the decision to give their babies up for adoption. A woman facing this trauma may need a third or fourth month shower of gifts she can use for the rest of her pregnancy. At the shower, celebrate the new life that is growing in her and pray for the parents who will be raising this special child.

## BABY GIFTS

Be creative here. There are a lot of gifts that take little money and add tremendously to the lives of the new parents. I know one completely broke medical student who threw a shower for his best friends. He gave them a handful of "Free Baby-sitting Tickets." Not only was his gift worth a financial fortune at today's baby-sitting prices, it represented a creative approach to gift-giving. And, think what a gift like this would mean to a single mother.

You might want to consider giving one large shower gift rather than individual small ones. The single gift takes only minutes to open and allows more time for interaction with the couple and others at the party than does the time-consuming opening of single gifts.

Sometimes buying one large gift can be a problem. Again be creative. I had one friend who was so excited about the baby that by shower time, she had bought everything the new child could possibly need. So the shower guests all contributed money to a baby bank account and presented the savings book at the party.

Here's my suggested order for a Ma and Pa Initiation shower. Cut and add things that would make the party perfect for your group and the honored couple.

## INITIATION MIMES

Mime comes from the Greek word "to imitate." In a mime, a person acts out an action or experience without using words. Mime allows us to use our facial and body expressions to communicate the meaning of the occasion.

The host should announce that a number of authorities on baby care are going to mime

**INVITATION IDEA**

# MA AND PA
# INITIATION

---

Shower for _____ and _____,
the soon-to-be parents

WHEN:

WHERE:

We'll be dedicating this evening to parent
training—giving the new parents a running
start on the next eighteen years!

different activities that would be helpful for expectant parents to know about.

You may want to assign these mimes before the party so people have time to practice once in front of a mirror. No props, unless absolutely necessary. Mimes are great photo opportunities.

You announce the topic, and the actor proceeds to demonstrate the activity. Encourage participants to be as funny as possible.

Here are some mime activities you might assign.

1._____ will now demonstrate how to change a diaper—a very dirty diaper. (The more hammed up the better! After all, anything for a little ma-and-pa education.)

2._____ will demonstrate how to get strained spinach down an unwilling baby's throat.

3._____ and _____ will show the new parents the proper routine to follow when baby starts crying in the middle of the night.

(For this, the couple may want to set two chairs in front of the group. The chairs represent beds. The humor will come as each person does his or her best

to make the other get out of the bed to take care of the baby's needs.)

4._____ will demonstrate how to dress the baby to go out into the cold winter.

5._____ will show you how a parent looks as he or she is trying to coax baby to take a first step.

6. _____ and _____ will demonstrate what happens the first time you take baby to a restaurant. (You might want to use chairs. Set them facing each other as if there were a table between them. The miming couple should pretend their baby is in a high chair. Other imaginary people would include the waitress and customers.)

7. Your baby will have to learn to enjoy many different people. Let's suppose the proud parents have taken him for a walk through the park. _____ will play three different people who come by to look into the buggy. First, a sweet, little grandmother. Next, a tough teenage boy. Finally, a mother with a baby about the same age. _____ will demonstrate how you'll feel at night when you look at the little darling fast asleep in the crib.

(Use this as the final mime. The actor should simply stand, sigh in pure joy, and sit down again.)

## GIVE THE PARENTS-TO-BE THE GIFTS

Plan a little initiation ceremony for the parents. Ask them to come up to the front of the room. Explain that this initiation will help them get ready for the great things to come—a preview of what babying is all about.

You'll be handing the parents various things throughout this initiation. Explain each one as you add it to the load the parents are holding. When you have completed the initiation, you should take a picture of the couple. It will look great in a baby book.

1. Hand the father something that weighs twenty pounds. Explain that before long, he'll be able to carry this weight for miles without thinking twice.

2. Present the mother with a well-spotted apron. Point to each spot and explain what it is. For example, "This is plum pudding. The baby burped at the wrong time. And this is red nail polish. You were trying to rock the baby with one hand and put polish on the other two hands and the fourth hand got flustered when you rubbed the apron! And this yellow spot with the strange smell—well, that's something else!" Really get into this. Finally, ask the mother-to-be to put the apron on. (Make sure it's big enough.)

3. Bring someone up from the watching guests, and ask that person to pull the mother's hair just a little but rather continuously. Babies have a way of doing this, and it's good to be prepared.

4. Give the father a large damp towel. Explain that drippy babies are the norm, and a wise father gets used to the slightly damp, uncomfortable feeling.

5. Present the father with a number of pins and ask him to hold them in his mouth. Explain that this is how many people keep track of the pins while they are changing the damp youngster. After a few months, assure him, the father will find his lips toughened to pinpricks.

6. Give the mother a book about child rearing. Have her hold it open. Explain that this is a book on practically anything she wants to know about her baby.

It's as comforting as it is important to know what the book says each step of the way. (You might want to pick a good book, and add this to the parents' presents for the evening.)

7. Give the mother a pacifier to hold in her mouth. Explain that this is usually for the baby, but there may be days when she wishes she had one too.

8. Give the father a bottle, and ask him to test it on his wife's wrist to determine whether the temperature is right for baby. If she turns red on that spot, it's too hot. If she turns blue, it's too cold. If she can hardly tell that she's being sprinkled, it's absolutely perfect.

9. Give the parents a banner on a stick that reads, "Now Ready for Parenthood!"

**PRAYER FOR
THE PARENTS-TO-BE**

Ask several parents to pray over the couple. Encourage them to be personal—praying specifically for problems and joys in the years to come. Here are two examples. Read them to the parents who will be praying to give them an idea of how personal you want them to be.

"Father, I remember how wonderful I felt when I discovered that I would be a father. I was scared to death. Babies are so little and seem so breakable. Be with (<u>the new father's name</u>) as he gets used to his new name and role. May he perform it with love and consideration. May he know that the gift of fatherhood comes from you, and it is among the most precious gifts you give."

"Dear Heavenly Father, when our baby was born, I didn't care if she was a boy or a girl or if her eyes were blue or her hair curly. All I wanted was for her to be whole. You answered my prayer. I pray your health upon this baby. May the child be perfect, mentally and physically. Thank you for your amazing gift of tiny life."

**REFRESHMENTS**

The mother-to-be would probably appreciate something light that won't show up on her next weigh-in at her doctor's visit. So how about:

### COTTAGE CHEESE LIGHT DESSERT
*1/2 package lime low-calorie
   gelatin*
*1-1/2 Tablespoons liquid
   calorie-free sweetener*
*1/4 teaspoon salt*
*3 eggs, separated*

*1-1/2 cups skim milk*

*3 cups cottage cheese*

*1 Tablespoon lemon juice*

*1 teaspoon vanilla*

*1 can crushed pineapple, drained*

Place gelatin, sweetener, and salt in top of a double boiler. Beat egg yolks with milk until blended. Mix with gelatin; cook, stirring constantly, until mixture is slightly thickened. Chill until partly set. Beat cheese in electric blender or with electric mixer until smooth. Stir in lemon juice and vanilla. Fold in gelatin mixture and pineapple. Beat egg whites until stiff but not dry. Fold into gelatin. Turn into a 9" x 9" x 2" pan. Chill until firm.

A few more calories, but maybe the mother-to-be will splurge:

## STUFFED PEACHES

*6 large, firm peaches*

*1/2 cup macaroon crumbs*

*1/2 cup almonds*

*4 Tablespoons sugar*

*1 Tablespoon candied orange peel*

*1/3 cup peach juice*

Halve the peaches. Combine macaroon crumbs, chopped almonds, 2 Tablespoons sugar, and candied peel. Lightly fill the peach halves. Place in baking dish. Pour peach juice over peaches. Sprinkle on remaining

sugar. Bake at 350° for 15 minutes. Serve hot or cold.

## AUNT LILLIAN'S FRUIT SALAD

*1 or 2 large cans of fruit cocktail*

*1 can crushed pineapple*

*1 jar maraschino cherries*

*1-1/2 cups tokay grapes*

*2 cups miniature marshmallows*

*6 bananas*

*4 ounces pecan meats*

*2 1-ounce cartons whipping cream*

*6 ounces cream cheese*

Open cocktail, pineapple, and cherries. Drain well. Cut cherries in quarters. Halve grapes and pit them. Add, with marshmallows, bananas, and chopped up pecans, to other fruit.

Whip cream—not too stiff— just until it is wavy. Cut up softened cream cheese and add in chunks as you whip the cream. Pour over fruit. If dressing is too thick, add just enough milk to reach the desired consistency.

And just in case you want to break the calorie bank, here are a few desserts your skinny guests will love:

## FUDGE BROWNIES

*2 ounces unsweetened chocolate*

*1/3 cup corn oil*

*1 cup sugar*

*2 eggs*

*3/4 cup sifted flour*

1/2 teaspoon baking powder
1/2 teaspoon salt
1/2 cup broken pecans

Melt chocolate with oil over hot water. Beat in sugar and eggs. Sift dry ingredients and stir in. Mix in nuts. Spread in greased pan and bake 30 to 35 minutes at 350°. Do not over-bake. When the brownie mixture is slightly cool, cut into 16 2-inch squares.

### THREE-LAYER FUDGE CAKE

2-1/4 cups sifted cake flour
1 teaspoon baking soda
1/2 teaspoon salt
4 ounces chocolate
1-1/4 cup milk
3/4 cup brown sugar
1 teaspoon vanilla
2/3 cup shortening
1 cup granulated sugar
3 eggs

Sift flour, soda, and salt all together. Heat chocolate and milk in top of double boiler until chocolate melts. Add brown sugar and beat until smooth. Cool and add vanilla. Cream shortening with granulated sugar until fluffy.

Add eggs one at a time, beating thoroughly after each. Add sifted dry ingredients and chocolate mixture alternately in small amounts, beating well after each addition. Bake at 350° in 3 round cake pans for about 1/2 hour. Top with favorite frosting.

### PEANUT BUTTER BANANA PIE

1 3-1/4 ounce package vanilla pudding and pie mix
1-1/2 cups miniature marshmallows
1/2 cup heavy cream, whipped
2 bananas, sliced
lemon juice
peanut butter crust

Prepare pie filling as directed on package, except using 1-3/4 cups milk. Cover with waxed paper; chill.

Fold in marshmallows and whipped cream. Dip bananas in lemon juice, place in crust. Pour filling over bananas. Chill several hours. Garnish with additional banana slices, whipped cream, and peanuts, if desired.

### PEANUT BUTTER CRUST

3 cups miniature marshmallows
1/2 cup crunchy peanut butter
1/4 cup margarine
4 cups cornflakes

Melt marshmallows with peanut butter and margarine in saucepan over low heat. Stir until melted and well blended. Remove from heat. Stir in cereal until well coated. Press onto bottom and sides of a greased 9" pie plate, and chill.

## Mini Ideas

You can build complete parties around the following ideas, or simply add them to whatever other shower ideas you have.

### NEW GROWTH ON THE FAMILY TREE

Do a little family research by contacting the parents and grandparents of the couple. Write a short history for the baby, and actually read it to "him" at the party. You might start like this. "Baby, you are being born into a wonderful family. Did you know that your great-grandfather on your mother's side was considered the best woodworker in Gap? And on your father's side, your great grandfather was a farmer who loved God so much that he was willing to give up his farm and move to a new country when his government tried to limit the amount of time he could spend in church . . ."

You might add a touch of "This Is Your Life" by having a few surprise guests appear as you read the baby's history. For example, the soon-to-be grandparents could remain in another room until it was time for them to suddenly "appear" and tell their part in the baby's history.

### BABY GUESS

Baby Guess is a perfect way to add a little excitement to the coming event when there isn't time or money for a shower. Or, perhaps it's not the first baby, but you would still like to do something a little special for the parents. (Our church had a rule that the church sponsored only first baby showers. Before the rule, we were feeling the crunch of buying several gifts a month.)

For a baby guess, find out when the baby is due and make up time sheets for the few days before and after that date. Ask people if they would like to guess when the baby will come. Charge $1.00 a guess. Larry and I were co-workers, and his wife Juanita was having their third baby. I displayed a time sheet on the employee's bulletin board, and was amazed at how seriously people took this game. Almost everyone asked questions before they would sign. "What was her pattern with the other two children?" "What did the doctor say on her last checkup?" We collected about $40, and the whole amount went to the couple. We also had a little prize for the person who guessed closest to the baby's actual birth hour. That prize was won by Brian who was about to become a father himself for the first time.

We set up our sheets like this:

### WEDNESDAY

1 A.M.

3 A.M.

7 A.M. Jim Townsend
10 A.M.

2 P.M. Brian Dill

5 P.M. Gabby Garcia
10 P.M.

And then on to the next day.

This little technique required very little time, and practically no money. But it generated a lot of enthusiasm and support for the parents. Everyone had a small, personal stake in the arrival of the new baby.

## AROUND-THE-CLOCK BABY GIFTS

(Also suggested for an engagement party)

Each person is assigned a time on a twenty-four-hour clock (all times don't have to be filled). He or she is supposed to buy a gift that could be used by the baby or baby's parents at that time of the day or night. For example, if Myra were assigned 4 A.M., she might give the parents a bottle warmer. And, of course, diapers would fit any slot.

## PICTURE GUESS

Everyone should bring one of his or her own baby pictures. The hostess should put the pictures on a table and number each. Everyone gets pencil, paper, and the job of guessing which picture goes with which adult.

## BABY SHOWER GAMES

There are a lot of silly games that can make a party more lively. Here are three suggestions.

*Diaper relay:* You'll need two life-sized dolls and two diapers. Both teams line up, and at the whistle the first person in each team rushes up to the baby and completely diapers it—two pins and all. The player runs back and tags the next person in line. That person comes up to the doll and undiapers it. That player goes back and tags the next person who diapers it, and so on until one line is finished.

You can add all sorts of extras—like a little mustard on the diaper!

*Baby Feeding Exhibition:* Blindfold the father-to-be and get a volunteer from the guests who is also to be blindfolded. (You might pick the last person to become a father.) Then have them feed each other. Pick a baby food that's a terrible color. The results are funny—if you like messy fathers.

*Baby Food Testing:* Divide the group into pairs. Blindfold one person in each pair. The other will give the blindfolded person one taste of a baby food, and the other must identify it.

The player should whisper the answer to his or her partner, who will keep track of correct answers. The person with the most correct answers wins—how about a jar of slightly used baby food?

You won't have to have more than one jar of each flavor because people don't have to be tasting the same food at the same time. Just pass the jars.

---

# Hospitality
*It just could become one of your favorite words.*

I love the story of the little girl who misquoted her favorite verse:

> ". . . *that whosoever believes in him should not perish, but have ever-laughing life.*"

That's the "version" I want to use when people are gathered at my home.

> —*May the time be filled with laughter . . . clear, fun, care-washing laughter.*
>
> —*May Jesus be present, and may the guests know it.*
>
> —*May seekers take those first steps that lead to ever-laughing life.*

---

# PARTY INDEX

# RECIPE INDEX